MW01128990

THE PSYCHOLOGY OF GUN VIOLENCE

How Smart Choices Can Save Lives

JANET SHIBLEY HYDE, PhD

Prometheus Books

Essex, Connecticut

Prometheus Books

An imprint of The Globe Pequot Publishing Group, Inc.
64 South Main Street
Essex, CT 06426
www.globepequot.com

Distributed by NATIONAL BOOK NETWORK

British Library Cataloguing in Publication Information Available

Library of Congress Cataloging-in-Publication Data Available

ISBN 978-1-4930-8997-0 (cloth)
ISBN 978-1-4930-8998-7 (ebook)

♾️™ The paper used in this publication meets the minimum requirements of American National Standard for Information Sciences—Permanence of Paper for Printed Library Materials, ANSI/NISO Z39.48-1992.

Contents

Preface

It was May 23, 2022, and I was thinking ahead to my retirement on July 1. I was considering what to do for a retirement project because I have a strong need to feel, at the end of the day, as if I've done something useful. The very next day, May 24, 2022, the massacre at Robb Elementary School in Uvalde, Texas, happened. I knew on that day what my project should be and I have never looked back. My project is to end gun violence in America. Yes, it's an ambitious goal, but as the Chinese proverb reminds us, a journey of a thousand miles begins with a single step.

From that day forward, I immersed myself in learning everything I could about guns, gun violence, and gun safety. I joined the local chapter of Moms Demand Action for Gun Sense in America and then became connected to the state chapter and the national organization. I read research reports on the website of Everytown Research and Policy, and I donated to Everytown and Moms. I completed the training for certification to offer the Be SMART educational program on how adults can keep children safe from guns, and I have given the program dozens of times in venues ranging from a PTO meeting, a gathering of a local ministerial association, to a church's dinner for needy people in the neighborhood. I have given away gun locks at a farmers market. I traveled to my state capitol with other Moms volunteers to talk with legislators about the importance of legislation for gun safety. And all the while, I have listened to how people respond to gun safety messages—what resonated for them and what they resist.

Of course, being an academic, I have read hundreds of scientific articles on gun violence and how to prevent it, and I have eagerly devoured relevant books. These resources proved invaluable as I wrote this book.

So many friends and colleagues have read chapters and given me expert advice that I worry about missing someone on the list. Special thanks go to Morton Gernsbacher, Luke Hyde (an expert on antisocial behavior and also my wonderful son), Ethan Kross, Steven Roberts, Amy Mezulis, Paula Niedenthal, Maryellen MacDonald, Judy Harackiewicz, Bill Sallak, Hazel Markus, and Mary

Anderson. Gun violence researchers who have shared their insights include Lois Lee, Nick Buttrick, Tom Heberlein, Dominic Erdozain, and Michael W. Austin. I also want to thank the hundreds of experts who pursue scientific research on gun violence and how to prevent it.

Fr. Andy Jones and Fr. David Hodges of the Episcopal Church have been enormously supportive of my efforts, as have Bishop Deon Johnson, Rev. Mary Haggerty, Rev. Meghan Ryan, and Jeff Wunrow. My partners in Be SMART presentations have helped to get the job done: Katie Smart, Donna Bernert, Lore Gross, and Diane Chalberg.

I am grateful to the St. Louis City chapter of Moms Demand Action for their monthly meetings, in which I have learned so much about urban gun violence and the toll it takes on individuals, families, and communities. Many of the stories I have heard during those meetings are heartbreaking, and yet they only serve to increase my motivation to end gun violence in America.

Janice Audet, who gave me the idea to write this book, has my deepest gratitude. A thousand thanks go to Nicole Bridge, who made swift and major contributions to technical aspects like Chicago style and permissions. Jake Bonar has been a wonderful editor at Prometheus. And Linda Kaplan, my agent, has skillfully introduced this college textbook author to the world of trade book publishing.

By way of giving back, I pledge to donate all royalties that I may earn from sales of this book to Everytown and Moms. These organizations head up major efforts to end gun violence in America and they are highly effective at what they do. I am focused on solutions and so are they.

CHAPTER ONE

Introduction

The Problem of Gun Violence in America and How Psychology Can Help

ON MAY 24, 2022, AN 18-YEAR-OLD ARMED WITH AN AR-15-STYLE RIFLE entered Robb Elementary School in Uvalde, Texas. He* shut himself in two adjoining classrooms and within minutes murdered 19 fourth graders and two teachers, while also wounding 17 others. The shooter carried with him seven 30-round magazines, so he could shoot 210 times. He had recently turned 18 so he could legally buy an assault weapon in Texas and that's just what he had done. Those who were trapped with him in the classrooms frantically called 911 or friends and relatives. Teacher Eva Mireles, in one of the classrooms, called her husband, Ruben Ruiz, telling him that she was shot and dying. Ruiz was actually just outside the school. When he tried to get in to save his wife, law enforcement stopped him and took away his gun. Eva Mireles later died, one of the two teachers who lost their lives, in one of the most horrific mass shootings in US history.

The statistics on gun violence are sobering. In the United States each year, roughly 43,000 people die by firearms.[1] That's more than 120 deaths per day. Of those deaths, 54 percent are suicides, 43 percent are homicides, and the remaining 3 percent are due to unintentional shootings, "legal interventions" (police shootings), and undetermined causes.

---

* Here and throughout the book, I follow the practice, advocated by many in the field, of not naming shooters, in the interests of not making them famous and not encouraging potential shooters to think they will become famous by committing a heinous act.

These gun deaths are not distributed equally across the US population. They differ by gender, age, and economic status. For gun homicides, 85 percent of the victims are males.[2] In 2020, for the first time in US history, guns surpassed automobile accidents as the leading cause of death for children under 18.[3] Every year in the United States, 4,000 children and teens die by guns, more than 10 deaths every day.[4] Of these deaths, 62 percent are homicides, 33 percent are suicides, and most of the remaining 5 percent are unintentional deaths; for example, when a child finds an unlocked, loaded gun in the home and accidentally kills themselves or others. Lastly, the rate of gun homicides for the poorest 25 percent of Americans is about four times higher than the rate for the wealthiest 25 percent of Americans.[5] The uneven distribution of gun deaths is one of the many reasons that the problem is so complex and why it demands a multipronged approach to solutions.

Gun violence levies an incredible cost on both individuals and society. One estimate puts the economic cost of gun deaths and injuries at $557 billion per year in the United States, $12.6 billion of which is paid by taxpayers.[6] Bills footed by taxpayers include the need for greater numbers of police to deal with gun crimes, the increased number of cases passing through the courts to prosecute shooters, and larger bills to Medicaid for medical care for those who are wounded.

The societal cost is a culture of fear and depression. And the individual costs—to the body, mind, and spirit—are life changing. Youth who are wounded often suffer disfiguring injuries.[7] In a study of 28,000 children who suffered firearm injuries, most of them between ages 13 and 18, 220 suffered an amputation and 191 were given a craniectomy (removal of a portion of the skull). For survivors of gun violence—family and friends of people who died by gun suicide, coworkers who survive a workplace shooting, children who survive a shooting in their school, victims of domestic violence who manage to get out before they are killed, and physicians in the emergency department who treat the victims—there are often overlooked effects. When we calculate the toll of gun violence, we must also consider and count the enduring psychological costs.

A PSYCHOLOGICAL APPROACH

If we are going to reduce gun violence in America, we must understand the psychology behind it, and then use strategies and interventions based on solid scientific evidence to halt the epidemic. These evidence-based strategies help us make smart choices, as individuals and as a nation. The psychology behind the issue is important because the act of shooting another human being is a behavior.

It's not a biochemical reaction or an astronomical event. As the science of behavior and mental processes, psychology is crucial in understanding the behavior of a shooter and the mental processes that led up to it.

Psychology is essential to understanding motivation. What motivates people to buy guns? To carry them? To use them?

A well-known slogan of the Gun Lobby is "Guns don't kill people, people kill people." In other words, it's all about the person and not at all about the environment. But psychology shows that the issue is a person-environment interaction; both the person and the environment contribute to the behavior. If a mass shooter had been in an environment free from guns, or at least with less easy access to them, they probably wouldn't have committed the mass shooting. Both the weapon and the person are required for a shooting.

Psychology has established powerful concepts about how to change behavior most effectively. That knowledge can help in the development of interventions to prevent gun violence. Psychological research has tackled and provided solutions for issues related to gender, identity, age, and economic status, and is crucial for solving this complex issue that takes a monumental toll on our society and individuals.

Consider the paradoxical phenomenon that occurs after a mass shooting in the United States. You might think that the horror of such an occurrence would propel citizens and legislators to pass a ban on assault weapons immediately. After a 1996 firearm massacre in Australia that killed 35 people, Australia enacted legislation banning semiautomatic shotguns and rifles.[8] In the 10 years following the legislation, there was not a single mass shooting in Australia! Why does similar action not occur in the United States?

The (admittedly oversimplified) answer is that we have a different culture in the United States. Another Gun Lobby slogan is "The only thing that stops a bad guy with a gun is a good guy with a gun"—that is, the solution to gun violence is more guns in the hands of presumably honorable "guys." The Gun Lobby has convinced many Americans to believe this. Many others, however, believe that the solution to gun violence is fewer guns, making them less readily available.

To see whether Americans' attitudes about gun control laws changed after mass shootings, researchers collected national survey data in two studies, one immediately after the 2016 killing of 49 people in Orlando's Pulse nightclub, and the other after the 2019 mass shooting at an El Paso Walmart.[9] In both studies, those who believed that more guns will reduce crime showed little support for stricter gun laws before the mass shooting and their attitudes remained unchanged following it. They don't believe that guns play a role in mass shootings and they support an armed citizenry. For those with the opposite point of view, who believe that the availability of guns is a major cause of mass shootings, support for stricter gun laws was already high before the mass shooting and support increased following the shooting.

This study illuminates the psychological processes involved with people's responses to mass shootings and why these horrifying events do not yield sensible gun legislation in the United States. A segment of Americans, including many members of Congress, simply don't believe that gun deaths can be reduced with stricter gun laws, despite the fact that the scientific data say otherwise. Their preexisting beliefs profoundly affect their cognitive processing of information about an event like a mass shooting.

In 2024, I was meeting with a state legislator about some gun bills that had been introduced. At the time, that state permitted schools to designate teachers or administrators as "school protection officers," allowing them to carry firearms in schools. The new legislation, HB 1440, expanded the list of employees who could carry in schools to include janitors, cafeteria workers, and more. It's a classic example of a weak gun law because it allows more guns in schools. What could possibly go wrong? When I asked this legislator what his position on the bill was, he said "I'll vote for it. Anything for more safety in the schools!" As I drew out the conversation, it turned out that he had grown up in a rural area and hunted, and had been a middle school teacher and superintendent of schools. He explained that small, rural schools don't have the funds to hire a full-time security officer, so his idea was that those schools could use other personnel as substitute security officers. I explained that research shows that schools with more armed personnel actually have more gun injuries than those with fewer armed personnel.[10] He was surprised by that and seemed to absorb the finding. Then he acknowledged that his plan would work only if the school protection officers had extensive training and certification to bring them up to the level of a professional security officer. None of that was in the bill. By the end of our conversation, he had pledged to introduce an amendment to the bill that would require the training and certification.

I give this example for two reasons. First, it shows that people can communicate across a divide about gun attitudes. Second, it illustrates how intuitively appealing it is to many Americans to think that more guns will make the nation safer. In most cases, the research shows just the opposite. I am a scientist and I believe in going with the scientific evidence, not with intuition or haphazard beliefs. This book is thoroughly science based.

Another response that comes up immediately after a mass shooting is the idea that "It's not a gun issue, it's a mental health issue." But the assertion that it's really a mental health issue is plainly contradicted by two sets of scientific data. First, it's very rare for people with mental illness to commit any crime, much less a violent crime.[11] Most persons with serious mental illness (schizophrenia, bipolar disorder, or major depression) are never violent. Researchers estimate that only 3 to 5 percent of all violence is due to mental illness.[12] There are, however, certain small subgroups of this population who are at higher risk to commit violence during certain times in their lives. Those who also have a substance use disorder (they are addicted to alcohol or other drugs) are more likely to be violent, but even then, it is a small minority of this group. People with psychosis also have a higher risk of committing violent acts, perhaps because during an episode they experience hallucinations (hearing or seeing things that aren't really there) or delusions (false beliefs). Among people with psychosis, though, only a small minority engage in any violent behavior. An analysis of a large database of mass shootings found that only 8 percent of mass shooters had ever experienced psychotic symptoms.[13] Mental illness is rarely the culprit in shootings.

Second, all Western nations comparable to ours have extremely low rates of gun homicide compared to ours. If it's true that gun deaths are really a mental health issue, the United States would have to have much higher rates of mental illness than other nations to explain why we have so many more gun deaths, but there is simply no evidence that's true. For example, the rate (prevalence) of schizophrenia is 0.30 percent (that is, a fraction of a percent) in the United States.[14] The rate is 0.30 percent in Canada, 0.25 percent in England, 0.23 percent in Italy, 0.33 percent in Australia, and 0.28 percent in Japan. In all countries, the rate is less than 1 percent. America is not exceptional when it comes to our rate of mental illness, so we can't use mental illness as a reason for our exceptionally high rates of gun violence.

The difference is that the Unites States has substantially more firearms in the hands of civilians. The United States has 120.5 firearms per 100 people in the population. We have more guns than people! The comparable figures are 34.7 for Canada, 28.8 for Norway, and 19.6 for France.[15] Those are just countries in the top 25. The UK, Spain, Japan, Italy, and Mexico have such low rates of gun ownership that they don't even make it on the list of the top 25.

Of course, we should have more resources to treat those with mental health issues, but it won't solve the gun crisis.

We can boost the effectiveness of the psychological approach to ending gun violence by pairing it with a public health approach. *Public health* is a field that seeks to improve the health of communities by collecting systematic data on the causes of disease and implementing changes in the environment to reduce or remove those causal factors. Public health interventions can be evaluated scientifically so that we can focus on implementing evidence-based solutions.[16] Applied here, the "disease" is gun deaths and injuries, and guns kill as surely as cancer does. The importance of a public health approach to gun deaths was underscored when, in 2024, US Surgeon General Vivek Murthy issued an official advisory, *Firearm Violence: A Public Health Crisis in America.*[17]

In this book, I will show you how psychology is essential for understanding and addressing the epidemic of gun violence in the United States and how a public health approach can boost the effectiveness of the psychological approach dramatically.

APATHY AND RESIGNATION ARE THE ENEMIES

When I told a woman in my exercise class that my new project was to work to reduce gun violence, she said, in a heavily ironic tone, "Good luck with that!" She is an intelligent, well-informed person, and clearly she thought that nothing could be done about gun violence in America. I strongly disagree. I know there are many steps we can take as a nation and as individuals to reduce gun deaths, if enough good people commit to the solutions. The problem is that too many citizens have become resigned to the situation and believe that nothing can be done. We have a Gun Culture in the United States, they say. End of discussion.

Two examples of major public health successes in the United States over the last 50 years demonstrate how a culture can transform in major ways that save lives. In our nation we have managed to reduce the number of deaths from motor vehicle accidents and deaths from smoking. Here I will focus on the former.

The dramatic reduction in deaths from motor vehicle accidents is one of the great public health success stories of the 20th century.[18] Beginning when cars were mass-produced, through the 1950s, thousands of people were killed in motor vehicle accidents every year.

Then beginning in the 1950s, public health researchers asked: What about the situation, what about the environment, causes the injuries and fatalities? Drivers were killed in crashes when their chest hit a hard, immovable steering wheel. Bodies were lacerated by the broken glass from windshields. In a crash, a passenger could be thrown out of the car and hit their head on the pavement, killing them.

The solution, then, was policies to address these causes. The federal government issued safety requirements for new vehicles, including requirements for seat belts, crash-resistant windshields, and energy-absorbing steering columns. Car seats for children became the norm. Between 1966 and 2000, fatalities per vehicle mile driven plummeted by 70 percent.[19]

An important takeaway from this example is that transformative cultural change—with corresponding changes in behavior such as wearing seat belts and putting children in car seats—can take place if the right policies are implemented, policies based on the best available scientific evidence.

If we can succeed in reducing deaths from motor vehicle accidents, we can succeed in reducing deaths from gun violence.

Figure 1.1. Rosie the Riveter from World War II. We could do it then and we can do it now!
WIKIMEDIA COMMONS

WHERE I'M COMING FROM

As a reader of this book, you might want to know where I'm coming from. Do I have any biases? An axe to grind? What is my point of view?

My single-minded goal is to reduce deaths from gun violence. I am putting my all into that effort. I grew up with a father who, for some years, worked for the National Safety Council, whose motto was "Prevention Is Better Than Cure," although it seems that Erasmus may have said it first. At any rate, I had that principle drilled into me from an early age, and now I am applying it to gun deaths.

I am a scientist by both training and inclination. Having spent decades of my life as a psychology professor, I believe that policy decisions should be based on the best available scientific evidence. That's how you get the best results, not by following someone's casual opinion. I also believe that people who hold uninformed views can learn what the science says.

I am not doing this work in support of a particular political party. We need bipartisan cooperation to solve this enormous problem in our country. My goal is to help find a middle ground of approaches that 80 percent of Americans can agree on. I firmly believe that with rights come responsibilities, and that was never more true than in the case of guns.

I do not own a gun, but I respect responsible gun owners and I hope that they return that respect to me. We will not stop all the senseless deaths unless gun owners and nonowners learn to talk with each other and cooperate. This book is written for people from both groups.

I hope that helps.

LOOKING FORWARD

The chapters that follow explore the complexity of the gun violence issue, on an individual and cultural level, and reveal what psychology can tell us about human beings, the ownership and use of firearms, and the deaths that result from them, always bearing in mind that these are problems that can be solved, just as our nation succeeded in drastically reducing deaths from motor vehicle accidents.

Chapter 2, on guns and emotion, details how fear and anxiety motivate people to buy and use firearms and how children and youth are responding to the epidemic of gun violence, including the anxiety created by active shooter drills in the schools. Anger and hatred are other strong emotions that motivate people to buy guns and kill, and gun owners' identities are often vested in their firearms. At the end of this chapter and all the ones that follow, I offer an evidence-based solution to the problem, a recommendation for ways to make smart choices.

Chapter 3 is about the toxic link between guns and masculinity. More than 98 percent of mass shooters are boys or men, a fact that often remains invisible in media reports. What accounts for this striking gender effect? Here I draw on my decades of research on gender roles and psychological gender differences to explain why boys and men are much more prone to shooting and killing. Patterns of domestic violence are also highly gendered and when guns enter the equation, domestic violence can turn deadly.

The topic of guns and race is the focus of chapter 4, including a consideration of the race of gun owners, shooters (as well as their victims), and the role of racism and implicit bias in incidents such as police shootings. Some mass shootings like the one in the Buffalo, New York, supermarket, are committed by White nationalists, and I review what is known about the psychology of White nationalists and their commitments to guns and killing. Race issues gained force in our nation's history with the enslavement of Black people, but arguably, American Indians were the first objects of enslavement and gun violence. I draw out these strands of history and their implications for the psychology of gun violence today.

Chapter 5 explores the link between religion and guns, including evangelical Protestants' remarkable affinity for firearms. I review biblical passages that might be used to justify violence or nonviolence and how other religious groups—such as Jews and mainline Protestants—view guns and violence. Religion powerfully shapes culture and socializes Americans—whether believers or nonbelievers—about how to think and feel about guns, and we need to recognize that socialization force.

In the United States, suicides account for 54 percent of gun deaths, and suicide is the topic of chapter 6. Moreover, some mass shootings are actually "suicide by cop," as in the case of the Louisville bank shooting in April 2023. What psychological factors lead to suicide attempts and what role do guns play? How can friends and loved ones recognize that a person is suicidal? On the policy front, Extreme Risk Protection Orders (ERPO, or Red Flag laws) are an important tool in preventing suicide by gun.

In chapter 7, I take up the Gun Lobby, which includes not only the National Rifle Association (NRA), but also gun manufacturers and sellers. Research indicates that following a mass shooting gun sales increase. In short, gun manufacturers profit from mass shootings. The Gun Lobby became powerful in America over many decades, gaining power that is not only political but also psychological. I explore the many ways in which the Gun Lobby has socialized a great swath of Americans to believe that they need guns for protection and that the Second Amendment is more important than any other principle.

Chapter 8 summarizes the legal state of affairs regarding firearms, beginning even before the framing of the US Constitution and the Second Amendment, and the role that slavery played in its passage. I review the major Supreme Court decisions on guns, as well as current laws at the state level. Research shows that the 10 states with the strongest gun laws have a much lower rate of gun homicides per capita than the 10 states with the weakest gun laws. Research also shows us which gun laws are the most effective at reducing gun deaths. Gun rights activists have a number of arguments they are encouraged to make to those who favor reasonable gun legislation, and table 8.1 lists some of their arguments and how you could respond based on scientific evidence. I introduce the concept of the right to freedom from gun violence.

The concluding chapter provides numerous ideas about what individuals, parents, communities, and the government can do to end the epidemic of gun violence. An important distinction is made between interventions based on scientific evidence (evidence-based interventions), those that have been tested and found to be ineffective, and innovative ideas that have not yet been tested. The implications of the successes with automobile safety and smoking cessation are drawn out. To give just three brief examples here, on the individual level, if you are a gun owner, be a responsible gun owner and practice safe storage. For parents, I explain the relevant findings in psychology on how to raise a child who will not become a mass shooter. At the community level, there is evidence that several community violence interventions are effective. Regarding policy, I review the consensus among experts about which aspects of gun legislation are the most important for stopping the carnage.

This is fundamentally an optimistic book by an optimistic author. The book is not designed to depress you about a huge problem that seems to be insoluble. Instead, it is intended to give you the information that every American should have about our gun problem and "arm" you with the tools—peaceful, nonviolent ones—to work to bring an end to the epidemic of gun deaths. I offer evidence-based, smart choices to get us out of the stranglehold that guns have on our nation.

> *The world will not be destroyed by those who do evil, but by those who watch them without doing anything.*
>
> —Albert Einstein

CHAPTER TWO

Emotions Make Us Buy Them

IN SEPTEMBER 2023, NEW MEXICO GOVERNOR MICHELLE LUJAN GRISHAM, responding to recent shootings including the death of an 11-year-old outside a baseball stadium, declared a public health emergency that suspended the right to carry firearms in public in Albuquerque and the county surrounding it. The words were barely out of her mouth when Second Amendment activists sued to block the order and, a few days later, a federal judge issued a temporary restraining order doing so. A couple of state legislators called for the governor to be impeached. Threats against the governor and her family proliferated on social media.

The question for us here is, why did Second Amendment activists immediately stage protests, file lawsuits, and threaten the governor? After all, she wasn't banning gun ownership, she was just restricting open carry. Photos of the protesters show them uniformly carrying guns, most of them AR-15s,* and most wore masks to hide their identity. These activists were not constitutional law scholars committed to the preservation of the Bill of Rights. Instead, they were people with a strong emotional attachment to their guns, who became extremely upset at the thought that anything might come between them and their security blankets. To understand Gun Culture and the current state of gun violence in the United States, we must understand the strong emotions that some Americans attach to guns.

In the United States, people who are fearful because they see or imagine threats all around them soothe those fears by buying a gun and, if they constantly

---

* I will explain the origin of the AR-15 semiautomatic rifle in chapter 7 on the Gun Lobby. A variety of terms are used, including AR-15, AR-15-style rifle, semiautomatic rifle, assault rifle, and so on. To avoid linguistic clutter, I will use "AR-15" as a generic to encompass all of these semiautomatic rifles.

fear threats, carrying the gun with them on a daily basis for "protection." When we are feeling strong emotions like fear or anger, it diminishes our ability to make smart choices. A very different set of emotions motivates mass shooters. And then there is the emotional toll on survivors, such as the mother whose son died by suicide with a gun. We must understand the deep emotions linked to guns and gun violence if we are to take the dozens of steps needed to get the epidemic of gun deaths under control. Until then, we will have activists threatening a governor who simply wants to restrict open carry following numerous shootings, with a goal of saving lives. But first, we need to recognize diversity among gun owners.

Not All Gun Owners Are Alike

One sunny summer day, I was at the local farmers market, wearing my red T-shirt proclaiming "Moms Demand Action for Gun Sense in America." I want to spread the word, and I hope that the shirt will stimulate some conversations. At one vendor stand, the seller, having read the shirt, said "I belong to the NRA, but no civilian needs an assault weapon." Essentially, he was agreeing that we need some commonsense gun laws. He went on to tell me that he had a rifle for deer hunting and he was a veteran. He complained that some of the guys who insist on their right to AR-15s have never volunteered for the military. They want to own weapons of war but they aren't willing to serve.

That conversation drove home to me the important point that not all gun owners are alike. Psychology can help us understand the details about the diversity among gun owners and the different motivations that drive people to own guns. Based on a survey of legal gun owners, researchers concluded that they fell into these categories.[1]

- family protectors, who believe that they should own a gun so that they can protect their family; they feel empowered by the gun
- self-protectors, of whom 51 percent are women, who believe that they need a gun to protect themselves
- Second Amendment activists, who engage in multiple gun-related activities and resist any social change
- target shooters
- hunters

Interestingly, the Second Amendment activists constituted only a small minority (18 percent) of this sample of gun owners. Of course, this study did not include illegal gun owners, who are another category altogether. They may be members of organized crime or gang members or a person with a domestic violence restraining order who nonetheless manages to buy a gun.

Some categories of legal gun owners seem to pose little threat to public safety. Hunters are a good example. Sociologist Marc Boglioli conducted an in-depth study of deer hunters in rural Vermont, using a research technique called ethnography.[2] Boglioli had, in fact, been part of hunting culture from a young age, having acquired an air rifle at age nine. His father, a former Marine shooting champion, gave him shooting lessons and stressed safety.

For the study, Boglioli interviewed hunters, participated in nine different deer hunting camps over many weeks, and worked as a clerk in a local sporting goods store. In short, he immersed himself in the culture. He concluded that one of the issues in our society is that urban-dwelling Americans don't have a clue about rural America, and most hunters are rural, white Americans. Hunters are demonized, but in fact many of them hunt to put food on the table for their families, and they have respect—indeed, deep affection—for the animals they hunt.

Aside from bringing home the venison, hunting also creates social communities. Going back to the same deer camp each year, hunters spend time with old friends and neighbors, including rituals such as game dinners. Parents hunt with their kids, and both mothers and fathers see hunting as a good, solid activity for youth, an activity that keeps them out of trouble. At home, the great majority of hunters practice safe storage of their firearms—keeping them locked up and unloaded—and teach their children to follow these practices.

Within these social groups, there are norms for behavior. In the hunting culture in Vermont, hunters are criticized by their peers if they do not follow game laws or if they are unsafe with their guns. Generally, there is a prohibition against bringing a loaded firearm into the camp cabin. Hunters are wise enough to know that you should never have a loaded gun in the house with your family and friends. In one case, a man brought a loaded handgun into camp and refused to unload it; he was asked to leave, even though he was a friend of the camp's owner. These are strong norms.

The community distinguishes between hunting and killing. Those who are there just to enjoy a kill—who engage in indiscriminate shooting, illegal killing, or failing to retrieve wounded animals—are treated as outlaws and are ousted from deer camp and other community activities. Among these Vermont deer hunters, hunting game for food is considered legitimate, but "trophy hunting" is seen as disgusting.

Some experts have even suggested that hunters and hunting regulations could serve as a model for what we could do about the problem of guns in America.[3] It turns out that if you let folks hunt as much as they want, the deer population plummets, potentially to a point where they are decimated. No more venison for the family. By 1776, the year of our nation's founding, 12 of the 13 colonies had hunting regulations to deal with this problem. These early colonists plainly saw the need for gun regulations. Conversely, if no hunting occurs, deer quickly overpopulate and, because there isn't enough food for all of them, they all starve together in the winter. Without regulation, everyone loses.

GUNS AND FEAR

As noted earlier, protection is one of the main reasons why people purchase guns, and these folks are, psychologically, in a completely different category from hunters. According to a 2021 Gallup poll, among gun owners 88 percent own a gun for protection against crime. That 88 percent is a dramatic increase from 65 percent in 2000. When someone says they buy a gun for protection, they are saying they feel fearful and the gun will reduce their fear and anxiety.

Firearm purchasing accelerated sharply during the Covid pandemic of 2020–2021.[4] On the face of it, that makes no sense. A gun can't protect you against being infected with Covid, being hospitalized with it, or dying from it. Psychologically, though, it does make sense. Many people felt anxious during the pandemic. It was a time of massive social upheaval, including racial violence such as George Floyd's murder by police. It was unsettling. And many Americans believe that a gun will keep them safe. They feel afraid and they buy a gun, although it won't help them a bit against a deadly virus.

University of Wisconsin psychology professor Nick Buttrick[5] has proposed a coping model of protective gun ownership, as shown in figure 2.1.

Compared with nonowners, gun owners—and here I mean protective gun owners, not others such as hunters—are more likely to believe that the world is a dangerous place and getting more so. To make matters worse, they believe that institutions such as the government and the police will not protect them from these dangers.

These perceived threats are stressors to the individual, and humans are built to cope with stress, sometimes adaptively and sometimes maladaptively. In the coping model of gun ownership, three major categories of stressors are present: threats to safety, threats to one's sense of control, and threats to belongingness.[6]

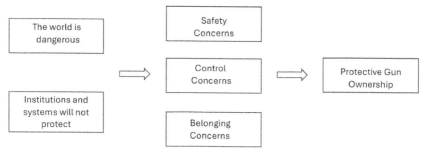

Figure 2.1.   Protective gun ownership as a coping mechanism.
ADAPTED FROM BUTTRICK 2020

Threats to safety involve things that make a person feel less safe, whether it's news of a mass shooting or fear of a tyrannical government taking over the country. *Threats to control* make a person feel like they have little control over their environment, and feelings of control are essential to mental health. *Threats to belongingness* challenge the human need to have others whom we trust and who understand us, and the threat involves a feeling that others are unwilling or unable to provide us with support.

Gun owners, especially handgun owners, perceive the world as dangerous, with many *threats to their safety*. Owning a gun helps them cope with these fears. The problem is that gun ownership is a maladaptive method of coping with safety concerns because it makes the owner's world more dangerous, not less dangerous, as explained below.

Research even shows that loss of the gun makes the owner feel more fearful. As one owner said about what it would mean to lose their gun, "I would have to live back in that fear, being afraid to walk, being afraid to go out. If you take it away from me, now I've got to walk a little faster, look over my shoulder a little bit more."[7]

All of us have a need to feel like we're in *control* of our lives, our environment, and our actions. We feel anxious when things seem out of control. The problem is that if you believe the world is a dangerous place and that the government will not protect you, then you have to figure out how to feel more in control. Gun owners cope and gain a sense of control by owning a gun.

Supporting these ideas, researchers found, in a well-sampled study, that economically distressed gun owners felt more empowered by their guns, compared with those who didn't feel economically distressed.[8] The sense of economic precarity creates feelings of loss of control, and guns make these folks feel empowered and more in control.

Popular press books have begun to take advantage of this belief that owning a gun will give you more control. Take, for example, Susan Czubek's *Arm up Ladies: Handguns 101 for Her: Empowering Women Through Every Step of Gun Ownership* (2020). It sells the idea that women can empower themselves by owning a gun—and not to worry about other issues like threats to their reproductive freedom or environmental hazards to their health. The gun will solve everything.

Threats to belongingness play an important role as well. All of us have a need to believe we are part of one or more social groups where we feel we belong and other members of the group recognize and appreciate us. If you believe you can't trust many elements of society, you will seek out groups where you feel you do belong, such as online progun groups or White supremacist groups. Owning a gun and subscribing to the ideologies of the online group make you feel you belong. Often these groups go on to radicalize their members.

Research shows conclusively that when humans feel uncertainty they are motivated to become zealously identified with some group, often extremist groups.[9] Now they belong to something. Many of these extremist groups have guns for their centerpiece. Think of the Proud Boys, an all-male, far-right, heavily armed group that played a major role in the insurrection at the US Capitol on January 6, 2021. As part of the initiation into the group, new members must take a loyalty oath that states, in part, "I'm a proud Western chauvinist." Members definitely gain a sense of belonging, not to mention pride, and a powerful attachment to guns is a must for being part of that brotherhood.

Overall, then, according to the coping model, protective gun owners gain a sense of power, control, community, and safety from owning a gun. Of course, there are other, safer ways to cope with threats. Certainly, folks in other countries face threats to their safety and sense of control, but a surge of gun purchasing doesn't follow. Why does it happen in America? One major reason is the easy availability of guns. Heck, if I can buy a handgun for $300 on Armslist and it makes me feel calm and in control, it's a good deal.

There is a tragic irony to all of the hundreds of thousands of acts of purchasing guns for self-defense. Guns actually do not protect, and in general they make the home more dangerous, not less. Data from the National Crime Victimization Survey shows that in crimes where the perpetrator and victim were both present, self-defense gun use occurred in less than 1 percent of the cases.[10] That is, in less than 1 percent of incidents did a victim actually use a gun for self-defense, to attack or threaten the offender, and this was true whether the event occurred in the home or away from home. Moreover, in only 18 percent of the incidents did the offender actually have a gun. Using a gun to protect yourself or your property is, in fact, very, very rare. People are buying guns to protect themselves from something that will never happen.

Not only do guns not protect, they actually make the home a more dangerous place. Multiple studies have found that the presence of a gun in the home increases the chances of both homicide and suicide.[11] Compared with those who live in a home with no gun, people who live with a gun have three times the odds of dying by suicide and two times the odds by homicide.[12]

Interviews with individuals who routinely carry guns for protection most of the time indicate, surprisingly, that they understand their chances of victimization are small.[13] However, they imagine a brutal attack on themselves or their family and it is so horrendous that it doesn't matter that the probability of it happening is tiny. Such an attack would be a consequence of not carrying a gun, they believe. What they don't think of is the potential negative consequences of carrying the gun all the time, such as unintentionally shooting themselves or another person.*

Could we mount a psychological intervention to help owners rationally understand the dangerous consequences of gun ownership? Sadly, it would be a tough sell. Over several decades, psychologists (and behavioral economists, who borrow heavily from psychology) have documented how human decision-making is not always rational. All of us have cognitive biases that make us feel good, often by not facing the truth.[14] *Cognitive dissonance theory* tackles one of these biases.[15] "Dissonance" occurs when two cognitions (ideas) we hold conflict with each other, or when our attitudes conflict with (are inconsistent with) our behavior. Dissonance makes us feel uncomfortable, and we do something to reduce the dissonance. For example, pregnant smokers certainly hear warnings about the dangers of smoking to themselves and the fetus, all based in solid science, yet research with this group indicates that they convince themselves that the evidence linking smoking to harm to the fetus is inconclusive.[16] They have reduced their dissonance and feel better about their behavior.

I don't mean to be a killjoy, but an intervention to convince gun owners about how dangerous their weapon is would be an uphill battle, although it might succeed with a subset of owners who are more open to scientific evidence.

---

* In pointing out these facts, I do not intend to disparage or dismiss the very real fears that drive people to purchase guns. You might, for example, be a woman who has been sexually assaulted once and you fear that it may happen again, so you want a way to protect yourself. Your fear is reasonable. The point is that, statistically, a gun is unlikely to protect you, and a potential attacker might even grab it and point it at you. Think about trying to find some other way to protect yourself, such as buying mace or taking martial arts classes.

For most, though, guns are so tied up with emotions that logical reasoning can fly out the window, and gun owners are likely to discount the dangers of their weapon, just like the pregnant women who discount the dangers of smoking. That said, we can still seek a middle ground that would make possible some reasonable gun regulations in ways that would not fire up cognitive dissonance in the gun-owning public.[17] We just have to be aware of the cognitive dissonance issue.

In addition to the question of why Americans own guns, we can ask an unexpected and provocative question—why do most Americans *not* own guns? The publicity about the high rate of gun ownership in America—400 million guns for just 340 million people—could easily lead a person to think that all Americans own guns, but that's not true. In fact, only 32 percent of US adults own a gun, and an additional 10 percent live in a household with a gun but don't own one themselves.[18] So gun owners are in the minority. How, then, do we get to the 400 million guns in America? It's individuals who own a lot of guns—perhaps 10 or 20. In one well-sampled survey, 70 percent of gun owners owned two or more guns.[19] But the fact remains that the majority of Americans don't own guns.

One reason that has been suggested for nonownership is sensitivity to harming others.[20] Folks who are high in sensitivity to harm are averse to hurting others. If a person buys a gun for protection, they must be willing to use it to harm or even kill another person. For those who are high in sensitivity to harm, concerns about the damage that guns can do could outweigh concerns about their own personal safety. In one study, researchers measured harm sensitivity with statements such as, "If I saw a mother slapping her child, I would be outraged." Sure enough, those who scored high in harm sensitivity were less likely to own a gun. Harm sensitivity also predicted the number of guns owned; those who had little sensitivity to harm owned the most guns.

Overall, then, the leading reason why Americans own guns is for "protection," although research shows that guns actually make the home more, not less, dangerous. For these protection owners, a gun eases their fears, particularly if they believe the world is a dangerous place and that institutions such as the government and police will not protect them from these dangers. According to the coping model, those fears stimulate basic human concerns about safety, control, and belonging, and gun ownership soothes all those concerns. And yet it is important to recognize that the majority of Americans do not own a gun, a major reason being their well-placed concern about harming others.

THE MOTIVATIONS OF MASS SHOOTERS

"Mass shooting" is usually defined as an incident in which four or more people, not counting the shooter, are killed by a firearm.[21] Typically it means a public mass shooting, that is, one that occurs in a setting such as a school, the workplace, outdoors, or a place of worship. It may occur in more than one location as the shooter moves about, seeking all the victims on the list, but all incidents must occur within a 24-hour period to qualify. The term *rampage shooting* is sometimes used for mass shooting.

By far the most common motive is revenge for perceived mistreatment.[22] The shooter may have been bullied at school and wants to get back at the bullies and others who did nothing to stop it. In another scenario, the shooter believes they were fired at work unjustly. Or the shooter may believe that members of a certain religious group are causing harm to society as well as himself. Consider these well-known mass shootings.

- Columbine High School, Colorado (1999): Two seniors gunned down 12 students and one teacher and injured many more. Their motivations have been debated, but one of them seems to have been revenge for being bullied.[*] Bullying by "jocks" was common at the school, and both shooters had been called "faggots." In a journal entry, one of them said "I hate you people for leaving me out of so many fun things." The pair were also avid fans of shooter video games such as *Doom, Duke Nukem 3D,* and *Postal*. I will return to shooter games later in the chapter.

- Edmond Post Office, Oklahoma (1986): A postal worker shot and killed 14 coworkers before committing suicide in the deadliest workplace shooting in US history. The shooter had been reprimanded by supervisors on multiple occasions and had previously threatened revenge. This tragedy was the source of the phrase "go postal."

- Tree of Life Synagogue, Pittsburgh, Pennsylvania (2018): The shooter went to the synagogue during morning services and killed 11 worshippers. The congregation participated in the Hebrew Immigrant Aid Society (HIAS), and the shooter had earlier posted on Gab, "HIAS likes to bring invaders in that kill our people. I can't sit by and watch my people get slaughtered."

---

[*] It's tough for researchers to gather good psychological data in these cases because, in many instances, the shooters kill themselves at the end of their rampage. That is precisely what happened at Columbine. There's just no chance to interview them.

Research has found that there is more than one kind of mass shooter and they tend to fit one of three psychological profiles.[23] One type is traumatized shooters—their parents had drug abuse and criminal problems and they were physically abused in childhood. Later, they turn to violence. A second type are those with psychosis, who have a diagnosis somewhere on the schizophrenia spectrum and may not always have a good grasp on reality. Those in the third category are psychopaths. They had not been abused, but they display narcissism, a lack of empathy for others, and no conscience.

Mass shooters typically plan their attack weeks or months in advance. During that time, they often exhibit one or more *warning behaviors*.[24] These behaviors yield powerful clues that could be used to stop the person before the shooting happens.

An analysis of the manifestos of 23 mass shooters found five warning behaviors before the attack, listed from the most frequent to the least.[25]

- Leakage, which is the term for indirect communication to someone else about the plans for an attack. For example, the perpetrator in the Eaton Township, Pennsylvania, shooting used Twitter and leaked the date of the attack, saying, "You probably won't sleep for a week after Wednesday . . ."

- Pathway warning behavior, which refers to planning for the shooting, creating a pathway toward it, such as identifying a location or stockpiling weapons. Shooters take great care in planning the date and researching the best location.

- Identification warning behavior, indicating that the perpetrator strongly identifies with previous mass shooters. The gunman often idolizes these previous shooters because they committed their acts for what the shooter believes is the good of society. One perpetrator named his gun Arlene after the shotgun used at Columbine. In some cases, the shooter seems to be seeking fame like that of the person they identify with.

- Fixation warning behavior, which refers to becoming preoccupied or fixated on particular ideologies, such as White supremacy. The shooter believes they are righting a wrong, the wrong being dictated by the ideology they have swallowed.

- Last-resort warning behavior, indicating that the shooter thinks they have no option for resolving their grievance other than carrying out the mass shooting. For example, the White supremacist who committed the

Charleston church shooting in 2015, murdering nine Black individuals during Bible study, said this,

I have no choice. I am not in the position to, alone, go into the ghetto and fight. I chose Charleston because it is [the] most historic city in my state, and at one time had the highest ratio of blacks to Whites in the country. We have no skinheads, no real KKK, no one doing anything but talking on the internet. Well, someone has to have the bravery to take it to the real world, and I guess that has to be me.

It is crucial that members of the public learn about these warning behaviors, and if they observe even one of them in someone they know, they should report it to the police or FBI. Powerful psychological research has identified these behaviors, and we could prevent many mass shootings if persons who display any one of the behaviors are reported. All you have to do is report. Law enforcement can take it from there.

EMOTIONAL DAMAGE TO SURVIVORS

Marsha Baldwridge is a dignified, older Black woman whose story as a survivor of gun violence is harrowing. A resident of Wisconsin, she had one child, a son. She lived in Madison and he lived in Milwaukee, a ninety-minute drive away. Her son, Sydney, was a wonderful, kind person. As Marsha says, "He could always make me laugh and gave the very best hugs." He was in his 30s and married when he started showing signs of psychological distress; Marsha was worried about him. He had a gun and it was taken from him on the grounds that he was a danger to himself. Then his wife left him, wanting a divorce. He became more despondent and Marsha worried constantly, but she was somewhat comforted by the fact that his gun had been taken away. A few weeks later, he died by suicide, using a gun that he had legally purchased just two days earlier.

Marsha was devastated. A solid churchgoer, she questioned her faith and God. Today, 15 years later, Marsha has made peace with her son's death; she has returned to church and has turned her agony into efforts to reduce gun violence. She joined Moms Demand Action for Gun Sense in America, an activist organization that I will discuss in chapter 9. Moms has a Survivors' Network and Marsha is a member.

While most of the research and policy debates focus on gun deaths—homicides and suicides—what is easily missed is all those survivors and their gut-wrenching experiences. Survivors include people like Marsha—family and friends of those who died by gun suicide; coworkers who survive a workplace shooting; children who survive a shooting in their school; children who are shot but not killed; victims of domestic violence who manage to get out before they are killed; and physicians in the emergency department who treat the victims. The list goes on, but the point is that for each gun death, there could be 10 or more additional individuals who are traumatized psychologically. When we calculate the toll of gun violence, those folks must be counted.

Here we will look at several categories of survivors: children following a shooting at their school; people exposed to incessant gun violence in their neighborhood; and medical personnel who treat those who have been shot.

The Effects on Schoolchildren
In the school shooting in Uvalde, Texas, 19 fourth graders and two teachers were shot and killed. The physical violence was horrific, but what about the psychological damage to the children who survived? Perhaps they were in one of the classrooms that became a battleground but managed to survive by pretending to be dead. Perhaps they were a second grader whose older sister was killed, or maybe they were the next-door neighbor of someone who was killed. How do these survivors fare psychologically? (For moving first-person accounts from child survivors, see John Woodrow Cox's book *Children Under Fire*.[26])

Scientists have used a variety of ingenious research designs to look at the effects on children. In one study, researchers studied the locales around 44 school shootings that occurred between 2006 and 2015. The outcome was a real-world one: youth antidepressant use. The research team collected data on prescriptions for antidepressants by providers close to the school (within 5 miles of the shooting), as well as by providers 10 to 15 miles away for a control group, both before and after the shooting.[27] The results indicated a 21 percent increase in youth antidepressant use in the two years following the shooting for those close to the school. From this it is clear that child survivors of school shootings experienced increased rates of depression.

Educational outcomes have been the focus in other studies. In one analysis using data from Chicago, a homicide in the neighborhood within a week before a standardized test reduced children's performance substantially.[28] Using data from Texas, researchers compared students at schools that had a shooting with students at matched control schools that had not had a shooting.[29] They found that school shootings increased absenteeism, which is never good for learning.

School shootings also reduced high school graduation rates, college enrollment, and earnings at ages 24–26. Talk about long-term impact!

Another study used data from the highly regarded National Longitudinal Study of Adolescent to Adult Health ("Ad Health"). Ad Health originally recruited a representative sample of more than 14,000 adolescents from across the nation in 1994–1995 to collect data. They contacted the adolescents again in 2001–2002 and then again in 2007–2008, when they were 24 to 32 years old. At each wave, participants were asked numerous questions including items about their symptoms of depression and about their exposure to gun or knife violence (the two are merged in this study). Professor Sara Jaffee, from the Psychology Department at the University of Pennsylvania, extracted the relevant data from this large dataset and designed a clever analysis in which she compared siblings who had or had not been exposed to gun or knife violence.[30] The design is clever because, by comparing siblings, she controlled for a multitude of other variables that might be alternative explanations, such as race and family socioeconomic status. Exposure to gun or knife violence included seeing a shooting or stabbing, someone pulling a knife or gun on them, or actually being shot or stabbed. Overall, a disturbing 32 percent of the sample had been exposed to gun or knife violence over the 15 years of the study, and this was a representative sample of American teens. Importantly, exposure predicted depression symptoms in early adulthood, and this was true regardless of race.

I could go on with other, similar studies, but the point is that we have solid scientific evidence that exposure to school shootings or other kinds of gun violence has serious psychological consequences for the children and adolescents who survive. The effects of school shootings are clearly not limited to a few weeks of mourning after the killings—they extend for years. And the effects are serious, including depression and failure to graduate from high school.

If we look not just at school shootings, but at mass shootings more broadly, they, too, have serious psychological consequences for both the children and the adults who survive. These include posttraumatic stress symptoms and depression.[31]

Another group to consider are children who are shot but survive. In one study, child/adolescent survivors experienced a 59 percent increase in psychiatric disorders and a 96 percent increase in substance use disorders compared with a control group.[32] They experienced a major trauma and it shows.

We also have to reckon with the consequences of some of the prevention strategies that have been implemented, such as active shooter drills in the schools. One impressive study collected data pre and post drills in 114 schools across 33 states.[33] The results indicated that anxiety and depression increased by 40 percent after the drills and that the effects lasted for at least 90 days. The drills upset children.

Do these drills actually save lives? Here things get complicated. There is a distinction between lockdown drills and active shooter drills. With a *lockdown drill*, staff lock up the school, including, especially, each classroom door, they turn out the lights, and everyone moves to a space that is out of sight. Kids and teachers practice how to do that. A lockdown might be necessary for any number of reasons, including an active shooter or a toxic fire at a chemical plant five blocks away. There is evidence that these drills actually save lives, according to a study published in the *Journal of School Violence*.[34] For example, with the Columbine school shooting, the attackers never succeeded in breaching a locked classroom door, but instead murdered in areas like the cafeteria, which could not be locked down.

Active shooter drills, in contrast, simulate—to a greater or lesser extent—a situation in which there is a mass shooter in the building and practice what to do in this situation. These drills are not standardized or regulated and some get much too intense, such as having an unannounced drill in which a masked man enters the building and pretends to threaten everyone with a gun. Of course, children are frightened by such drills, and there is no evidence that they are effective.

A reasonable conclusion, then, is that lockdown drills are backed by scientific evidence and are likely to save lives, while not frightening children very much.[35] Active shooter drills, however, are not backed by scientific evidence and are much more disturbing to many children and adolescents. In fact, active shooter drills are considered so distressing that the American Academy of Pediatrics has issued a policy statement cautioning against them, especially the high-intensity variety.[36] The American Federation of Teachers and the National Education Association do not recommend them, and the National Association of School Psychologists advises that drills should be used to train adults, not students.

If you are a parent, check on which kind of drill is used in your child's school. The Standard Response Protocol Extended, from the I Love U Guys Foundation, is a widely used lockdown drill and was the protocol in the schools in the evaluation studies described above. If the school is using an active shooter drill, try to talk them out of it and persuade them to use lockdown drills instead.

ᔐ

In 2021, US Surgeon General Vivek Murthy issued an advisory, *Protecting Youth Mental Health*, which documented the dramatic increases in mental health problems for youth in the United States and pointed to causes such as social media and media coverage of traumatic events. It offered numerous recommendations for addressing this mental health crisis, including providing greater access to mental health care. The advisory made good points, but it reminds me of the old saying about "closing the barn door after the horse has bolted." Greater access to mental health care after the problem—the mental health problem—has occurred is a good idea, but it would be much better if we could prevent the problems before they happen.

A few years later two psychiatrists contributed a provocative article titled "Addressing the Mental Health Crisis in Youth—Sick Individuals or Sick Societies?"[37] Much of the conversation about the mental health crisis has focused on individuals—what may have caused their problem and how to treat that individual. Surely we need that, but we must also consider whether our society has created an environment in which youth are likely to experience these crises, including depression, anxiety, and suicidal behavior. Yes, the media play an outsized role, but so too do school shootings and the easy availability of guns for an adolescent contemplating suicide. We will not get the epidemic of youth mental health problems under control until we put an end to the epidemic of gun violence.

Exposure to Neighborhood Gun Violence
School shootings are not the only situation in which children are exposed to gun violence. Some children live in low-income, urban neighborhoods characterized by the incessant drumbeat of gunfire. Much of this is what researchers call "indirect exposure" to community gun violence, which includes witnessing gunfire or hearing gunshots in public places (e.g., streets, parks), knowing a friend or relative who has been shot or who carries a gun, or being aware of gun violence in the community.[38]

Multiple studies have shown that exposure to community violence is linked to trauma symptoms and other symptoms of psychological distress.[39] Gun violence may have these effects in multiple ways: by reducing a child's sense of safety; by causing mental distress to parents, who then communicate it to their child; and by creating general instability in the neighborhood. Researchers believe that, compared with other forms of violence, violence that involves a firearm triggers a stronger stress response in the body and more severe psychological distress. Exposure to neighborhood gun violence has been linked not only to psychological symptoms, but also to physical symptoms such as high blood pressure. It's just not good for you.

The severity of the effects on the youth depends on many factors, including frequency of exposure, age of exposure, and how close the youth was to the event. For example, a study that used geospatial analysis of community gun violence in 20 large US cities found that the closer gun homicides were to adolescents' homes or schools, the worse their anxiety and depression symptoms.[40] This study is a good example of the power of combining psychological and public health approaches.

Medical Personnel

I have a friend whose husband is a physician in an emergency department. One evening at dinner, I asked him to tell me about some of the cases of individuals with gunshot wounds he had treated. He deftly changed the subject. He is a laidback, positive person, but he implicitly refused to think or talk about the cases of gun violence he had seen up close. It was too painful.

Medical personnel can find themselves on the front lines when a mass shooting or neighborhood gun violence occurs.[41] The psychological toll on them has been documented and may include posttraumatic stress disorder (PTSD). Not only must they treat bodies lacerated by bullets, but in many cases they watch victims die and then must deliver gut-wrenching news to family members.

As we tally up the psychological cost of gun violence, it is important to remember the effects on medical personnel and first responders.

THERE'S NOTHING AS PRACTICAL AS A GOOD THEORY

Famed social psychologist Kurt Lewin once said that there is nothing as practical as a good theory. We tend to think of theories as . . . theoretical, that is, not necessarily useful in the real world. So Lewin's assertion comes as a surprise to many. But decades of research have shown that Lewin hit the proverbial nail on the head. A good psychological theory helps us understand human behavior, predict future behavior, and design interventions to prevent problem behavior.

One of those good theories is social learning theory, proposed by Stanford psychology professor Albert Bandura[42] and building on B. F. Skinner's learning theory. Three principles are central to the theory. (1) Behavior that is positively reinforced will become more frequent in the future. "Positive reinforcement" refers to something pleasant or rewarding that follows the behavior. (2) Behavior that is punished will be less frequent in the future, although punishment is not nearly as consistent in its effects as positive reinforcement. (3) People tend to imitate or model the behavior of others, especially if the other is powerful or admirable, or the person strongly identifies with them.

In a classic experiment, Bandura and colleagues had children watch an adult behaving aggressively toward a Bobo doll, which is an inflated plastic doll that bounces back up if it has been knocked down and is about the size of the children in the study.[43] The adult struck the doll with a hand, kicked it, and yelled aggressive things at it. The children were then given time to play with the doll. Sure enough, the children behaved aggressively toward the doll, often engaging in the same behaviors they had observed from the adult (as seen in figure 2.2). Children in a control group who did not see the aggressive adult rarely behaved aggressively toward Bobo. This experiment and many others like it demonstrate the effects of observing aggressive behavior and then imitating it.

Social learning theory can explain many aspects of what is happening with guns and shooters in America. For now, let's chew off just one piece: the effects of media exposure and violent video games on potential shooters.

Many mass shooters have a history of playing violent video games extensively. The Columbine shooters are a prime example. From the standpoint of social learning theory, the player is repeatedly practicing the behavior of shooting someone (on the screen), and they receive positive reinforcement for killing successfully. They also observe characters in the game shooting others. That leads to more shooting during the game, and it's just a stone's throw from there to using a real gun on real human beings.

Research has repeatedly shown that youth who frequently play violent video games are more violent in later years. For example, in one study, a sample of high-risk second, fourth, and ninth graders were recruited in Flint, Michigan.[44] Flint has a high poverty rate and a high crime rate, so the kids were at risk. When the children first started the study, they were asked to name their three favorite video games and how often they played them. They were asked the same questions one year later and again a year after that. Ten years later they were asked questions that were the outcome measures: whether they had carried a gun, and whether they had shot a gun at someone or threatened to shoot at someone. The video games were coded for violence. The results showed that cumulative exposure to violent video games (cumulated over the first three years of data) significantly predicted carrying a gun and using a gun 10 years later. For the icing on the cake, the researchers obtained official arrest reports from the Michigan State Police. Exposure to violent video games in childhood predicted whether the person had ever been arrested for a weapons crime!

Figure 2.2. The Bobo doll experiment. The top row shows the adult behavior that children saw, and the other two rows show actual children in the study.
WIKIMEDIA COMMONS

Social learning theory explains why this occurs and it also provides ideas for solutions. Parents should carefully monitor their kids' video game use. There are plenty of games that are not violent. Saying "But my kid really wants to play that violent game" just won't cut it. Parents have a responsibility to keep their kids—and other people's kids—safe.

SOLUTIONS: USING A PUBLIC HEALTH APPROACH

Back in 2000, I had an extraordinary opportunity. I was invited to be one of the scientific advisors to then-Surgeon General David Satcher for a project to promote sexual health in America. The result was the *Surgeon General's Call to Action to Promote Sexual Health and Responsible Sexual Behavior* (2001). Dr. David Satcher is one of the most brilliant, charismatic, courageous people I have ever met. When I was in the room with him as he spoke it seemed like the words were coming straight from God.

Dr. Satcher is the person who first introduced me to the public health approach, and he is passionate about it. He told the story of John Snow, anesthetist to Queen Victoria and a founding member of the London Epidemiological Society (epidemiology and public health go hand in hand, and I will define both below).[45] It was 1854 and London had been experiencing cholera outbreaks for several years, killing thousands. Snow traced 500 cases of cholera and saw a striking pattern: all of the victims used a particular well for their drinking water, known as the Broad Street pump. Similar Londoners using a different well were not coming down with cholera. Snow had the insight that the water from the Broad Street pump was contaminated. He persuaded officials to remove the handle from the pump so that no one could use it. The cholera epidemic disappeared in days and legislation was passed mandating water filtration. A monumental breakthrough, Snow's work is a perfect example of the *public health approach*, which seeks to promote health and prevent disease in populations of people (in contrast to traditional medical approaches, which treat disease in individuals). It's also worth noting that Snow's scientific research led to a discovery that was followed by legislated regulations so that the whole population would benefit.

Public health is all about prevention. Ideally, we want *evidence-based public health*, that is, public health that is based in scientific evidence and its interventions evaluated scientifically.[46]

Epidemiology has been called the basic science underlying public health.[47] Epidemiologists study epidemics—when there is an outbreak of disease, they want to know where it occurs and what the people who become sick have in common, all with a goal of figuring out what is causing the epidemic. Usually, we think of epidemics involving infectious diseases like Covid, but we can extend the concept to the epidemic of gun deaths in the United States. Guns can cause death as surely as viruses do.

For many Americans, getting the epidemic of gun violence under control seems like an impossible task. I don't think it is, and here I give the example of an equally impossible epidemic that was tackled and solved: the epidemic of smoking and deaths from lung cancer in the United States.

In the 20th century, cigarette smoking rates rose dramatically from 1900 to 1964, and declined gradually thereafter.[48] Smoking causes cancer, which causes fatalities. Prevent smoking and you save lives. It's just that simple.

It's difficult to describe how pervasive smoking was in the mid-20th century for those who did not live through the era. I remember sitting in faculty meetings in the 1970s, in a small, packed room, with multiple colleagues smoking. I remember hating to have to inhale their smoke, but it's just the way it was. We nonsmokers had no rights, although it didn't occur to us to think of it that way. We had a Smoking Culture in America.

The history of America and tobacco goes back much farther than the mid-20th century, though. The tobacco plant was domesticated by the Indigenous peoples of the Americas before Columbus ever arrived on the scene.[49] Tobacco was an important crop in 1600s colonial Virginia. Growing and harvesting it required enormous amounts of labor, contributed by enslaved persons. Tobacco grew up hand in hand with the growing nation, just as guns did.

Fast-forward to 1953, when 47 percent of American adults smoked cigarettes, as did half of physicians.[50] How did such widespread tobacco use come about? The major force was systematic mass marketing campaigns by the tobacco companies encouraging smoking in various ways: smoking makes you seem cool and glamorous, smoking is masculine, smoking is pleasurable (see figure 2.3).

To give you more of a feel for these marketing campaigns, consider the following example. In the 1960s, a huge billboard in New York's Times Square featured an ad for Camel cigarettes, with the Camel Man blowing exceptionally perfect actual smoke rings into the sky.[51] It was eye-catching, to say the least. The Camel Man had already been there for a couple of decades. During World War II, he wore a military uniform. In 1989, faced with declining sales among middle-aged adults, manufacturer RJ Reynolds created a cartoon character, Joe Camel, to appeal to 14- to 24-year-olds, a market they wanted to cultivate. Joe took over the billboard. Scientists were quick to conduct research showing that recognition of Joe Camel was high among high school students and that Camel's share of this underage and illegal market had jumped from less than 1 percent to 33 percent since the beginning of the ad campaign.

In the 1950s, scientific research began to appear linking smoking to lung cancer. Manufacturers cleverly responded with filter-tip cigarettes and advertised them as reducing health risks, although the evidence indicated that smokers of the "healthy" versions still inhaled as much of the bad stuff (tar, nicotine, and gases) as those smoking traditional cigarettes.

By 1957 the scientific evidence linking smoking to lung cancer was strong, and the US Public Health Service issued a statement to that effect. What did the tobacco industry do at that point? They could have said, "Gosh, we're terribly sorry. We'll stop manufacturing cigarettes. We certainly don't want people to die of lung cancer. And don't worry about us. We'll find something else to manufacture." But that's not what they did. Instead, they hired a public relations firm to create a media campaign arguing that the scientific evidence was actually inconclusive, reassuring smokers that it was safe to continue smoking.

The tobacco industry also engaged in audacious lobbying. It formed the Tobacco Institute in 1958 to serve as the juggernaut for lobbying.[52] When tobacco regulations were introduced in Congress, they were regularly thwarted by the lobby. Those wanting to get smoking under control couldn't begin to compete with the hard-hitting financial resources of the tobacco industry.

Figure 2.3.   Advertising for Camel cigarettes in the 1950s, including endorsement by a doctor. Through the 1960s, America had a Smoking Culture and thousands were dying from it. We cleaned up that culture, and we can do the same with Gun Culture.

A watershed moment occurred in 1964, when the US Surgeon General issued a major report on the dangers of smoking, based on more than 7,000 published scientific articles. The report concluded that smoking was a cause of lung cancer in men and probably a cause in women (but women hadn't been studied as much). With dramatic media attention given to the report, public attitudes began to shift, as did patterns of smoking. As noted earlier, in 1953, 47 percent of adult Americans smoked. In 2011, less than 20 percent did. What an inspiring public health victory!

Many things happened after the 1964 Surgeon General's report that also contributed to the decline in smoking.[53] Beginning in 1966, regulations required manufacturers to put a label on cigarette packs stating that cigarette smoking "may be hazardous to your health." In 1967 the Federal Communications Commission (FCC) ruled that television stations must broadcast one antismoking ad for every cigarette ad, and cigarette ads were completely banned from TV beginning in 1971. Today, you still see antismoking ads on TV, often sponsored by the CDC. In movies made before the 1970s, heartthrob actors smoked profusely. Think of Humphrey Bogart in *Casablanca*. All of their smoking contributed to an aura that smoking was glamorous. Today, we don't see actors smoking in movies. The glamour has been erased.

A *nonsmokers' rights* movement also emerged, demanding smokefree environments in public places like restaurants, and the movement gained traction first at the local and state levels and later at the national level.[54] Today, smoking is not permitted in most public places, so nonsmokers are not forced to inhale secondhand smoke. Nonsmokers have some rights.

There are many more details to this story, but you get the point. A massive cultural shift was accomplished—albeit over several decades—and it has saved hundreds of thousands of lives. A combination of scientific research, public health approaches, and application of psychological principles was essential to moving the needle. The tobacco companies lied and poured millions of dollars into prosmoking campaigns, but in the end truth and health won. Between 1950 and 2000, America was transformed from a lung-destroying Smoking Culture to one in which smoking is marginalized and stigmatized.[55]

What lessons can be drawn from this success story and how can they be applied to the epidemic of gun deaths in America?

1. It is possible to change a deeply entrenched, unhealthy culture into a more sensible, healthy one. It can take decades, though, of scientific research, public health initiatives, and persistent activism to accomplish the goal. If

we succeeded with cigarettes and deaths from lung cancer, we can succeed with guns and deaths from them.

2. Corporate greed combined with a remarkable lack of business ethics can push a whole culture around to practices that kill people. The tobacco industry and the gun industry have a lot in common.

3. Imitation, a key principle in social learning theory, is an extremely powerful force and it acts not just on children but on adults as well. If you watch glamorous actors smoking, you're more likely to do it yourself, whether you're an adolescent or an adult. If you watch glamorous actors—and now, video game characters—shooting and killing, you're more likely to purchase a gun and use it. Just as the television and motion picture industries restrained themselves from showing routine smoking by actors, so too could the media rethink their whole approach to showing guns and shooting.

4. Cigarette sales did not have to be banned completely to achieve good results. Individuals were persuaded, in a variety of ways, not to start smoking, and they were helped to quit if they wanted to. Most folks came to understand the dangers of smoking and most gave up the habit. How can we create parallel circumstances with guns? For example, physicians and psychologists started clinics to help people quit smoking. Could we create clinics to help people give up guns? I'm serious.

There are two big differences between the smoking problem and the gun problem, though. First, smoking was not a partisan issue, with one political party advocating smoking and the other opposing it. Sadly, guns have become a partisan political hot potato, which makes it more difficult to accomplish the goal of saving lives. Second . . . the Second Amendment. It is not an impenetrable barrier to progress, though, as we'll see in chapter 8, "The Second Amendment Does Not Doom Us."

One of the factors that was crucial in stopping the smoking epidemic was scientific research—a lot of it. As noted earlier, the 1964 Surgeon General's report was based on 7,000 published scientific articles that linked smoking to cancer. We need a deluge of similar research on fatalities from the epidemic of gun violence. However, when Congress passed the appropriations bill in 1996, under pressure from the NRA it added the Dickey Amendment, forbidding the CDC from using funds to "advocate or promote gun control."[56] This was interpreted as a ban on funding firearm research. Similar restrictions were extended to other federal agencies such as the National Institutes of Health (NIH). The result—a drastic decline in firearm research, so that we don't have as large a base of evidence as we did about smoking. Moreover, during that period, young scientists were less likely to go into firearm research because there was no funding, so a whole generation of potential researchers was lost. The good news is that, in 2020, Congress again allocated funding to the CDC and NIH for research on gun-related deaths and injuries. The research area is showing every sign of rebounding, but during the ban we lost 20 or more years of what would have been highly informative research.

If we could turn around the Smoking Culture and save lives, we can turn around the Gun Culture and save lives.

CHAPTER THREE

A Gun Will Make You a Real Man

I WAS TALKING WITH A MIDDLE SCHOOLER AND I ASKED HER ABOUT THE KIND of lockdown drills they had at her school. She gave me great detail about how the drills were conducted and how the teachers received a lot of training in the procedures. She was proud of the teachers' training, and she was clearly describing well-conceived lockdown drills. Then she added an interesting observation, that a bunch of the kids didn't take the drills seriously, talking and making jokes during them. She was plainly exasperated with those kids because, to her, the drills were serious and important for safety. I couldn't help but ask whether those who weren't taking the drills seriously were mostly boys, mostly girls, or some of both. She replied that they were boys, in a way that implied that surely I should have known that. Why did I even have to ask?

She then asked me why anyone would joke about the drills. My immediate answer? Masculinity. These puny, 12-year-old, seventh grade boys felt the need to perform masculinity for their peers, to laugh in the face of danger.

Masculinity is at the heart of so many aspects of Gun Culture and gun deaths in the United States. More than 98 percent of mass shooters are boys or men.[1] That stark gender effect speaks volumes. Psychological research over several decades provides insights into the demands of masculinity and the way that masculinity and guns feed on each other. We will not solve the crisis of gun violence in America until we understand the role that masculinity plays in it.

TRADITIONAL MASCULINITY IDEOLOGY AND ITS DISCONTENTS

The male role changed dramatically over the last century in the United States and many other Western nations. In the late 1800s and early 1900s, institutions strictly controlled the roles of men and women.[2] Men worked in all-male industries, attended all-male colleges, drank at men-only saloons, and presided

35

in all-male boardroom. Men occupied one distinct sphere and women occupied another.[3]

With the *traditional male role*, a man held a job and was the breadwinner in the family. He had a gun for hunting and nothing else. He was strong and could lift the little woman, throw her over his shoulder, and carry her in case of calamity. Today those practices seem ridiculous and restrictive, and yet there was one advantage to them. Men knew exactly what they were supposed to do. There were no ambiguities, and that is comforting to many.

The traditional male role began to fall apart during the Great Depression of the 1930s.[4] Droves of men were unemployed and therefore unable to fulfill the male role of breadwinner. The male role gradually became less well defined and more uneasy.

With the *modern male role*, success on the job, climbing the corporate ladder, and earning boatloads of money are the defining features, but of course few can achieve that. The modern man should be emotionally sensitive with his romantic partner, but otherwise emotionally in control.

These shifting sands of expectations for men have left many feeling threatened and uncertain because of *gender-role strain*.[5] Add to that economic insecurities and the decline in manufacturing jobs, and you have a would-be army of men needing additional ways to shore up their masculinity. The gun manufacturers are happy to help with that, as they use a host of marketing strategies that appeal to men needing a boost to their sense of masculinity. In chapter 7, we will take up the Gun Lobby's use of psychology to sell their product.

Some aspects of the male role have stood the test of time: husband, father, and protector. The responsibility to protect one's wife and children is deeply rooted in the psyches of many men and, to many, that means owning a gun. As one man recalled from the time when he and his wife were expecting their first child, "You know, I've got a newborn child that is relying on me to not only protect him but to protect myself and his mother."[6] That man got a concealed carry license and began carrying a handgun everywhere.

Despite, or perhaps because of, the shifting definitions of the male role, some men adopt an extreme and dysfunctional version of it. *Toxic masculinity* is characterized by a strong drive to dominate others, devaluation of women, antigay attitudes, and violence.[7] Psychology researchers measure toxic masculinity with questionnaire items such as "In general, I will do anything to win," "I would be furious if someone thought I was gay," and "In general, I control the women in my life."[8] Boys and men who score high on toxic masculinity tend to lack empathy for others.

You can see how toxic masculinity contributes to gun violence, as well as domestic violence. Experts believe that we need both a social-psychological explanation and a cultural explanation for the link between masculinity and gun violence.[9] The social-psychological approach addresses why masculinity—and threats to masculinity—can lead to violence; the cultural approach seeks to explain what it is about American masculinity specifically that links it to guns, given that the link doesn't exist in other Western nations, where there is also plenty of masculinity.

What is the evidence for this theorizing? In a series of experiments, researchers have demonstrated that threats to men's sense of masculinity lead to a variety of aggressive political attitudes including more support for war, more antigay attitudes, and more dominance.[10] In one of the experiments, researchers brought both women and men to the lab. They took a test of masculinity-femininity and then were randomly given feedback that they scored in the "masculine" range or the "feminine" range, regardless of their actual score. After that, they completed questionnaires on their attitudes about war and about LGBT issues. For women, it made no difference whether they were told they scored masculine or feminine. Women just don't experience threats to their femininity the way men do to their masculinity. The men who had been told they scored in the feminine range—their masculinity had been threatened—showed more support for war and more antigay attitudes, compared with the men who had not been threatened. That's all it took—telling men they scored feminine on a questionnaire—to make them more enthusiastic about war and more antagonistic on LGBT issues.

In another series of experiments, men's masculinity was threatened in various ways—by telling them that they scored feminine on a questionnaire, or by leading them to believe that they were physically weak.[11] Compared with the control group, those whose masculinity had been threatened expressed more politically aggressive attitudes such as support for stand-your-ground gun laws, for war, and for the death penalty.

In an experiment most directly related to the topic of guns, the same paradigm of a threat to masculinity for men and to femininity for women was used.[12] Participants were then shown photos of two handguns, one bolt-action rifle, and one military-style assault rifle, and asked how much they wanted to own each gun. Compared with the control group, men in the masculinity threat condition expressed significantly more desire to own each of the weapons.

In yet another set of studies from a different lab, men's masculinity was threatened in the same way, but this time the outcomes were attitudes about sexual violence.[13] Men whose masculinity had been threatened reported a greater likelihood to sexually harass and greater acceptance of rape myths.

I could continue with more studies, but the pattern is clear. Men, on average, react to threats to their masculinity with aggressiveness—whether politically aggressive attitudes, desire to buy a gun, or support for sexual violence. Masculinity and threats to masculinity are a major piece of the puzzle of why more than 98 percent of mass shootings are committed by boys or men.

And about the pattern that threatening men's masculinity leads to aggressive outcomes, but threatening women's femininity seems not to affect them—psychologists have coined the terms *precarious manhood* and *fragile masculinity* to describe the phenomenon.[14] The two terms are pretty much synonymous. They derive from the consistent findings that women's femininity is not easily threatened, but it doesn't take much to threaten men's masculinity. Not for all men, but for quite a sizable proportion.

It's also worth noting that nostalgia for the traditional male role has emerged in some sectors. A prime example is Sen. Josh Hawley's (R, MO) book *Manhood: The Masculine Virtues America Needs* (2023). In it, he argues that all is not well with American men, many of whom have forsaken the traditional male role and masculine virtues, and this is bad for the nation. Who is responsible for this weakening of American manhood? The political left, according to Hawley, because they blame problems like domestic violence on toxic masculinity. Hawley's solution is a return to traditional masculinity and its virtues: responsibility, bravery, fidelity (marriage to a woman is assumed), and leadership. Bible study is essential, too. He urges men to adopt six male identities: Husband, Father, Warrior, Builder, Priest, and King. Right up there on his top six list is Warrior, and warriors need guns. I just checked the *New York Times* Bestseller list and Hawley's book is not on it. It looks like his retro movement is not catching on.

Understanding toxic masculinity and its antigay component helps to make sense of why LGBT folks have been the targets of mass shootings. For example, in 2016 a gunman entered the Pulse nightclub in Orlando, armed with two automatic weapons, and began firing, killing 49 people. In 2022, an LGBTQ nightclub in Colorado Springs was targeted by a mass shooter who killed 5 people and injured 25 others. One of the key components of toxic masculinity is antigay attitudes, and toxic masculinity can be so extreme that it turns a bad attitude into a murderous rampage.

Another manifestation of toxic masculinity is the *incel movement*, incel referring to heterosexual men who are involuntarily celibate.[15] They want to have sex with a woman but can't seem to find a partner. When you hear about their attitudes, you can see why. They blame their situation on women, whom they hate, as well as alpha men who monopolize all the good women. They congregate in the internet's "manosphere," where far-right extremists can recruit them. The 2014 Isla Vista killings, which occurred near UC Santa Barbara, are a prime example. The killer first stabbed to death three men and then went to a sorority house and shot three women. The shooter had posted a video on YouTube saying that the killings were his revenge. He wanted to punish women for rejecting him, as well as sexually active men, whom he envied. Toxic masculinity, hatred of women, and violent extremism all feed on each other.

To be fair, the Isla Vista case is probably a bit more complicated than just the incel movement.[16] The killer had a developmental disability as a child, was small for his age, and was extremely shy and withdrawn. He had no friends. His parents had conscientiously recruited therapists for him. But in the months before the shooting, everyone around him had missed some warning signs. That said, he still had a sense of entitlement to women and a resentment that none of them were interested in him, and that fueled the pattern of his killings.

It is important to recognize that, although 98 percent of mass shooters are boys or men, the great majority of men never engage in gun violence, despite all the cultural pressures of masculinity.[17] Those twin facts—the preponderance of male mass shooters and yet the fact that most men do not commit violent acts—present a puzzle for psychologists to solve. Much of the answer lies in socialization in childhood and adolescence. Some parents demand that their sons conform to masculine norms and excel at masculinity, whereas other parents have more flexible views and want their children to be healthy, happy, decent human beings, regardless of whether they are boys or girls. And, of course, it isn't just parents who wield influence, it's teachers and coaches and youth group leaders and peers, and the list goes on. Less demand for masculinity from all these sources will help to reduce the number of boys and men who use a gun to kill.

Masculinity and Emotions

Virginia Military Institute (VMI) is a state university supported by taxpayer dollars. It was founded in 1839 for men only and that policy continued for more than 150 years, but it began to be questioned in the 1990s. When the men-only policy was challenged in court, it went all the way to the Supreme Court. One expert testified in favor of keeping it all-male, saying VMI "was not suitable for most women, because, compared with men, women are more emotional, less aggressive, suffer more from fear of failure, and cannot withstand stress as well."[18] The Supreme Court was not persuaded by this and other arguments and ruled that VMI could not discriminate against women in admissions. The part that's relevant here, though, is the statement that women are more emotional. That is one of the classic gender stereotypes: women are emotional and men are about as emotional as a block of granite.

Beyond the broad stereotype about emotionality, there are gender stereotypes about specific emotions. In one study, Ashby Plant and I gave a list of 19 specific emotions to participants (college students and adults from the community) and asked them to rate how much men are expected to experience each emotion in our culture and how much women are expected to experience them.[19] If men were expected to experience an emotion significantly more than women, we categorized that emotion as "male," and if women were expected to experience an emotion significantly more than men, we categorized it as a "female" emotion. If there was no significant difference between ratings for males and females, the emotion was called gender neutral. The results of the study are shown in table 3.1.

As you can see, the list of "female" emotions is long—13 of them—which syncs with the stereotype that women are more emotional than men. Men are allowed only three emotions: anger, contempt, and pride. All of them are power and dominance emotions. The person expressing them is exerting power over others. The stereotype that anger is a male emotion is notable, because men are taught to channel their anger into aggressive behavior. Sympathy is strongly

Table 3.1 Americans' Gender Stereotypes of Emotions

"Female" Emotions	"Male" Emotions	Gender-Neutral Emotions
Awe	Anger	Amusement
Disgust	Contempt	Interest
Distress	Pride	Jealousy
Embarrassment		
Fear		
Guilt		
Happiness		
Love		
Sadness		
Shame		
Shyness		
Surprise		
Sympathy		

Source: Plant, Hyde et al. 2000; table created by Janet Hyde.

stereotyped as a female emotion, and it is sympathy and empathy for potential victims that restrain people from acting violently, but that is not supposed to be part of the male repertoire. Gender stereotypes of emotions, then, yield up a lethal cocktail for men of anger but no sympathy. We should not be surprised when that cocktail fuels violence.

Boys are socialized from a tender age not to express emotion, especially vulnerable and caring emotions.[20] One psychologist termed the result "normative male alexithymia," alexithymia being the inability to put emotions into words, that is, an inability to label one's emotions. Being glued to screens, where boys spend more time than girls do, has only exacerbated the situation. The pattern is so serious that a manual for psychologists has recently appeared, titled *Assessing and Treating Emotionally Inexpressive Men*.[21]

Americans hold gender stereotypes about many other qualities besides emotions, of course. Most relevant for a discussion of violence are the stereotypes that men should be physically strong and aggressive.[22] Women, in contrast, are supposed to be submissive and caring. With stereotypes like that, it is not surprising that almost all the mass shooters are boys and men. Shooting others, in a twisted way, fulfills the male role, whereas shooting another person is a major violation of the female role.

MALE SOCIALIZATION

How are these gender stereotypes etched on the hearts and minds of boys? The answer is gender-role socialization, a process that has been studied extensively by developmental psychologists.

Parents are the first agents of gender socialization of children, and parents plunge enthusiastically, if often unwittingly, into these efforts. The popularity of "gender reveal" parties before the little one is even born testifies to a cultural belief that the baby's gender will be its most important quality.

Developmental psychologists have found that parents engage in gender socialization in multiple ways.[23] Parents create a gendered world for their offspring through the toys they buy, the activities they choose for the child, and so on. It could be a football as a toy for a baby boy, although his tiny hands couldn't begin to grip it. A quick internet search just informed me that I could start my son in flag football at age 4 and tackle football at age 6. Boys are encouraged in physically aggressive activities from a young age. Tackle football, of course, carries a risk of concussion and other head and neck injuries. In fact, the American Academy of Pediatrics issued a policy statement about tackling in youth football, urging leagues to delay the age at which tackling is introduced, and encouraging the expansion of nontackling leagues.[24] "Toxic masculinity" is an apt term. Football is so masculine and yet can inflict serious physical injury on a boy or man.

In addition to creating gendered environments for their children, parents behave differently with sons and daughters. Today in the United States, the differences are usually pretty subtle, but they are still there. For example, fathers engage in more physical, rough play with sons than with daughters.[25] Boys learn how to be physically rough and to accept it as a normal part of the way the world works.

Some of the gender messages that parents convey are more intentional, such as saying "boys don't cry." I sympathize with the frustrated parent who can't take any more agonized tears. I've been there myself. But one could deal with it in a gender-neutral way. Telling a son that boys don't cry is setting him up to believe that men can't express emotions—except, of course, anger, contempt, and pride. It can lead him to the alexithymia described earlier.

Actions speak louder than words, and parents are constantly modeling the behaviors that are appropriate for men and for women. For example, in hunting culture, boys are socialized, usually by their fathers, to become hunters, with the father serving as role model and mentor.[26] Based on interviews with hunters, researchers concluded that children in hunting culture progress through four developmental stages. As a prehunter, they are taught stealth and sitting still and they carry an unloaded gun. In the neophyte stage, they are taught safety and beginning gun skills, they carry a loaded gun, and they participate in their first hunt. When they reach apprentice, they sharpen their skills and go on their first solo hunt. And finally, in the competent stage, they have solid expertise and can begin serving as a mentor to other hunters. Boys may participate as prehunters, sitting quietly beside their father and practicing self-control, as early as 6 or 8 years of age. Notice that safety training is embedded from an early stage, as part of hunting culture. That leads to a tantalizing idea: Could we make gun safety training part of national policy?

Socialization within the family is evident in various rituals, such as gift-giving at Christmas. An analysis of Christmas gift advertising from 1911 to 2012 in *Boys' Life* magazine, the official publication of the Boy Scouts of America, found numerous ads for firearms in the December issues (figure 3.1).[27] Remington and Winchester were the most frequent advertisers, and the .22 rifle—but never handguns—was featured as the appropriate gun for the American boy. Readers were told that the gun could help with varmint control, eliminating pesky squirrels that ate birds' eggs, and weasels that attacked the family's chickens. Self-defense was never part of the message. The ads portrayed fathers giving

Figure 3.1.   Rifles as Christmas presents for boys, 1902

firearms to sons, with mothers at most in a supporting role, perhaps because many mothers had doubts about the wisdom of giving a firearm to a child. All of these activities were intended to develop manliness in a boy. One Remington ad was explicit when it claimed "You'll give him a big lift toward manhood when you hand him this modern repeater." In these ads, the gun manufacturers are intentionally encouraging fathers and sons to purchase their product, all in the interests of cultivating masculinity.

Parents are not the only agents of socialization. Youth organizations can play a powerful role. The NRA has in fact actively collaborated with the Boy Scouts of America for decades. The NRA Foundation has provided training material and "equipment" to local councils, and NRA staff participate in national Jamborees. Many men had their first experience of holding and firing a gun as a Boy Scout.[28] You would think the NRA was using the Scouts as an agent of socialization into Gun Culture.

As children reach elementary school age, peers take on a major role in socialization, as do teachers and other adults, and the influence of peers increases with age. One large-scale study found that the single best predictor of whether an adolescent carried a weapon was the proportion of friends who carried weapons.[29] Socialization continues throughout adolescence and into adulthood, as people are molded by forces such as the media and peers.

The media is a powerful force socializing adolescents. Hundreds of studies have found that exposure to media violence is a risk factor for aggressive behavior.[30] The evidence is solid. The aggressive behavior in those studies might be getting into a fight with someone on school grounds. More extreme than that is criminal violence (e.g., homicide) and, again, exposure to TV violence has a significant effect on criminal violence.[31] If we look specifically at exposure to violent video games, multiple studies link it to increased aggressive behavior and decreased empathy.[32]

GOOD NEWS

When parents set limits on children's media use, it protects against aggressive behavior.

The good news—and I imagine that you could use some—is that when parents set limits on the amount and content of children's media use, it protects against aggressive behavior.[33] And it's free! You have to use some skill in implementing limits though. If you use a dictatorial parenting style and just order the kid not to watch, it can backfire and they want to watch more, not less. The seeds of rebellion are sown. Ideally what you want to do is have a set of rules and enforce them consistently (inconsistency wrecks everything), while being supportive to the child by explaining the reason for the rules and respecting the child's point of view.[34] The goal is to have the child understand the rules and internalize them, encouraging self-regulation. Eventually they have to learn to be good on their own, without you enforcing everything. If you face a bit of resistance, explain again. "We (your parents) have decided that you can't play this video game because there's violence in it. Our family doesn't believe in violence." Or, "We don't watch TV like this because it isn't good for kids." You can make up dozens of variations on these statements, depending on the age of the child.

In addition, if a child or adolescent does view a violent scene, you can use it as a teaching moment.[35] Ask: What are other ways of resolving that conflict besides shooting? Why is that scene unrealistic? Explain that guns are dangerous even if it doesn't look like it on TV.

GUNS AND IDENTITY

A favorite saying in the NRA is, "The only thing that stops a bad guy with a gun is a good guy with a gun." We could debate whether "guy" here is generic, referring to both men and women, but humor me, and let's assume that "guy" means a male human being. I think it's a pretty safe bet.

"Good guy with a gun" is presented as an identity. A gun-owning real man would like to think of himself as a good guy with a gun, and this is an identity that many American men have adopted.

This book is devoted to scientific approaches, so let's first examine whether the slogan is actually true, that good guys with guns are invariably the ones to stop bad guys with guns. The *New York Times* analyzed data from 433 active shooter attacks, as shown in figure 3.2.[36] In 184 (42 percent) of the incidents, the denouement occurred after the police arrived, that is, the police handled it, contradicting the view of some that the police don't protect us. In the other 249 cases, the event ended before the police arrived, but in only 22 cases (5 percent) did a bystander actually shoot the attacker. It was almost twice as likely (42 cases) for a bystander to successfully subdue an attacker by means other than a gun, such as tackling. In the remaining cases, the attacker died by suicide or fled the scene. Bottom line: in an active shooter situation, it is very rare for that person to be stopped by a good guy with a gun. As a marketing tool for the gun industry, it's a great slogan, but it isn't accurate.

And yet we have tens of thousands of American men who think of themselves as good guys with guns. It's part of their identity, an identity called *citizen*

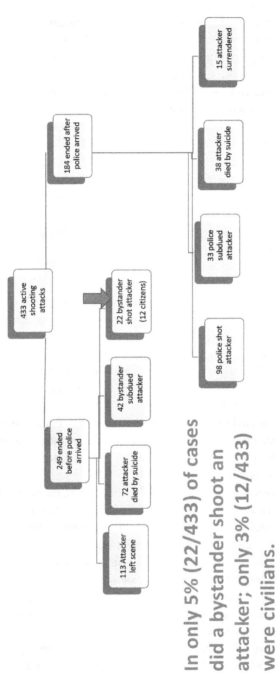

In only 5% (22/433) of cases did a bystander shoot an attacker; only 3% (12/433) were civilians.

Figure 3.2. Who actually stops a bad guy with a gun?

protectors.[37] This identity is particularly appealing to men in the postindustrial era in the United States, when so many manufacturing jobs have been moved overseas, making the traditional breadwinner role feel precarious to them. The NRA has sold this identity in multiple ways, as we'll see in chapter 7 on how the Gun Lobby uses psychology. Citizen protectors believe that carrying is a civic duty, a kind of moral imperative. The police are not capable of controlling crime, much less responding immediately to assaults, they say, and threats are everywhere. The only solution is to have tens of thousands of citizen protectors on hand, all carrying handguns daily, who can intervene immediately if a violent crime occurs. These gun owners' fantasies of violence justify the need to carry a gun and to use it.

But racial issues raise their ugly head. A White guy with a gun is a good guy with a gun. A Black guy with a gun is . . . a criminal.[38] The meaning of ownership and carrying a gun are very different depending on the color of your skin.

Guns are an essential component of masculine identity in a different sector of society: street gangs.[39] Gangs thrive in neighborhoods characterized by poverty, general social disorganization, and the easy availability of drugs and guns. Youth join gangs for a number of reasons.[40] For most, it is normative in their neighborhood so they join, just as the White suburban kid joins the football team because that's what the cool guys do. Youth also join for "protection," believing that they will be safer in a gang than outside it, despite the fact that gang members are actually much more likely to be victims of violent crime than comparable nonmembers. The protection theme surfaces yet again and, again, it is contradicted by the data. Gang membership is predominantly male.

When adolescents do not have strong family relationships or school success, they lack a positive identity, so they search for one.[41] A gang provides an identity—a social identity shared by all members. A gang also provides a sense of belonging and a set of norms for how to behave and think. Moreover, a gang provides a concrete "pathway to manhood," a way to establish your masculinity. Participation in violence—preferably extreme violence—is essential for proving yourself within the gang and gaining respect. Any challenge to a member's masculinity is interpreted as disrespect, and retaliation is an absolute requirement. Gang members typically live in neighborhoods that contain many threats to personal safety, and these threats motivate members to identify even more strongly with the gang.

Gangs socialize their members into norms about masculinity and gun violence.[42] They teach that the way to settle a dispute is with violence and that is also the way to defend one's identity. Some researchers have argued that violence establishes an adolescent's masculinity when other opportunities (e.g., becoming a breadwinner) are denied.

To earn respect and maintain identity within the gang, a member must engage in outward displays of masculinity such as gun violence.[43] Members carry guns not only for protection, but also to project a tough, masculine image. Today, it is standard for youth to post photos of themselves holding a gun on social media such as Twitter/X.[44] An AR-15-style rifle is especially impressive for photos.

The good news is that adolescent boys do not stay in the gang forever. Interviews with former gang members show that a process of "masculinity maturation" occurs for many.[45] These men believed in masculine values of respect, honor, and integrity. In adolescence, the gang seemed to uphold these values. But as the boys matured into men, the gang didn't seem to embody those values so much, and in the meantime, the men had become involved with family, work, and religion. That is, they had other identities, and the gang was not needed anymore. They grew out of it.

HONOR CULTURE

You may have seen news reports of women in faraway places being stoned to death for an offense—usually adultery. Such a case occurred in Sudan in 2022. The woman's name is Maryam and she was just 20 years old at the time. Men are not stoned to death for adultery, and it's not even clear that Maryam did commit adultery. The extreme human rights violation inherent in her court conviction and inhumane punishment makes us wonder. Why would such a sentence be handed down, by a court no less? The answer is honor culture, which is prevalent in many parts of the Middle East and North Africa.

A *culture of honor* refers to a set of cultural norms in a geographic region or an ethnic group that insists that an insult or threat to the reputation of a person—a threat to their honor—must be met with immediate, violent retribution.[46] Honor culture is highly gendered. It is men whose reputations can be threatened, and men who engage in the violent retributions. That is why an adulterous woman must be stoned, because her husband's honor and reputation have been sullied. Moreover, threats to an individual's honor may also be seen as threats to the family's honor. In this cultural mindset, a violent response is the honorable thing to do. It is morally correct.

In an honor culture, men must maintain a reputation for toughness and a capacity to respond aggressively to perceived threats, and they must protect their family.[47] These matters should be handled on the spot by the man himself, no police involvement needed. A real man is expected to be a one-man SWAT team.

As it turns out, honor cultures are not limited to faraway places. Many parts of the southern United States have a culture of honor. Among Whites, the homicide rate for male perpetrators is three times higher in the South than in New England. According to the theory of honor cultures, that is due to Southern White men seeking retribution for perceived insults to themselves or their family. Survey results show that, compared with men from New England and the Midwest, Southern men are twice as likely to approve of punching a drunk who bumps into him and his wife. Would you take that as an insult? Do you think it deserves an aggressive response?

Another analysis indicated that when homicides by White men are separated into argument-related murders versus other murders, Southern men have about the same rate of perpetration as men from other regions for nonargument situations, but they have more than twice the rate for argument-based murders. Arguments generate insults, and the response must be swift and violent.

Researchers in psychology have devised a way to measure an individual's commitment to masculine honor ideology using a questionnaire.[48] Respondents indicate the extent to which they agree or disagree with statements such as "A man has the right to act with physical aggression toward another man who slanders his family" and "A real man will never back down from a fight." In one study, men who scored high on this scale were four times more likely to report they had gotten in trouble for violent behavior and that they had been accused of domestic violence. White men who were born in the South had higher scores on the scale than White men born in the Midwest or Northeast. These findings support the idea of a culture of honor tied to masculinity in the South. Many experts say these same principles are prevalent for men from Western states, too.

Psychologists have argued that a culture of honor is a risk factor for intimate partner violence as well. A woman's infidelity or rejection of a man as a romantic partner threatens that man's honor, in the logic of honor culture, and that justifies aggression against her. For example, compared with men from the Northern United States and Canada, men from honor cultures (Southern United States as well as South America) perceive a woman's infidelity as more damaging to the husband's reputation and hold a more positive view of the husband who aggresses against her.

In the United States, a culture of honor is found not only among White Southerners. It is also found among Black men and boys, particularly in low-income urban neighborhoods. In a national sample, Black men scored higher than White men on the masculine honor ideology scale.[49]

In inner-city neighborhoods, there is a set of cultural norms termed *code of the street*.[50] In the face of a police and judicial system that fails them, Black youth in these neighborhoods believe they must be prepared to defend themselves and their families; projecting this aura of aggressive masculinity leads to respect. Disrespecting someone is a serious offense that justifies a violent response. You can see the parallels to honor culture.[51] Violations of honor are similar to disrespect and both merit violent responses. And you just can't count on the police. You have to settle it yourself, whether you're a White Southerner or a Black adolescent in the inner city.

During the Academy Awards in 2022, Will Smith leaped to the stage and slapped host Chris Rock after Rock said something that could be interpreted as an insult to Smith's wife, Jada Pinkett Smith. I'm not trying to excuse Will Smith's behavior, but you can see how it was a glaringly public expression of honor culture.

INTIMATE PARTNER VIOLENCE, GENDER, AND GUNS

Intimate partner violence (IPV) is a scourge not just in the United States, but around the world. IPV includes physical violence such as punching the partner, sexual violence, stalking, and psychological aggression such as coercively controlling or humiliating the partner.[52] A spouse, romantic partner, or ex-partner all count in the category of intimate partners.

In the United States, the Centers for Disease Control and Prevention (CDC) conducts the National Intimate Partner and Sexual Violence Survey annually, administering it to a representative sample of Americans. It is crucial to have this monitoring of such a serious public health issue. According to the most recent round of the survey, 41 percent of women and 26 percent of men have experienced IPV during their lifetime.[53] By far the most common pattern is for a man to commit violence against his female partner and most of the research has been on that pattern, so that will be the focus here.

But wait, you say. Fully 26 percent of men have experienced IPV and that's not so different from 41 percent for women. Men are about as likely to be victims as women are. In response, first, there's still a big gap between those percentages, making women 58 percent more likely to be victimized than men. But there's also some insider knowledge that you need in order to evaluate the data. In these surveys, something as mild as slapping a partner is counted as physical violence just as much as punching a partner and breaking her jaw. Certainly, I don't condone slapping your intimate partner, but it's just not as serious as punching and breaking bones. Women are more likely to slap, and men, aided and abetted by their greater size and strength, are more likely to punch and break bones. For example, 13 percent of women need medical care for their IPV injuries, compared with 4 percent for men.[54] It's a lot scarier for women.

Intimate partner violence can start early in life in the form of dating violence during high school. Among women, 27 percent were 17 or younger when they first experienced IPV.[55]

It's horrifying, but pregnant and postpartum women have a heightened risk of intimate partner homicide compared with other women.[56] The pregnancy adds strain to an already fragile and abusive relationship.

Being the victim of domestic violence can be devastating psychologically. Posttraumatic stress disorder (PTSD) is common among victims, who may experience difficulty concentrating and making decisions, trouble sleeping, chronic pain, feelings of helplessness, and even blindness from their injuries.[57]

Lisette Johnson, a survivor of domestic violence, said this.

I narrowly survived being shot by my husband. I survived his suicide. Our children survived as witnesses. I survived my trauma and navigating my children through their trauma and grief journeys. I survived burying the beliefs of who I trusted him to be as I faced the undeniable truths of who he was, a controlling man who believed he had the right to use the guns he kept for our "protection" to murder me.

I cannot say that survival is any more than a day-to-day proposition. There is no mastery over trauma and PTSD after violence, no arrival at the day when it is left squarely behind.

Even within my hopefulness and optimism, a darkness lies, and only a sound, an event, a stress, fatigue, open the door for it to emerge. I suspect anyone who has survived violence experiences the same; it's just not something we talk openly about. Perhaps in our minds to acknowledge it gives it too much space to expand; perhaps we want to pretend it isn't there and we can be who we were before. But I'm not the person I was before. She is gone, and the aftermath of gun violence, with its physical, emotional, and financial reminders, are what I am left to re-create her with. [58]

Among women whose children live with them, 11 percent report that their child has actually witnessed physical violence against them.[59] Psychologists talk about the *intergenerational transmission of violence.* It is passed down from one generation to the next just like a family heirloom, and it comes from children growing up in a violent household and then becoming perpetrators or victims in adulthood.[60] Because of their childhood experiences, they come to believe that violence is acceptable and even normal in families.

Researchers have found that one risk factor for men engaging in IPV is holding a traditional masculine gender-role ideology.[61] When the man experiences stresses or threats to his masculinity, he restores his masculine self by dominating and controlling a woman.

When guns appear in these domestic dramas, homicides happen. Among cases in the United States in which a woman is murdered, approximately 50 percent are perpetrated by an intimate partner, and the majority of those are committed with a firearm.[62]

Experts have found the following as key risk factors for a man to commit intimate partner homicide[63]:

- Having direct access to a gun
- Having committed nonfatal strangulation previously
- Having previously raped the victim
- Previously threatening with a weapon
- Engaging in controlling behaviors
- Previous threats to harm the victim

If you are a woman in a relationship with a man who displays one or more of these risk factors, get out now before you become a homicide statistic.

The important point for a discussion of gun violence is that access to a gun is a key factor in intimate partner homicide. The gun can turn a garden-variety batterer into a murderer.

A surprising finding is that the majority of mass shootings (59 percent) are linked to domestic violence.[64] Domestic violence–related shootings also have a higher fatality rate than shootings that are unrelated to domestic violence.

Amid all this violence, there is still good news. Firearm regulations at the state and federal levels can reduce intimate partner violence and intimate partner homicide.[65] In one analysis across the states, those that had the most restrictions on firearms (e.g., Massachusetts)

GOOD NEWS

State and federal firearm regulations can reduce intimate-partner homicide.

had half the rate of intimate partner homicides compared to those with the fewest restrictions (e.g., Alaska).[66]

Which regulations are most important in preventing intimate partner homicide? This is one of those cases where the devil is in the details, and if the regulations have any loopholes, the bad guys will leap right through them. Also, we want to follow the scientific evidence. The effectiveness of many of these restrictions has been evaluated, and we should put our energy behind legislating restrictions that are proven to be effective. The ones I list here have solid evidence backing them.

Domestic Violence Restraining Orders (DVRO)

When an abusive man has access to a firearm, the chance of him killing his female partner goes up by 400 percent.[67] Any man with a legally issued DVRO is a high-risk individual and he shouldn't be able to purchase a gun. State regulations vary in how broad the DVRO coverage is. Do they include just current and former spouses? Current and former cohabitants? Current and former dating partners? The broader the coverage, the more effective the regulations are in reducing intimate partner homicides.

Another detail in the regulations concerns whether a person with a newly issued DVRO who already has a gun must relinquish it to law enforcement. That seems like a no-brainer. He shouldn't have a gun. But sometimes this relinquishment provision is missing from legislation. It, too, has been shown to reduce intimate partner homicides.[68]

The other flaw in the system is that many women who suffer abuse do not seek a DVRO. It takes a lot of courage to do it and it's risky because the abuser may escalate his firearm threats.[69] In a situation like this, the abuser can legally purchase a gun because there is no DVRO on his record. Even in those cases, though, research shows that in almost all intimate partner homicides of women, the police had been in contact with the victim prior to her death, typically on multiple occasions.[70] She had sought help. This means police have the opportunity to assess risk and, with the right laws, remove guns from high-risk abusers.

In June 2024, the US Supreme Court handed down an important decision in a disturbing case, *United States v. Rahimi*. Back in 2019, Zackey Rahimi assaulted his girlfriend and threatened to shoot her if she told anyone, so she sought a restraining order.[71] Smart move on her part, and the judge granted the order, which prohibited him from possessing firearms. Rahimi—this guy is really something else—flagrantly defied the order, threatened another woman with a gun, and opened fire in public on five different occasions. Those incidents led to a search warrant for Rahimi's home, where law enforcement found multiple weapons, and he was charged with violating the federal law that bans possession of firearms by someone with a DVRO. Rahimi brazenly challenged his arrest in the courts, saying that his Second Amendment right to possess firearms was being violated. SCOTUS ruled against Rahimi, saying that removing guns from someone with a DVRO did not violate the Second Amendment. That's a win.

Violent Misdemeanor Conviction

A person convicted of a violent misdemeanor—any kind of violent misdemeanor—is statistically at risk for future firearm offenses.[72] Any individual in this category should not have a gun, so they should not be able to purchase a firearm and they should be required to relinquish one if they have it at the time of the conviction.

Criminal Background Checks

Essential to enforcing these restrictions on dangerous individuals are criminal background checks. These checks are mandated by federal law, as I explain in the chapter on the Second Amendment. Right now, the process is far from perfect because the national database of domestic violence restraining orders and violent misdemeanor convictions needs improvement. It's a good place to put government resources. The other loophole has been that only licensed sellers were required to conduct background checks, and it's easy to purchase firearms from unlicensed sellers at gun shows or on the internet. The background check doesn't occur in those circumstances, and a dangerous individual can purchase a gun. Federal legislation in 2022 attempted to close this loophole, as explained in chapter 8 on the Second Amendment. Many states have also passed stricter background check laws that mandate *universal background checks*—no exceptions, no loopholes. We can reduce intimate partner homicides with these regulations.

SOLUTIONS: THE POWER OF SOCIAL NORMS

Social psychologists have conducted extensive research on humans' tendency to conform to social norms. Now as Americans, we think of ourselves as rugged individualists, having the right to do whatever we please. That belief in individualism and independence may mislead us into thinking we aren't conformists, but social psychology has evidence to the contrary.

Think of the ice bucket challenge of 2014, which was a fundraiser for the ALS Association. You could challenge another person to pour a bucket of ice water over their head and, depending on whether they did, they made a smaller or larger donation. It was an unbelievable success as it spread to every corner of the nation and the world. Photos and videos were posted on Facebook. Donations to the ALS Association reached such a level that they didn't quite know what to do with all the money, never having had so much before.

From the point of view of social psychology, the ice bucket challenge was a new social norm that popped up overnight and led millions of Americans to conform to it.[73] Sometimes conformity to norms leads to positive outcomes such as all the money raised for ALS, but sometimes conformity leads to the worst in human behavior, such as the masses of previously ethical Germans who, in the 1930s, believed Hitler's propaganda, which blamed Jews for the collapse of Germany's economy. The solution: obey Hitler and exterminate them.

Researchers have identified two basic types of conformity: informational conformity and social-approval conformity. *Informational conformity* occurs in situations that are ambiguous, when we don't have all the necessary information. Suppose that you live in a neighborhood where there are a lot of college students. At 10 p.m., you hear a woman out on the street scream. What should you do? Rush out and save her from an attacker? Or think that it's just a group of college students messing around and go back to watching TV? You don't have enough information. One solution is to see how other people are reacting to the scream. If there are others in your house, how are they reacting? Are they about to rush outside to save the woman? Are they dialing 911? If others are running to save her, you are likely to join in. If others just smile and say "it's the students again," you are likely to think there is no problem and you do nothing. In both cases, you sought information from others about the ambiguous situation, and in the end, your behavior conformed to theirs.

Social-approval conformity is rooted in the strong need that most people have to be well liked by those around them. We seek social approval for our actions. For example, in some high schools it is common for a group of boys to insult another boy by using antigay epithets such as "Dude, you're a fag."[74] If you're a new kid in the school, you want to belong to that popular group of boys, so to gain their social approval, you start saying "Dude, you're a fag," even though you had never said or thought it before.

Those boys in street gangs who post photos of themselves holding a gun on social media—they are seeking social approval by conforming to the norms of their group.

How can we harness the power of social norms for good, to tackle the problem of gun violence in America? There are dozens of possibilities. I'll give just two examples here and leave it to you to be creative and think of others.

One of the problems we have with moving forward with lifesaving gun legislation is the polarization—indeed, animosity—between gun owners and nonowners. A substantial majority of gun owners support enhanced gun regulations such as universal criminal background checks, so they agree with non–gun owners on that point. However, many gun owners believe, erroneously, that people in their group (gun owners) despise those regulations. Seeking social approval, the gun owners downplay their own support for the regulations and harp on how different they are from those naive, fuzzy-minded non–gun owners. In short, they believe that universal background checks are controversial when in fact they are not.

In a clever series of studies, researchers recruited online samples of gun owners and nonowners to answer questionnaires.[75] In the first study, respondents were asked whether they supported universal background checks. Fully 91 percent of gun owners (and 93 percent of nonowners) expressed support. But gun owners estimated that only 64 percent of owners supported that policy. They underestimated support dramatically. In the second study, each participant was randomly assigned either to read corrective information about gun owners' support for universal background checks (experimental group), or to read neutral information (control group). Those in the experimental group read this.

On February 14, 2018, a gunman opened fire at Marjory Stoneman Douglas High School in Parkland, Florida, killing 17 students and staff members and injuring 17 others. Following the massacre, many Parkland student survivors and members of the public began lobbying for legislative action on gun violence. A majority of American gun owners support such actions. For instance, a recent national poll found that 85 percent of gun owners support requiring background checks on all gun sales, and 77 percent support a federal mandatory waiting period on all gun purchases.

Participants then rated their support for universal background checks and whether they would be willing to express that support publicly. Compared with the control group, those in the experimental group, who had read accurate information about gun owners' support for the policy, showed significantly greater support for universal background checks and were more willing to express those views publicly. The information given to the experimental group seemed to shift their understanding about the norms of gun owners, which in turn led them to be more supportive of background checks.

Wow! By giving folks accurate information about the norms of their group, we can increase their support for crucial gun policies! Next stop: Congress and every state legislature. Politicians need to learn accurate information about how much consensus there is around universal background checks and other gun policies. They are following the will of the people when they pass this commonsense gun legislation.

There are many other possibilities to use social norms for the good in reducing gun violence. Here is one more example. Safe storage of firearms is essential to reducing gun deaths. That means storage not only in the home, but also in the car or truck. Thefts from motor vehicles are a major source of stolen guns that then go on the black market and end up in the hands of criminals who can't pass background checks. The key is to create social norms about safe storage. Hunters by and large already have these norms. Other gun owners need them, and especially gun owners with children in the home.[76] Estimates are that about 40 percent of American children—that's 31 million—live in a household with a gun.[77] For safest storage, guns should be locked and unloaded, with ammunition stored separately. In these households with guns and children, 44 percent are storing that way. Kudos to them! Only 15 percent are storing the most dangerous way, unlocked and loaded (the rest are in between, e.g., locked but loaded). That could become a social norms campaign, perhaps with ads on social media or posters in doctors' offices. The ads could include both information (for safe storage, it's crucial to have a gun locked and unloaded) and a message that conveys social norms for safety, such as, "Only 15 percent of parents store their guns unlocked and loaded. Don't be one of them!" Or, "64 percent of parents store their guns safely locked. Do you?"

To tackle the masculinity boost of owning a gun, we could also use a social norms approach with a message such as "60 percent of real men in America do NOT own a firearm." According to a well-conducted survey by the Pew Research Center,[78] that's the number. Psychological research on social norms could be used in a multitude of ways to reduce gun ownership and gun violence.

CHAPTER FOUR

The Volatile Mix of Race, Racism, and Guns

ON MAY 14, 2022, AN 18-YEAR-OLD WHITE MAN—BOY, REALLY—ENTERED A supermarket in Buffalo, New York, that served mainly Black customers.[1] He carried an AR-15 rifle, modified to accommodate high-capacity magazines, and he had several with him. Wearing body armor and a military-style helmet, he began his assault, killing 10 people, all of them Black, and wounding three others. In the midst of the killing, a security guard shot at him to try to stop him but because of the body armor, the bullet did not penetrate, and the shooter instead murdered the security guard. The shooter had written a manifesto proclaiming that he supported White nationalism and believed in replacement theory, an unscientific right-wing idea that Whites in the United States are systematically being replaced by people of color and that the trend must be stopped. The shooter actually lived 200 miles away and drove to Buffalo, having investigated where he could find a high concentration of Black people to kill.

In the wake of the disaster, the State of New York banned sales of assault weapons to anyone under 21, as well as some kinds of body armor. They actually did something!

The killer survived his own rampage and was convicted of murder, domestic terrorism, and hate crimes. He is currently serving 11 consecutive life sentences.

This story is a tale of racism and White nationalism, but it is also a story about the easy availability of guns in America and how an 18-year-old with tons of hatred and only ounces of judgment can access guns to commit a mass shooting.

Black Americans are not the only ones to be targeted in White nationalist shootings. On August 3, 2019, a 21-year-old White man killed 23 people and wounded 23 others at a Walmart in El Paso, Texas. In this case, the attack was against Latinos, and the shooter, who used an AK-47, had posted a manifesto with White nationalist and antiimmigrant sentiments shortly before the shooting. In response, employees in one division of Walmart threatened to go on strike if Walmart continued to sell firearms. Walmart agreed to stop selling ammunition for handguns and assault rifles.

Social psychologists have conducted research on racial prejudice for decades, arguably beginning with Gordon Allport's book *The Nature of Prejudice*, published in 1954.[2] That research can give us insight into these lethal incidents of gun violence based on race. Before we look at contemporary research, though, let's consider a bit about the history of racism in America and the brutal link between racism and guns. To understand where we are today, we must understand how we got here.

BLACK AMERICANS AND GUNS

Before the Civil War, the economy of the Southern states depended on growing labor-intensive crops like rice and cotton, which in turn relied on the intensive labor of enslaved people, captured in Africa and shipped across the Atlantic.[3] These Black people had to be kept in line with White people's guns, and a large stock of firearms was especially important in case of slave rebellions, which happened with some regularity.

A famous—infamous, really—Supreme Court case leading up to the Civil War was the Dred Scott decision in *Dred Scott v. Sandford* (1857). Although the case is well known, what is less known is that the decision involved statements about race and guns.

Dred Scott was enslaved by a man named John Emerson. Emerson moved around quite a lot, taking Dred Scott with him. In the late 1830s, Emerson and Scott moved to Fort Snelling in the Minnesota Territory, which was a free territory. While there, Dred Scott married Harriet Robinson, who was also enslaved. In 1838, Emerson returned to Missouri, a slave state, with Dred and Harriet Scott. Emerson died, and the Scotts were inherited by John and Irene Sanford (their name is misspelled in the court case). Dred and Harriet Scott were fed up with their situation and, in the late 1840s, sued the Sanfords for their freedom in state court, based on the argument that because they had resided in a free territory (Minnesota) they should be free. Dred Scott lost the case in state court and pursued it to the US Supreme Court, which also denied his claim in a decision full of appalling content.

The decision, written by Chief Justice Roger Taney of Maryland, a supporter of slavery, held that Dred Scott must remain a slave and, to rub salt in the wound, that slaves could not constitutionally become American citizens. Ever. As if that weren't enough, Taney's decision also held that Congress did not have the authority to ban slavery in American territories such as Minnesota.[4]

Taney's decision, for the 7–2 majority, stated that persons of African descent "had no rights which the white man was bound to respect." Bolstering his argument, Taney pointed out that if Black people were recognized as having rights they would have a right "to keep and carry arms wherever they went." Well, that clinched it, from Taney's point of view. It was unthinkable that Black people could possess firearms.

Many experts believe that the Dred Scott decision actually contributed to igniting the Civil War.

After the Civil War, during Reconstruction, White Southerners were even more perturbed because of the new empowerment of the Black people around them, and again, the solution was to arm themselves.[5] The Southern economy was in ruins following the war, and Whites were feeling oppressed; White leaders capitalized on this resentment by blaming the misery on freed Blacks and White Northern carpetbaggers. The South was not safe anymore. Weapons and groups like the Ku Klux Klan were needed to keep (White) folks safe.

All that is in the past, you might say. Why is it relevant today? University of Wisconsin psychology professor Nick Buttrick conducted a remarkable study in which he found that the prevalence of slavery in counties in the South in the 1860 census predicts the prevalence of firearm ownership in those same counties today, more than 160 year later.[6] The greater the prevalence of slavery in 1860, the higher the rate of gun ownership now.

In many ways, the finding is astonishing. How is it possible to predict gun owners' behavior today from what occurred 160 years ago? The study was designed very cleverly. First, how do you measure firearm ownership in all the counties in the United States today, when there is no federal register of firearms? Buttrick used a proxy measure, the rate of suicides per county. It turns out that the number of suicides is very highly correlated with the number of firearms. That in itself is an extremely important finding, which we take up in chapter 6 on suicide. But the point here is that the researchers had a good measure of the rate of firearm ownership per county across 1,123 counties. For rates of enslavement, they used the 1860 census, which enumerated both enslaved and free Americans in the count. Southern counties included not only those in the states of the Confederacy, but also Kentucky, Maryland, and Delaware, where slavery was also widespread. The bottom line is that the more intense the enslavement in 1860, the more guns today.

Psychologically, how can we understand this pattern? Buttrick—whose Coping Model of Gun Ownership we saw in chapter 2 on guns and emotions— argues that, following the Civil War, because Southern society was massively destabilized, Whites felt threatened to their core by their loss of power. They launched a systematic campaign both to regain power and to feel less threatened, the Ku Klux Klan being the example par excellence. To protect the Southern way of life, (White) men needed to own guns. The "Southern way of life" was a thinly veiled way of saying White supremacy. Flashy and frequent displays of guns intimidated Black residents, as intended, and one's sense of security depended on private ownership of firearms—at least if you were White. Et voilà, Gun Culture was created.

How then did Gun Culture come to pervade the entire country when it started in the South? The answer is *social diffusion* of beliefs, through which those in the enslavement counties transmitted their ideas to others across the nation over the period of a century or more. In fact, in this same study, the researchers used a measure of social connectedness between individuals of different counties across the country today as assessed by people from those counties being friends on Facebook.[7] They found another astonishing result—for individuals in the North and West today, the higher their connectedness to people in counties with higher rates of enslavement in 1860, the higher the gun ownership in the counties in the North and West! Today, the tentacles of slavery still grasp at us. Americans fear for their safety and buy guns for "protection," in psychological patterns stemming from the period of slavery and the aftermath of the Civil War.

AMERICAN INDIANS AND GUNS

While all those Europeans—mostly English, French, and Dutch—were landing on the eastern shores of North America, often bringing kidnapped Africans with them, the Spanish were busy colonizing on the west coast and they were doing it in the 1500s, long before the *Mayflower* set sail. There were, of course, Indigenous people on that land that Spain wanted for its own. Yale historian Ned Blackhawk has chronicled this history, including the role of guns, in his book *The Rediscovery of America*.[8]

Originally, the Indigenous communities of the Americas did not have guns. Europeans did, and brought them to North America. Europeans also brought diseases, such as smallpox, that decimated many Native communities. With no prior exposure to these diseases, Native people had little immunity to them and died.

The French explorer Samuel de Champlain claimed vast expanses of land in the Northeast, around the St. Lawrence River, for France, coming in contact with the Iroquois. Champlain believed that it was essential to assert French imperial authority over the land and the people, and he did so using violence supported by guns. Before the arrival of Europeans, there had, of course, been intertribal warfare, but European guns escalated the violence dramatically.[9]

In the 1600s in the Northeast, the Dutch and the Mohawk formed a trading alliance—Dutch guns in return for Mohawk furs. Gun trading became a major force in the colonial period. The Mohawk were so energetic on their side of the supply chain that the result was a great depletion of animal populations in the region. The Dutch had developed more advanced gun technology than the other European nations, so the Mohawk had guns that were superior to those of other tribes using French-supplied guns. The fatalities of intertribal warfare escalated.

The Iroquois (a confederacy, of which the Mohawk were one nation), with their Dutch-supplied guns, were highly successful at raiding French settlements, to the point that the French monarch, Louis XIV, sent more troops, with a mission to destroy the Iroquois completely. It was a historical tipping point, the shift from seeing the Native peoples as trading partners or colonial subjects to seeing them as pests to be exterminated—with guns, of course. Extermination became an all-too-frequent theme in the centuries that followed.

Meanwhile, in California, Spanish soldiers and priests claimed land on behalf of cross and crown, founding missions up and down the coast, authorized and encouraged by a papal bull (edict) of 1493 from Pope Alexander VI, authorizing the Spanish to colonize and enslave the Native populations of the Americas.[10] Known as the Doctrine of Discovery, it was finally renounced by the Vatican in 2023.

In the 1500s, Father Junipero Serra, the leader of mission building, described a common occurrence in which Spanish soldiers would use their lassoes to capture Native women and rape them. When husbands and fathers tried to intervene, they were shot down with bullets.[11]

Just as gun violence was used to enforce slavery in the South, so too was gun violence used to control Indigenous peoples across North America. The pattern repeated itself over many decades, including the forcible "removal" of American Indians from their lands, which were coveted by Whites, with the removal enforced by soldiers wielding guns. Perhaps the best-known example is the Trail of Tears, during which from about 1830 to 1850 the "Five Civilized Tribes" (Cherokee, Chickasaw, Choctaw, Muscogee/Creek, and Seminole) were forced to leave their homelands in the Southeast and walk to Indian Territory, in what is now Oklahoma. Thousands died along the way.

As you might imagine, there was resistance to these measures. The Seminole of Florida, for example, refused to go where they were told, and in 1835 they ambushed a US army company marching from Tampa to Ocala, killing all but a few of the 110 soldiers.[12] Both sides had guns. Florida militias asked the War Department for 500 muskets and waged war, a war that lasted roughly 10 years because of determined resistance from the Seminole, who were joined by some Black people who had escaped their bondage. In the end, some of the Seminole were exiled from their land and others retreated to the Everglades, where the army was impotent. Eventually the US government gave up, having spent about $20 million on the war.

The role of Indigenous people in the creation of the US Constitution is important to recognize as well. According to Yale historian Ned Blackhawk, "it is impossible to understand the making of the US Constitution outside the context of Native history."[13] In fact, references to Native peoples can be found in the Constitution, which does not contain the words "slave" or "Black."

At the time of initial contact between Europeans and Indigenous peoples, the Iroquois Confederacy was particularly notable. Extending from what is now New York state through eastern Canada, it was a confederacy of five nations— Mohawk, Oneida, Onondaga, Cayuga, and Seneca—and featured a well-conceived political organization. Doubtless the colonists absorbed some of these ideas about government, which then found their way into the US Constitution. The Iroquois also had a matrilineal society in which women held control of farming rights and the appointment of political leaders. Somehow, the Founding Fathers did not absorb those concepts.

Following the Revolutionary War, tens of thousands of former colonists— now US citizens—craved land of their own and the riches that would come with it. They rushed west across the Appalachians to places like Kentucky, to seize land for themselves. The problem, of course, is that the land was already inhabited by Native persons, and violent conflicts resulted.

The new US Constitution had to deal with these issues. Article I enumerates the powers of Congress, one of which is to "regulate Commerce with foreign Nations, and among the several States, and with the Indian Tribes" (this is the so-called Commerce Clause). Here the American Indian nations are treated as government units that are roughly equivalent to foreign nations or states. The Constitution therefore recognized American Indian nations as sovereign nations, and also asserted the power of the federal government (not the states) to govern relationships with them. Diplomacy and treaty-making rested with the federal government.

All of that sounds good on paper, but as massive numbers of settlers rushed west, the federal government lacked ways to keep order and govern the new territories. Many of the settlers were lawless and generally had little respect for treaties between the federal government and Native nations; treaties were ignored. Kentucky settlers, for example, crossed the Ohio River to the north and, using guns, raided villages in southern Ohio and Indiana, intent on seizing treasure troves of silver possessed by Native peoples. In reality, the principles specified in Article I of the Constitution were trashed. The new Constitution provided little protection for Native Americans from the flood of White settlers and their guns.[14]

In his books *Regeneration Through Violence* (1973) and *Gunfighter Nation* (1992), award-winning historian Richard Slotkin makes the case that in America we have myths, just as the ancient Greeks and Romans did. These myths inspire us in ways that shape our thoughts and actions or, in the terms of social learning theory, these myths conjure up role models whom we are inclined to imitate. For Slotkin, the most influential and persistent of these American myths is the Myth of the Frontier. As early as the 1600s, Europeans, to establish colonies on the new frontier of America, waged gun war against the non-European "natives." Through the 1700s and into the 1800s, the "civilized" settlers fought against "savages," and guns were a crucial part of the history and the myth.[15] By the early 1900s, geographical frontier was in short supply, but movies and then television moved in to fill the void with Westerns that perpetuated the Myth of the Frontier and its hero, the gunfighter.

With the demoralizing end of the Vietnam War in the 1970s, Westerns and gunfighters hid in the shadows. The Myth of the Frontier was magically revived in the 1980s, though, during the campaigns and two-term presidency of Ronald Reagan, who had himself acted in Westerns.[16] The Myth of the Frontier and its hero, the gunfighter, live on today in the myth of the "good guy with a gun," who is invariably White.

What's the matter with the Myth of the Frontier, you say? It's who we were and are. The problem is that the frontier belonged to the Native peoples and was "won" by guns that killed so many that we don't know the number, and those guns continue to kill today.

༈

White nationalism in contemporary America is the miserable descendant of the nation's history of gun violence, slavery, the Ku Klux Klan, and the expropriation of Native American lands.[17] Don't get me wrong. My goal is not to criticize my country. I love it and can't think of another place I would rather live. But just as individuals must face up to their mistakes, their sins, if they are to become better human beings, so too must nations face up to their past sins if they are to become better and stronger. We will not solve the problem of gun violence until we do that.

WHITE NATIONALISM TODAY

Charlottesville, Virginia, is a lovely town, home to the University of Virginia and its buildings designed by Thomas Jefferson. Its peace was shattered in August 2017, when a White nationalist group, Unite the Right, staged a protest over the removal of a statue of Confederate General Robert E. Lee. They came carrying Confederate flags and Nazi flags (shown in figure 4.1). A Ku Klux Klan rally had been held in Charlottesville just a month before. And you thought the Civil War was long in the past!

Peaceful counterprotesters were there, too, exercising their First Amendment rights. Suddenly, a man drove his Dodge Challenger at high speed into

Figure 4.1. White nationalists in Charlottesville, Virginia, 2017.
WIKIMEDIA COMMONS

the crowd, killing counterprotester Heather Danielle Heyer and wounding 35 others. The 20-year-old man had previously expressed neo-Nazi and White supremacist beliefs and had driven from Ohio to attend the rally. He was convicted of first-degree murder and numerous federal hate crime charges and sentenced to life in prison.

Then-President Donald Trump initially issued a statement blaming both protesters and counterprotesters and said there were "very fine people on both sides." Only after a lengthy delay did he clarify that the neo-Nazis and White nationalists should be condemned.

In this incident, the weapon was not a gun, it was a car. But that's not the point, which is to shine a spotlight on the continued, violent existence of White nationalists in America.

The killer had a history. He had threatened his mother with violence on multiple occasions. His family had a history of violence, too. His father died in a car crash before he was born, and his mother's parents had both died in a murder-suicide. While in high school, he applied to join the US army, encouraged by a teacher who thought the military would expose him to different races and help him get over his White supremacist beliefs. The killer did enter the army but was released just a few months later due to failure to meet training standards. This is exactly the kind of person who is attracted to White nationalism or White supremacy (I use the two interchangeably because they rest on the same ideology). Some experts say we should call it White male supremacy because male supremacy is embedded so deeply in White supremacy.[18]

THE PSYCHOLOGY OF WHITE NATIONALISM

While social psychologists have devoted an immense amount of research to race bias, they have paid less attention to radicalism and extremism. Let's consider those first, White nationalism being a prime example, and we'll take up the issue of garden-variety race bias in a later section.

White nationalism has been defined as an ideology that Whites are inherently superior to people from all other racial groups and to preserve their White, European, Christian identities, they deserve their own homeland, preferential treatment, and special legal protections.[19] White nationalism is not unique to the United States; there's plenty of it in Europe, too.

White nationalism idealizes and romanticizes what it sees as the America of the past, which was dominated by Whites, and condemns current American culture and its devaluation of the status of Whites.[20] For a White nationalist, their identity as a White person is extremely important and a source of pride.

Social psychologists have documented how people who identify with a particular social group display *in-group favoritism*.[21] All of us tend to think "My group is best!" even if the distinction among groups is trivial. I recently moved into an apartment complex that has a Building A, Building B, and Building C, and I am in Building A for no particular reason except that I liked the apartment that was available there. My new friends in Building A quickly pointed out all the advantages to be had in Building A. And I have to say they're right. That's in-group favoritism. Put us together in a group defined by living in the same building, and we immediately think that our group and our place are better than the others. White nationalists take in-group favoritism to a dangerous extreme.

Social groups also protect their group from outside threats. I have yet to experience that in Building A, but all the folks in it are awfully benevolent and I can't discern any threats to us. Not so for White nationalists, who perceive a multitude of threats to their group and are willing to engage in all kinds of extreme behaviors, including gun violence, to protect their group.

Researchers believe that a number of forces have contributed to White nationalists feeling threatened, including changing demographics that make Whites a smaller majority in the United States: the Great Recession of 2008 and loss of jobs to technology, and the presence of people of color in positions previously held by Whites (for example, the first Black president, Barack Obama, or the first Black woman vice president, Kamala Harris).

One psychological technique that a person can use when they are feeling inadequate, perhaps having lost their job, is to identify with a successful person from their group and *bask in their reflected glory* (termed BIRGing).[22] How is a down-on-his-luck White guy whose White identity is important to him supposed to do that when the president is Black? If he's psychologically healthy, he will find some other successful White man for BIRGing, but if he's already feeling oppressed, the Black president gives him just one more notch on his resentment belt.

We engage in BIRGing not only to soothe our own self-esteem, but we also do it on a group level. White nationalists engage in *racial BIRGing*, extolling the virtues of Whites, past and present, convincing themselves of racial superiority. Stormfront is a prominent White nationalist organization. Go to their website, stormfront.org, if you want to see some of the language they use.

The other side to BIRGing is *CORFing, cutting off reflected failure*, that is, distancing oneself from failures of one's group, again to bolster self-esteem.[23] In 2023, the state of Florida, led by Governor Ron DeSantis, withdrew credentialing from an AP high school course on African American studies on the grounds that it taught critical race theory, in a move designed to manipulate the College Board to change the course to make it more palatable—to Whites, of course. It's unclear that the course actually covered critical race theory, but it did cover slavery, Reconstruction, and other topics that show White folks behaving badly. The push to cut off this material is a good example of cutting off reflected failure, CORFing.

White nationalist groups deal with documented moral failures of Whites by ignoring them, reframing them, or removing them from the history of their group as in the case of the Florida AP course.[24]

Another important psychological concept in understanding White nationalists is *aggrieved entitlement,* which is a set of beliefs and emotions in which the person perceives injustice against themselves and feels victimized, threatened, and morally outraged.[25] For example, Sam (a fictitious White man) might believe that White men are entitled to high-paying blue-collar jobs. When men of color are hired for these jobs, often at lower wages that benefit the employer, Sam feels a grave sense of injustice and believes he is a victim. He was entitled to that job. Mass shooters often have a sense of aggrieved entitlement, as do White nationalists. It can be difficult to mount an intervention to reduce folks' sense of aggrieved entitlement because it is so deeply rooted in feelings of injustice.

Individuals become White nationalists through a process of recruitment and radicalization.[26] People who are attracted to these groups tend to be socially isolated, feel a need to do something about a grievance, or are seeking a sense of belonging and importance. They are potential recruits, and White nationalism is there for them, often through the internet. Once affiliated with the group, they are progressively radicalized. White nationalism is but one example of far-right extremist groups that recruit new members through a combination of internet messaging and in-person gatherings at places such as mixed martial arts (MMA) events.[27] Newbies are radicalized into a set of ideologies that include violence.

Journalist Seyward Darby chronicled these processes in her book *Sisters in Hate: American Women on the Front Lines of White Nationalism* (2020).[28] When we think of White nationalists, we think of White men, but it turns out that plenty of White women are involved, too, and they were the subjects of Darby's investigation. One of the women she interviewed was Corinna, who lives in Tacoma, Washington. Corinna works as a professional embalmer. She hadn't finished college and spent a few years at home with her two daughters, but when she needed an income, she decided to pursue professional embalming, which does not require a college degree. As a person, she did not relate easily to others, and she was understandably traumatized when her younger brother, Harley, accidentally died in a boating accident at age 20.

Trying to understand her brother after his death, she did an internet search for "skinheads"—she thought maybe that's what he had been—and found herself on the website of Stormfront, the White nationalist group I mentioned earlier. As she read the posts, she thought some were awful, but others talked about White pride and heritage, which seemed reasonable to her. According to the website, Whites were maligned and misunderstood. It was so easy to join online. And she was searching for meaning in her life.

Soon she was posting comments such as "white people are generally more hard-working, honest, decent, dignified, and intelligent than nonwhites. . . . What is wrong with seeing our race as superior to that of the blacks? Don't we all?" She received lots of responses on Stormfront and they were highly affirming. In psychology, we would say that she received loads of positive reinforcement for her White supremacist comments.

When leaders met her in person, they saw her as a White woman with two White daughters—automatic credentials for advancing the White race. Soon she was the leader of a neo-Nazi group in Portland and got a tattoo of Hitler's face on her leg. She traveled to Arizona with other neo-Nazis to demand that the government halt the immigration of non-Whites. Later she became a broadcaster on far-right radio. And she, a person who had trouble connecting with others, *belonged*. In short, she was recruited by Stormfront, starting with its website and later in person, and over time, she was socialized by its members and became radicalized.

Pinpricks began to appear in her happy bubble, though. An anti-racist activist named Luke was shot while leaving a club in Portland. He survived but was paralyzed from the waist down. Suspicion immediately fell on White extremists. When the police interviewed Corinna, they wanted to know how she could associate with such bad people, and she didn't have a good answer. More important, she failed to tell them she knew who the shooter was, that she had actually given him the gun as a gift, and that, after the shooting, he had asked her to help him conceal the gun. The shooter was never identified by law enforcement.

Eventually Corinna became disillusioned with the extremism of the group and the violence, especially an attempted bombing at a Martin Luther King Jr. Day parade, and she took an astonishing step—she contacted the FBI! She became an informant within the White nationalist movement.

Corinna's story tells us a great deal about how—and who—White nationalists recruit and how they radicalize them. It is also a remarkable story of personal strength: the strength that Corinna mustered to get out of the movement, which is a dangerous undertaking, and refocus herself on doing good.

THE PSYCHOLOGY OF RACISM AND IMPLICIT BIAS

Racism is a form of *prejudice*, which refers to a negative attitude toward people from some identifiable group, such as Black people or LGBTQ people, based solely on their membership in that group.

Psychologists have defined *racism* as a system of advantage based on race that results from a combination of psychological factors (e.g., prejudiced thoughts and emotions) and social/structural factors (e.g., biased laws and policies, such as redlining so that Black people couldn't get mortgages to buy homes, which are necessary to build family wealth).[29]

Multiple psychological processes contribute to the flourishing of racism and, in turn, racism enhances these psychological processes. One of these processes involves categories and the human tendency to categorize things, whether it's cats versus dogs or Blacks versus Whites. According to developmental psychologists, humans learn, from early childhood, to categorize by race (and also by gender) because (a) there are differences in appearance between racial groups—kids can see the differences; (b) racial categorization appears in the environment in tangible ways, such as housing segregation; and (c) adults verbally label the categories, for example, "Black people."[30] Once children have learned the categories and the labels for them, they come to believe that the differences are essential or natural. (They also do this with gender.) Racial hierarchies therefore seem natural, too.

Kids also start to identify with their own racial category and favor it (in-group favoritism, discussed earlier) while expressing negativity toward other racial groups (out-group bias).

Segregation contributes to these psychological processes. Housing segregation means that Black folks and White folks live in different neighborhoods in most American cities. With neighborhood schools, that means that schools tend to be racially segregated. As a result, Black kids and White kids in many areas of the country have little contact with each other. It is much easier to stereotype when you don't know anyone from the group.

Social psychologists have an evidence-based antidote to racial prejudice, expressed in the *contact hypothesis*, which states that contact between people from different groups will reduce prejudice.[31] The more we segregate, the less contact we have with those of other races, and racism flourishes. The more that contact occurs—and I'm not talking about the White CEO exchanging a few words with the Black custodian, but equal-status contact—the more we reduce racism.

The media also contributes to racism, by both underrepresenting and misrepresenting people of color.[32] For example, American Indians are nearly invisible on television and other media, and in the rare instances when they are shown, they are usually portrayed in stereotyped ways, such as chiefs, warriors, or princesses.[33]

Experts make a distinction between old-fashioned racism and modern racism. Back in the 1950s and earlier, *old-fashioned racism* was prevalent and consisted of blatant, crude behaviors such as yelling racial slurs. Today, most of that is gone and has given way to *modern racism*, which refers to subtle forms of prejudice.[34] Psychologists measure these types of prejudice on questionnaires with items such as "If a black family with about the same income and education as I have moved in next door, I would mind it a great deal" (old-fashioned racism) and "Over the past few years, the government and news media have shown more respect to blacks than they deserve" (modern racism). Modern racism involves denial of continuing discrimination against Black people and resentment about perceived special favors given to them. Modern racism is prevalent in America, but you can still find old-fashioned racism in some sectors, such as among White nationalists.

Implicit Associations and Implicit Bias

With the trend toward more subtle forms of race bias, psychologists have devised clever ways to measure the subtlest of our prejudices, our implicit associations. These measures rely on our reaction times. We react quickly to the pairing of two words that are strongly associated in our minds, and more slowly to words that aren't as strongly associated.

The mostly widely used test to measure implicit, nonconscious associations is the IAT, which stands for Implicit Association Test. To take it, you sit at a computer screen as shown in figure 4.2. To measure the association between race (Black and White) and good traits versus bad ones, you first have a series of practice trials in which you place the index finger of your left hand on the E key of the keyboard and the index finger of your right hand on the I key. You are told to press the left key (E) if the face that flashes on the screen is Black, and the right key (I) if it is White. The instructions are to respond as fast as you can. After 8 or 10 of these practice trials, you proceed to the real task, which is more complicated and proceeds through several stages in various orders. I will give one as an example here. In stage 1, press the left key if you see a European American face or a word that is good (e.g., joyous) and the right key if you see an African

Figure 4.2.   The kinds of stimuli that are shown for a race Implicit Association Test.

American face or a word that is bad (e.g., evil). Again, you are given about 20 trials with these instructions and your reaction time is measured on each. In stage 2, the instructions change and you should press the left key if you see an African American face or a good word, and the right key if you see a European American face or a bad word. Again, there are about 20 trials and your reaction times are measured. Most of us react faster to the pairing of White/good and Black/bad, than we do to the pairing of White/bad and Black/good, indicating a preference for Whites, or a mental association between White and good, and Black and bad.

If you haven't ever taken the race IAT (there's also a gender IAT and many others), try it to see what it's like and test yourself. You can do it on the Project Implicit website at www.implicit.harvard.edu. Don't be upset with yourself if your score indicates that you have a moderate or strong preference for Whites, even though you think of yourself as unbiased. Each of us has experienced years of conditioning to pair White and good, and Black and bad. Every time you watch the news and they show a photo of a Black man arrested for a crime, you are being conditioned to associate Black with bad. But it's important to recognize these implicit associations.

Hundreds of scientific papers have been published showing that most individuals have implicit associations with race categories, with gender categories, and so on. One piece of good news is that, based on those taking the IAT on the

Project Implicit website, implicit race bias declined from 2007 to 2020.[35] We are making progress—sometimes uneven progress, but still progress—as a nation.

In work that is highly relevant to race and gun violence, researchers have used the IAT to discover whether there are implicit mental associations between race categories (Blacks and Whites) and weapons versus harmless objects. The studies show that many folks implicitly associate Black men and weapons.[36] Another study found that 63 percent of Americans associate Black women with handguns and White women with cell phones.[37]

These implicit biases are more than just mental quirks. They have real-life consequences, some of them deadly. In Kansas City, 16-year-old Ralph Yarl, who is Black, had been sent by his mother to pick up his two younger siblings.[38] Confusing the address, he knocked on the wrong door. It was opened by an 84-year-old White man who shot Ralph in the head. At trial, the shooter said that he was terrified by the stranger and acted in self-defense. In nothing short of a miracle, Ralph survived and has recovered for the most part, although the psychological wounds will stay with him for a long time. Why would the White man shoot immediately, without asking questions? The answer is because Ralph's skin is Black and the man doubtless held implicit associations between Black people and criminal violence. Objectively, Ralph posed no threat. In split-second decisions like this, our implicit associations bias our reactions in ways that can kill.

Police shootings of unarmed Black men are another arena in which implicit bias plays a tragic role. It is important to recognize that there are two types of errors that police can make in these situations; for example, with a traffic stop. They can mistakenly shoot a man who is unarmed; or they can hold fire, only to learn that the suspect has a gun, which he uses to shoot and kill the officer. Either error is costly, and accuracy in making the decision couldn't be more crucial.

Researchers in psychology have figured out a way to bring this one into the laboratory so it can be studied scientifically. They use a first-person shooter task (FPST), sometimes in a video game format and sometimes with images appearing on a computer screen and respondents pushing one button if their decision is to shoot and a different button if they decide not to shoot.[39] And the decision must be made in less than a second. The images are of either a Black man or a White man, holding either a handgun or an innocuous object such as a wallet or Coke can.

The FPST has been used to test both police officers and community members.[40] As it turns out, police officers—much though they have been criticized—are much more accurate than community members. That is, they make fewer errors than community members. The hours of training that police undergo seem to pay off.

Race bias occurs when the subject shoots at a Black man holding an innocuous object and that error rate is higher than the rate of shooting a White man holding an innocuous object. Community members display this race bias, but at least in one study, trained police officers do not.[41]

The extent of race bias in shooting is influenced by context and environmental factors. For example, when community members first read a simulated newspaper article about Black criminals, they show a sizable race bias on the FPST, but when they first read an article about White criminals, their race bias disappears.[42] These biases are not hardwired in the brain. They are a result of learning, and they can be unlearned.

In another study, researchers used the IAT to measure associations between weapons (vs. harmless objects) and Black versus White people, among respondents from 350 US metropolitan areas.[43] They also obtained objective measures of the extent of racial segregation versus integration in neighborhoods in those areas. Respondents from more segregated neighborhoods showed a strong association between Black people and weapons, whereas respondents from more integrated neighborhoods showed only a weak association. There are many reasons to favor racial integration of neighborhoods, but this is an unexpected one—integration reduces implicit bias when it comes to race and guns, and that could make the difference in the shooting of an unarmed man.

Following the January 6, 2021, insurrection at the US Capitol, Senator Ron Johnson (R, WI), who fled for safety with other members of Congress, later said that he never felt threatened as rioters broke into the Capitol because they were citizens who loved their country. What he didn't say is that almost everyone was a White man. Johnson went on to say, "Now had the tables been turned, . . . had the tables been turned and President Trump won the election and those were tens of thousands of Black Lives Matter and Antifa protesters, I might have been a little concerned."[44] In short, he would have felt threatened if the protesters were Black. White rioters were fine. His implicit bias was hanging out a bit too explicitly.

Breaking the Prejudice Habit

University of Wisconsin psychology professor Patricia ("Trish") Devine is one of the originators of the IAT. Once she and others found evidence of implicit race bias, she set her sights on trying to reduce it. She approaches prejudice as a bad habit, not something evil about a person.[45] In her view, the prejudice habit can be broken if a person has sufficient motivation and awareness and puts in the effort.

In the habit-breaking intervention, participants first take the race IAT.[46] Next, they receive information about implicit bias, how it is measured, and the consequences of implicit bias for racial minorities. They receive feedback on their own IAT scores. Then they go through a training session in which they are taught five strategies for reducing bias: stereotype replacement (identify a stereotyped thought or action and think about how to replace it with a non-stereotyped thought in the future, for example, that Black man walking toward me probably has a gun, replaced with that Black man walking toward me probably has a cell phone); counter-stereotypic imaging (imagine individuals who contradict the stereotype); individuating (think about members of the group as individuals who are not all alike); perspective taking (imagine yourself as a member of that group and how it would feel, for example, how it would feel to be a Black man walking down the street with others assuming you have a gun and are violent); and increasing opportunities for contact with members of the group. Participants complete measures assessing their racial attitudes and their concerns about discrimination against Black people. They are contacted again two weeks later, and in one study, two years later, to test whether the effects are lasting. In these studies, long-term changes did occur in individuals' knowledge and beliefs about race-related issues. In short, evidence-based interventions are available that reduce racial prejudice.[47]

GUN VIOLENCE IN CITIES

On July 2, 2023, folks were having a neighborhood block party in Baltimore, Maryland, celebrating the Fourth of July weekend. Suddenly gunfire rang out. In the melee that ensued, 30 people were shot, two of them killed and several others critically wounded.[48] Police analysis at the crime scene indicated that multiple guns had been used, and eventually five adolescent boys, aged 17 and 18, were arrested.

One of those who was murdered was 18-year-old Aaliyah Gonzalez, who had just graduated from high school.[49] Her mother, Krystal Gonzalez, said that with her daughter's death she was experiencing more pain than she had ever experienced in her life. This is the scourge of street gun violence—the lives lost and the pain experienced by the survivors.

Baltimore mayor Brandon Scott spoke of the need to address the "over-proliferation of illegal guns on our streets, and the ability for those who should

75

not have them to get their hands on them." And that is exactly the issue—the easy availability of guns.

On the same day, July 2, 2023, a mass shooting occurred in Philadelphia, leaving five people dead.[50] The shooter, apparently firing at random, wore body armor and used an assault rifle. On July 3, 2023, 11 people were shot in a parking lot in Fort Worth, Texas; three of them died. These are the patterns of gun violence in cities across the country, and these are just the mass shootings that make the headlines. They don't recognize the day-to-day shootings in many urban neighborhoods.

Racial disparities exist for different categories of gun violence. An analysis of 104 mass shootings in the United States found that Whites were overrepresented as shooters in mass shootings with a high number of victims, typically using legally owned assault rifles.[51]

The pattern for individual gun homicides is very different. Black boys and men between the ages of 15 and 24 have an astronomically high rate as victims of homicides, compared with other race, gender, and age groups.[52] The homicide rate for that group is three times that for Latine and Indigenous youth, and 10 times that for White and Asian American youth. For Black youth, the great majority of these homicides occur in urban areas, whereas the rates are more even between urban and nonurban settings among White youth. In short, inner-city gun violence—street shootings—take their greatest toll on Black boys and men between the ages of 15 and 24, followed by Latino boys and men in that same age group.

These street shooting homicides are tragic for the person who died, but they also have tragic consequences for the survivors, those who are part of the collateral damage—the relatives and friends of those who died, as well as everyone in that neighborhood. Black and Brown children living in urban areas have disproportionately high exposure to gun violence, and the psychological consequences can be severe.[53] The evidence consistently shows that exposure to firearm violence in the community is highly distressing to children in the immediate aftermath and can have lasting effects on mental health. The effects are particularly serious for those who experience poly-victimization, that is, exposure to multiple incidents of firearm violence. Black children are exposed to four times more neighborhood firearm violence than White children, and Latine children experience twice as much as White children.[54]

Direct exposure to firearm violence is a traumatic event that can be so serious that it overwhelms the child's stress-response system (the HPA axis, involving the hypothalamus, pituitary, and adrenal gland, and secretion of the

hormone cortisol). Exposure to later stressors can then have serious consequences for mental health. After direct exposure such as this, youth may develop
symptoms of PTSD, including upsetting dreams, strong emotional and physio-
logical responses to seemingly small cues that evoke the trauma, irritability, and
difficulty concentrating.[55]

We may wonder why Malik is having trouble with reading in his third-
grade class today. Perhaps it is because his cousin was shot six months ago, and
he could hear the sounds of gunfire in the neighborhood as he tried to fall asleep
last night. Even though he wants to, he simply can't concentrate.

To be sure, there are many factors that contribute to street shootings besides
the psychological ones I have described. Poverty, unemployment, and structural
racism contribute mightily. In these settings, Black youth cannot envision a
future for themselves and instead devote themselves to the thrills of the moment.
The White high school boy in the suburbs who aims to go to Yale and then
medical school isn't going to buy a gun to settle a score with another kid because
it would bring down the whole wonderful future that he envisions for himself.

The major problem, though, is the easy availability of guns. I was watching
a news story on a community violence intervention program in Baltimore and
the words of the middle-aged Black man who is in charge of the program still
stick with me. Having grown up in the very neighborhood where he now heads
the intervention, he said that back in the 1990s, if you had a beef with another
person, you met and punched each other a few times, and walked away, the issue
having been settled. The damage was at most a few bruises. Today, with the easy
availability of guns on the streets, the two guys meet, shoot each other, and at
least one dies.

I met Precious Jones at a meeting of Moms Demand Action. Precious lives
in St. Louis and is determined to reduce gun violence in her community. When
Precious and I talked, she said several things that really struck me and express
how urgent the problem of urban gun violence is.

- "We are tired of burying our kids." Parents shouldn't ever have to bury
  their children, but it is common in her community.
- "Any fifth grader in my community can tell, from a distance, what kind
  of gun a person is holding and what ammo it takes, but they can't tell
  you what 7×8 is, much less what an Ivy League school is." The kids are
  smart and they are learning, but they aren't given the right material to
  learn.

- "If a White cop kills a Black kid, protests happen and it makes national news. If a Black kid kills a Black kid, no one notices." Everyday community violence deserves outrage and attention.

SOLUTIONS: COMMUNITY VIOLENCE INTERVENTIONS

For a solution to problems covered in this chapter, I will focus on urban gun violence and a promising approach called *community violence intervention (CVI)*. The city of Baltimore is leading the way.

In 2007, Baltimore instituted Safe Streets Baltimore, a community violence intervention, in neighborhoods that had high rates of homicides and nonfatal shootings. In 2023, researchers from Johns Hopkins University evaluated the program and found that it was effective! That's good news! Specifically, over four years of implementation of the program, homicides were reduced by an average of 32 percent, and nonfatal shootings were reduced by 23 percent.[56] Lives were saved and bodies were kept whole and not maimed by gunshot wounds.

Safe Streets has therefore been scientifically evaluated and shown to be effective. It is an evidence-based intervention. In fact, the evidence is so strong that the CDC—the Centers for Disease Control and Prevention in Atlanta, the nation's public health agency—has designated Safe Streets as an "evidence-based practice." As we seek solutions to the problem of gun violence in America, we must put our energies into evidence-based solutions. Folks throw out plenty of ideas for solving the problem, but many don't work or haven't been evaluated. Safe Streets Baltimore is an evidence-based intervention. What goes into it? What's the magic sauce?

GOOD NEWS

Community violence interventions are effective at reducing the number of homicides and nonfatal gun shootings.

Safe Streets is based in a public health approach, and there is a lot of psychology in it, too. The program hires staff who have similar life experiences to those who are at high risk of committing violence, and perhaps even grew up in that neighborhood, which gives the staff credibility with their clients. These frontline staff are called "violence interrupters."

Violence interrupters get to know the high-risk youth in their neighborhood. They learn about simmering disputes and they mediate them, finding a solution that does not involve guns.

They also help high-risk youth learn to reframe their thought processes using techniques from cognitive behavioral therapy (CBT). Imagine the following scenario. Sixteen-year-old Dewayne is walking down the street in his neighborhood. He's carrying a handgun because everyone does. You have to. He sees 16-year-old Tyrell walking toward him on the opposite side of the street. He knows Tyrell a little bit, but not well. Dewayne thinks, "Tyrell sure has a mean expression on his face. He's gonna shoot me. I have to shoot him first." Dewayne shoots and kills Tyrell, who did not actually have a gun and had no intention of harming Dewayne.

In the program, Dewayne and other high-risk youth learn skills for risky situations so they don't end in gun violence. They learn to pause and count to 10 before doing anything in a situation like this where they feel threatened. That gives them time to think and question the assumptions they are making. Do I actually know that Tyrell has a gun? Do I actually know he means to shoot me?

Safe Streets partners with neighborhood nonprofits that provide additional services to participants in the program, including employment training, help finding jobs, mental health services, and drug abuse treatment. The approach is comprehensive and that's what is needed. This aspect of the program, especially the employment training, gives youth an alternative to a life of violence and gives them hope for the future.

Now you may say, this program reduced homicides by "only" 32 percent. Why can't we get a program that reduces homicides by 90 percent? The answer is the easy availability of guns. Until we solve that problem, which I will address in later chapters, we will have to be happy with a 32 percent reduction. And a life saved is a very good thing.

What about the 2023 mass shooting in Baltimore, described earlier? Where was Safe Streets? The City of Baltimore launched intense scrutiny of Safe Streets and the police department following the shooting. The police were faulted for not responding to multiple 911 calls made before the shooting. Safe Streets outreach staff had been at the event at 9 p.m. and had deescalated several fights, none of which involved firearms. Unfortunately, they were not there at 12:30 a.m. when the shooting broke out because their shift ended at 11 p.m. Following the investigation, Safe Streets modified its protocol for events such as the July 2 party so that staffers must share information about large community events (those holding the event in question had not obtained a permit from the city) and violence intervention resources can be increased. Safe Streets staff have to walk a fine line: they must bring in the police if things are getting out of hand

and violence may occur, but if they bring in the police too early or too often, they will lose credibility in the community.

Community violence interventions are not unique to Baltimore. Similar programs have been launched and found to be effective in Chicago, where it is called Cure Violence, and Philadelphia. The evidence of the effectiveness of these interventions is strong.[57]

A related approach is *hospital-based violence intervention programs* (HVIPs).[58] Here's how they work. An adolescent or young adult comes to a hospital emergency department with a nonfatal gunshot wound. That person is now a gun violence survivor, with long-term hits to their mental and physical health, as well as a statistically heightened risk of reinjury. They also might have retaliation on their mind. Hospital staff could just patch them up and send them back on the street again, but that does not lead to good long-term outcomes. The survivor would be going back to the same conditions that led to the gunshot wound in the first place. With HVIPs, the individual immediately receives crisis support while in the hospital, and then long-term follow-up for six months or more, including housing assistance, job training, and victims' services. HVIPs take advantage of a critical window of opportunity, while the person is in the hospital, to intervene so they do not become involved in gun violence again.

GOOD NEWS

The Department of Homeland Security provides funding for projects that tackle violence prevention in communities.

There's good news! The Department of Homeland Security, out of their Center for Prevention Programs and Partnerships (https://www.dhs.gov/CP3), provides funding for projects that tackle violence prevention. Could your city use some funding for community violence intervention?

CHAPTER FIVE

The Tortured Relationship Between Religion and Guns

I was listening to live reporting on a National Rifle Association (NRA) convention and heard not one, but two, speakers assert that owning guns was their "God-given right." I was surprised by the claim, to say the least. I have studied the Bible a fair amount, and I don't recall reading anywhere that God gives humans the right to guns. In this chapter the focus is on the psychology of the link between religion and guns, including the role of Christian nationalism, and what the Bible actually says about whether violence is justified. I also examine cases in which religious groups have been the targets of gun violence, such as the murders at the Tree of Life Synagogue in Pittsburgh, Pennsylvania.

But first, let's refresh ourselves on the Declaration of Independence and its list of God-given rights. They are life, liberty, and the pursuit of happiness. Hmmm . . . no mention of guns there.

THE PSYCHOLOGY OF RELIGION AND GUNS

Americans of different religious persuasions have different rates of gun ownership and attitudes about firearms, as shown in table 5.1. *Evangelical Protestants* (e.g., Southern Baptists, Assemblies of God, and many nondenominational churches) lead the pack with the highest rate of gun ownership. They also lead the pack with the lowest rate of support for—that is, most opposition to—passing stricter gun laws. To understand the link between religion and guns in America, we must understand the Evangelical Protestants, who make up 25 percent of the US population.[1]

Evangelical Protestants—and here I mean White Evangelicals, who are the largest group of American Evangelicals—are fundamentalists, meaning they

81

Table 5.1 Percentage of Americans Owning Guns and Favoring Stricter Gun Laws, as a Function of Religious Affiliation

Religious Affiliation	Self or someone in household owns gun (%)	Favors passing stricter gun laws (%)
Evangelical Protestant	57	37
Mainline Protestant	49	48
Black Protestant	30	76
Catholic	32	64
Other religions	45	46
None	37	61

Source: Merino 2018.

take the Bible literally and believe that it contains no errors. The Bible is God's word. Coupled with this is a commitment to the Bible as the most important source for how you should live your life.

Evangelicals tend to be strongly individualistic and oppose government "interference."[2] Because of this belief that individuals can and should take charge of their own lives and solve their own problems, Evangelicals tend to make personal rather than situational attributions for wrongdoing. That is, they blame a crime on the perpetrator and ignore the situational context, such as neighborhood poverty or the easy availability of guns. The emphasis on individualism and lack of trust in government implies that individuals should own guns and solve problems themselves, with firepower as needed.

Evangelicals hold to traditional gender roles, so traditional masculinity becomes a factor in their support for gun ownership.[3] Suspicious of science because of their belief that the Bible contains all truth, they are difficult to persuade about supporting gun restrictions based on scientific research showing that restrictions save lives. Evangelicals believe that social problems would be solved if everyone went to church and followed God's guidance in their lives.

It is also true that some leaders within the Evangelical community are calling for reform. In *Losing Our Religion: An Altar Call for Evangelical America*, former Southern Baptist minister Russell Moore[4] makes the case that Evangelical Christians have lost their authority, their identity, and their integrity. Moore held a major position in the Southern Baptist Convention. Then he refused to endorse Donald Trump for president and was reviled by the Southern Baptist leadership. At about the same time, reporters uncovered evidence of hundreds of people having been sexually abused in Southern Baptist churches, which the churches had covered up. Clearly Moore has good reason to call for reform. His main concerns are the fusion of Southern Baptists with Christian nationalism, the racism, and the radicalizing of members using conspiracy theories.

Award-winning journalist Tim Alberta reaches strikingly similar conclusions in his book *The Kingdom, the Power, and the Glory: American Evangelicals in an Age of Extremism.*[5] With a father who was an Evangelical minister who devoted his life to that cause, Alberta grew up inside evangelicalism. And yet when he returned to his Michigan hometown for his father's funeral, some members of the church accosted him for his critical portrayal of Donald Trump in a previous book—all while his father lay in a coffin within eyesight. One man who had been a family friend handed him a chilly note at the funeral, saying how disappointed he was in Alberta, whom he saw as part of an evil plot to undermine God's anointed leader of America, Donald Trump. It wasn't the same church he grew up in. Members had been radicalized to believe that America was God's kingdom, and that they, as Christians, should seize power over it. Any departure from those beliefs was evil. Alberta also tells the story of a talented Evangelical minister who was in trouble with his congregation because he was a Democrat and didn't like guns.

This mixture of evangelicalism, Christian nationalism, and guns is as volatile for the nation as it is volatile psychologically. One thoughtful Evangelical minister observed that Americans like to think of the rights in the Bill of Rights as "God-given," but there is a distinction between God-given and culturally given.[6] In other nations of the world, including predominantly Christian nations such as the UK, the right to keep and bear arms is not seen as a God-given right but as a culturally given right. The troubling fact is that in America, a substantial segment of the population—Christian Evangelicals—believe firmly that God gives them the right—indeed, the duty—to carry concealed firearms. That is not an easy belief to change, although in the Solutions section at the end of the chapter, I present some techniques developed to change such deeply rooted beliefs.

Evangelicals are distinct from *mainline Protestants*, such as Presbyterians, Episcopalians, Methodists, and Congregationalists. These groups tend to be more liberal on social issues, and more educated than Evangelicals.[7] In the Episcopal Church, for example, the bishops have formed a group called Bishops United Against Gun Violence, which calls for sensible gun restrictions to save lives.

American Catholics, who make up 21 percent of the US population, also follow a different path from the Evangelicals. After the mass shooting in Uvalde,

Texas, both the Pope and the US Catholic Bishops called for gun control measures to save lives.[8] Chicago's Cardinal Blase Cupich was quite clear when he stated "The Second Amendment, unlike the second commandment, did not come down from Sinai."[9] The Catholic bishops support universal background checks and a total ban on assault weapons. Both Evangelicals and Catholics are Christians, but they come to very different conclusions about God and guns.

Reform Jews also advocate for Congress to pass stricter gun laws, including universal background checks and a ban on assault weapons.[10] The Rabbinical Assembly of Conservative Judaism has a similar position.[11]

In one well-sampled survey, respondents were asked what they thought was the most important solution to mass shootings. Response options were "stricter gun control laws and enforcement," "better mental health screening and support," "stricter security measures for public gatherings," "allow more private citizens to carry guns for protection," and "put more emphasis on God and morality in schools and society." Which would you pick? For Evangelicals, the top choice was to put more emphasis on God and morality in schools and society. The top pick for mainline Protestants was better mental health screening and support. For all other groups (Black Protestants, Catholics, other religions, or no religion), the top solution was stricter gun control laws and enforcement.

Evangelical Protestants—a large group but still only 25 percent of Americans—have an outsized role in determining US gun policy and blocking stricter gun regulations. In fact, in October 2023, Mike Johnson, an Evangelical Southern Baptist, was elected Speaker of the US House of Representatives. In his acceptance speech, Johnson said "God is the one that raises up those in authority."[12] And to the 2023 mass shooting in Lewiston, Maine, Johnson responded "The end of the day, the problem is the human heart. It's not guns. It's not the weapons. At the end of the day, we have to protect the right of the citizens to protect themselves, and that's the Second Amendment."[13] It's a textbook Evangelical Christian response—blame the shootings on the perpetrator's heart, ignore the easy availability of weapons, and insist that Americans are rugged individualists who must have guns to protect themselves. It is worth noting that the Lewiston shooter was not stopped by a good guy with a gun. He escaped and later killed himself.

Christian Nationalism

Christian nationalism refers to a belief system that asserts that Christianity was central to the founding of the United States, and should continue to be, and fuses national identity with Christian identity.[14] Christian nationalists advocate for government policies that align with conservative Christianity, and they frame opposition to their views as evil. In 2016, 2020, and 2024, Donald Trump cannily said that he embraced their views and won their enthusiastic support. Christian nationalists seek to preserve and expand gun rights. Many, though not all, Evangelicals also adhere to Christian nationalism.

In the Christian nationalist belief system, an idealized vision of Christian society is seen as constantly under threat from groups like Muslims and immigrants (although immigrants from Latin America tend to be Catholic and therefore Christian, so much of the thinking is not especially logical). This bias toward seeing threats everywhere gives rise to conspiracy theories and beliefs that political liberals are evil.

All these perceived threats and conspiracies mean that you should own a gun to defend yourself.[15] Guns are needed to protect not only yourself and your family, but also your religion and your government, which is threatened by a liberal takeover.

Researchers measure Christian nationalism with items such as "The federal government should declare the United States a Christian nation" and "The success of the United States is part of God's plan." Christian nationalist beliefs are correlated with ownership of semiautomatic weapons, handguns, and guns owned for protection. Right-wing conspiracy thinking also correlates with gun ownership. Interestingly, Christian nationalism is not associated with ownership of hunting rifles. So Christian nationalism is associated with ownership of guns used for protection and for violence, but not those used for recreation or sport.

Christian nationalism is linked not only to gun ownership, but also to attitudes about guns and gun policy. To give you a flavor of how deeply engrained these beliefs are, here are the words of Wayne LaPierre, then executive vice president of the NRA, following the mass shooting at Marjory Stoneman Douglas High School in Parkland, Florida, in 2018: "[The right to keep and bear arms] is not bestowed by man, but granted by God to all Americans as our American birthright."[16]

There's the answer to the question I posed at the beginning of the chapter, about where the God-given right to own guns comes from. It's not in the Bible; it's simply an assertion of the NRA and Christian nationalists.

Analysis of back issues of *The American Rifleman*, the NRA's official magazine, shows that the term "God-given" appeared only once or twice a year in the 1970s, 1980s, and 1990s.[17] A surge in use occurred beginning in 2008, when it appeared nearly 20 times a year. Essentially the NRA began to use religious language to transform the Second Amendment into a matter of absolute,

God-given rights, not just a part of the Constitution. It also incorporated Christian nationalist rhetoric to turn defense of the Second Amendment into a religious obligation. There lies the crux of the tortured relationship between religion and guns, as captured in the title of this chapter.

With this kind of rhetoric in the winds, it is not surprising that people with the highest scores on the Christian nationalism scale show the least support for the federal government enacting stricter gun laws.[18] "Least support" doesn't really do justice to their feelings. They are strongly opposed to stricter gun laws.

Results from a nationally representative survey show that, compared with other Americans, Christian nationalists prioritize gun rights, religious freedom, and states' rights, but they don't care so much about freedom of speech, freedom of the press, and the right to a speedy and fair trial.[19] In short, they are not dedicated to the entire Bill of Rights, much less the whole Constitution, only the parts that protect Christian nationalists' interests, particularly their interest in guns.

Gun Identity

The psychological concept of "identity" generates even more understanding of Evangelical Protestants and their ties to guns. Each of us has multiple social identities. What are yours? Democrat? Republican? Church member? Small business owner? Teacher? A social identity reflects a person's self-understanding as well as their psychological investment in belonging to a particular social group.[20]

In a national survey, the Pew Research Center asked those who were gun owners "How important is being a gun owner to your overall *identity*?" rated on a scale from "not at all important" to "very important."[21] Among gun owners, 42 percent said that gun ownership was somewhat important or very important to their overall identity, and Evangelical Christians scored higher on gun identity than people from all other religious categories. With social identities, we are prone to in-group favoritism and out-group disparagement, so a person with a strong gun identity is likely to have warm, fuzzy feelings about other gun owners, and unfavorable, prickly feelings about nonowners, which contributes to polarization between gun-owning and gun-free groups.

Belief in Supernatural Evil

Some people believe in supernatural evil, such as the devil or Satan, and others don't or believe only weakly. The concept of supernatural evil is found in most of the world's religions.

Research with national samples shows that strong beliefs in supernatural evil are associated with higher levels of anxiety and paranoia.[22] If you believe that the devil is out there to get you, of course you would feel more anxious and paranoid. Satan makes the world a more threatening place.

These ideas quickly attach themselves to guns. Following the mass shooting at Columbine High School, narratives appeared implying that the shooters had been captured by evil forces, in language eerily reminiscent of the Salem witch trials.[23] One Christian Columbine student who survived said, "You could feel evil in the room. You could just feel the kind of battle going on." A student who was shot but survived observed, "We are not fighting against humans, we are fighting against forces and authorities, against rules of darkness and spiritual powers in the heavens above. . . . When I look back at the events that took place that day, I see Columbine at the mercy of a spiritual war."[24] One politician opined that the shooters didn't need a mental-health counselor, they needed an exorcist. The Christian students who died were portrayed as martyrs and were embraced by Evangelical teens.

The NRA got behind all these interpretations. An analysis of issues of *The American Rifleman* showed that references to evil forces accelerated following the terrorist attacks of September 11, 2001, and accelerated out of the ballpark following the Columbine shootings.[25] The NRA promoted the idea that demons are in our midst and they can't be stopped by the rule of law, so the only solution is to arm yourself.

Consistent with this sales pitch, research shows that the stronger individuals' beliefs in supernatural evil, the more they oppose a ban on semiautomatic weapons and high-capacity magazines.[26] And White Evangelicals have a stronger belief in evil than any other religious group in the United States.[27]

The Bottom Line

As you can see, Evangelical Christians and Christian nationalists pose an obstacle to enacting simple, lifesaving gun restrictions, especially because these groups are very powerful politically. Are there solutions? An appeal to rationality and to scientific data showing that the states with the strictest gun laws have the lowest rate of gun deaths is unlikely to convince this crowd. What we need are culturally sensitive messages that speak the language of Christian nationalism. I don't have a perfect answer, but I think it lies in making arguments based on the Bible. With that in mind, let's look at what the Bible has to say about weapons and violence.

VIOLENCE IN THE BIBLE: THE HEBREW SCRIPTURES (OLD TESTAMENT)

As I have throughout the book, here I use an approach to the Bible based on the best available scholarship. Today, the top biblical scholars use the *historical-critical method* to understand the text of the Bible. That method rests on the belief that the ancient texts of the Bible mean what their authors originally intended in the context of their culture, and not what a 21st-century reader might intuitively think of the texts as they have been translated into English.

There is plenty of violence in the Bible. What does God have to say about it? Professor Michael W. Austin has analyzed the biblical passages related to the use of violence in his important book, *God and Guns in America*.[28] According to Austin's analysis, God repeatedly warns against trusting in violence. People should instead trust in God. These are a few examples.

- God does not allow the mighty King David to build the temple, saying "You shall not build a house for my name, for you are a warrior and have shed blood." (I Chronicles 28:3). Instead, David's son Solomon—a man of peace and wisdom—is chosen by God to build the temple.

- In Psalm 44, "For not in my bow do I trust, nor can my sword save me. But you (God) have saved us from our foes."

- In Proverbs 3:31, "Do not envy the violent and do not choose any of their ways." And Proverbs 24:1–2, "Do not envy the wicked, nor desire to be with them; for their minds devise violence, and their lips talk of mischief."

- As King Hezekiah is frantically building fortifications around Jerusalem to protect it against an attack by foreign invaders, the Prophet Isaiah chides the King for not trusting in God (Isaiah 22:8–11). God will take care of punishing the marauding Assyrians.[29] King Hezekiah should have more faith.

Overall, then, the Hebrew Scriptures record many episodes of violence, while also recording God's disapproval of it.

VIOLENCE IN THE BIBLE: THE NEW TESTAMENT

Trijicon is a company that manufactures sighting devices for firearms, supplying them to the US military and civilians. In 2010, ABC News reported that Trijicon was engraving references to Bible verses on its sights: 2COR4:6 and

JN8:12. The first refers to Second Corinthians, "For it is the God who said, 'Let light shine out of darkness,' who has shone in our hearts to give the light of the knowledge of the glory of God in the face of Jesus Christ." The second refers to the Gospel according to John, "Again Jesus spoke to them, saying, 'I am the light of the world. Whoever follows me will never walk in darkness but will have the light of life.'" When ABC reported on these practices, many in the religious community were outraged at the pairing of the Bible with gun parts. According to Austin,[30] there is no legitimate interpretation of these New Testament passages that makes them appropriate for guns. Moreover, the verses imply that God is on the side of the American military, a principle that reflects Christian nationalism but not Christianity.

In the midst of the controversy, Trijicon stopped inscribing its sights and even offered kits to remove the inscriptions. Good for them. The point, though, is that individuals and businesses have often manipulated passages from the Bible to suit their own purposes.

The essential question for the New Testament is, what did Jesus teach about violence and weapons? For the crucial passages, it is astonishing how different the interpretations are from gun-rights activists compared with biblical scholars.

First, let's look at what the gun-rights folks have to say. If you go to the website of the Gun Owners of America, for example, you will find a fact sheet titled "The Bible, Guns, and the Second Amendment."[31] It looks at a critical passage in Luke, when Jesus, nearing his crucifixion, says to his disciples, "But now, the one who has a purse must take it, and likewise a bag. And the one who has no sword must sell his cloak and buy one" (Luke 22:36). The Gun Owners of America (GOA) emphasize that Jesus "told his disciples to acquire swords, which were the ultimate fighting weapon of the day."

What the GOA neglects to mention is that a mere two verses later the disciples say "Lord, look, here are two swords." He replies, "It is enough." He didn't encourage the purchase of 100 swords or even 12. Two was enough. Show some restraint.

The GOA website goes on to a passage many verses later, when Judas, betraying Jesus, leads the high priests to him. The GOA switches to Matthew's telling of the story. "Suddenly, one of those with Jesus put his hand on his sword, drew it, and struck the slave of the high priest, cutting off his ear. Then Jesus said to him, 'Put your sword back into its place; for all who take the sword will perish by the sword.'" (Matthew 26:51–52; also John 18:11; Mark doesn't record any of this). The GOA author makes much of the fact that Jesus said to put the sword away, not get rid of it. There are at least two problems with this argument. First, it rests on an inference from what Jesus did not say, and how do we know he didn't say it? Those who wrote the Gospels probably didn't get every single word down, and they wrote years after his death. Second, in Luke, Jesus doesn't say to put away the sword, but instead says "No more of this!" No more violence. The GOA somehow misses this command.

Biblical scholar Michael W. Austin writes that there are three primary ways to interpret all this swordplay.[32] One is that these words of Jesus authorize the use of weapons for self-defense, the argument made by the GOA. The second is that Jesus was speaking symbolically or metaphorically, to warn his disciples about the persecution that was to come. They will soon face hostility themselves. Austin notes that Jesus is not authorizing them to respond to hostility with a sword because Jesus rebukes the disciple who cut off the ear of the high priest, "No more of this."

The third interpretation of the passage is that Jesus is marking the fulfillment of a prophecy in Isaiah (53:12), "and he was counted among the lawless." Arming the disciples with swords makes them transgressors of the law, fulfilling the prophecy. And two swords are enough to fulfill the prophecy. This third interpretation is the one favored by biblical scholars. Austin concludes that the first interpretation, that Jesus believes that the disciples (and Americans) should buy weapons to commit violence against others or for self-defense, is without merit.

I have devoted so much space to dissecting this passage because it is the one that the gun rights folks and Christian nationalists like to use to justify their enthusiasm for gun ownership. If we look at the best biblical scholarship, though, that is not what the passage means. As Dr. Serene Jones, president of Union Theological Seminary, put it, "The 'God-given right' to guns is a cash-fueled sham."[33]

Robert Schenck is an ordained, conservative, Evangelical Christian who had a dramatic change of heart about guns. Originally, like other Evangelicals, he had been a supporter of guns and gun rights. Then his brother told him about a product sold by a company named Garrison Grip.[34] Have a look at their website. The item in question looks just like a Bible with faux leather covering, and Holy Bible is emblazoned in gold letters on the cover. Inside, however, are not the books of the Bible, but rather space for a medium-to-large pistol, such as a Glock 17. This nifty product allows you to carry your pistol into church or any other place you want, while leading others to believe that you're virtuously carrying a Bible. Talk about concealed carry! It hit Schenck that Evangelicals had made idols out of guns. As he said so clearly, "By venerating the Second Amendment, we evangelicals were in danger of violating the Second Commandment."[35] The Second Commandment states "Thou shalt not make any graven image. . . . Thou shall not bow down to them or serve them." That is, do not engage in idolatry. Worshipping guns is a form of idolatry.

I should note that, according to the website, the faux leather covering on the gun Bible is vegan. I guess that's something. Actually, it's terribly funny that the website would court those who don't want to see animals killed in the making of the product but are happy to carry a pistol, the purpose of which is to kill people. Alternatively, the website may be using "vegan" sarcastically. You can judge for yourself.

RELIGIOUS GROUPS AS TARGETS OF GUN VIOLENCE

In the past decade, two mass shootings aimed at members of particular religious groups captured media attention.

One was the 2019 mass shooting of Muslims at two mosques in New Zealand by a White supremacist, killing 51. New Zealand has a bit of a Gun Culture itself, although it doesn't come close to America's. In response to the incident, which was classified as terrorism, the government of New Zealand passed the Arms (Prohibited Firearms, Magazines, and Parts) Amendment Act, 2019. It bans semiautomatic firearms, large-capacity magazines, and parts that can be used to assemble prohibited firearms. The government also created a buyback program in which gun owners could turn in the firearms and ammunition that were now prohibited. One mass shooting and they passed the needed legislation. Because our focus is on the United States, I will leave it there for the New Zealand case, but we could learn something from them.

The other incident was made in America. The Tree of Life Synagogue is located in the Squirrel Hill neighborhood of Pittsburgh, a neighborhood that has a large Jewish population.[36] In 2018, on a Saturday morning when worshippers would be there, a gunman entered the synagogue carrying multiple semiautomatic weapons and killed 11 people, the largest attack on Jews in US history. In a cruel twist of fate, several of those killed were Holocaust survivors. They survived Hitler, only to be killed in America. The shooter had posted anti-Semitic comments online, and the Anti-Defamation League (ADL; an organization created to oppose the defamation of Jews) had recorded an increase in anti-Semitism online in the months leading up to the incident. The ADL hypothesized that the increase in hate speech was related to the run-up to the 2018 midterm elections, with far-right extremists using hate speech to rally their troops for the election. A similar spike in anti-Semitism had occurred before the

2016 election. It was reported that the shooter told a SWAT officer who assisted in his capture that he wanted Jews to die and that Jews were committing genocide against his people.

Analysis of his online postings indicated that the shooter had been radicalized by White nationalists. He had a warm relationship with neo-Nazis and posted the assertion that "Jews are the children of Satan." All these dangerous forces came together in one person—the White nationalism, the belief in supernatural evil—and the result was the mass shooting of Jews in their synagogue.

This shooter and his online pals are just the latest manifestation of two myths that have been around for more than a century.[37] Both involve conspiracy theories. One is that Jews control all the financial markets and the other is that Jews want to control the whole world. These ideas are ridiculous, but with the internet, they spread like wildfire and some folks are gullible enough to believe them.

In 2023, when the terrorist group Hamas attacked Israel, and Israel responded by invading Gaza, anti-Semitism bubbled up in the United States on social media and in person. At Cornell University, online threats appeared, specifically talking about violence against the Center for Jewish Living.[38] Campus police stepped up security at that building and offered enhanced protection for Jewish students. It doesn't take much for anti-Semitism to seep out of its dark caverns into the daylight.

The National Opinion Research Center (NORC) at the University of Chicago conducted a national survey on anti-Semitism in 2023.[39] The researchers measured respondents' level of anti-Semitism by their agreement or disagreement with seven statements reflecting negative stereotypes about Jews, such as "Jews in business are so shrewd that other people do not have a fair chance at competition" and "Jews have too much power in the United States today." The results indicated that highly anti-Semitic individuals (estimated at about 10 million Americans) are much more likely to support political violence than are members of the general public. For example, 21 percent of the highly anti-Semitic believe that the use of force is justified to preserve the rights of Whites (compared with 8 percent of the general public). Anti-Semitism has a lot in common with anti-Black racism, except in this case the hate is directed at a religious group instead of a racial group.

SOLUTIONS

Here I explore two different avenues for addressing the support of Evangelical Christians and Christian nationalists for Gun Culture in the United States: deep canvassing and promoting the Christian tradition of nonviolence.

Deep Canvassing

As we have seen, not all gun owners are alike. Some are hunters, some are citizen protectors, some are Evangelical Christians, and some are Christian nationalists. The focus here is on Evangelical Christians because of their potent political power in the gun debate. *How could we persuade Evangelical Christians to practice gun safety and support gun safety legislation?* One potential strategy is called *deep canvassing*.

We know that Evangelical Christians are strongly motivated by the Bible and they are motivated to follow biblical teaching in both their behavior and their thinking (attitudes). The problem is that the Gun Lobby has inundated them with marketing messages saying that owning guns for protection is authorized by the Bible, when the best biblical scholarship says it isn't. How can we help them change their minds?

Deep canvassing involves people (canvassers) going door to door.[40] Someone opens the door and is willing to have a conversation with the canvasser, who then has a long—10 to 20 minute—conversation with them. This is not just thrusting a flyer in someone's hand and saying "Vote for Proposition 7." It takes time, but the results can be transformative. And it has been effective with some issues that are as controversial as guns, including prejudice against transgender folks and immigration policy.

The canvasser asks the respondent to explain their views on the issue at hand. Let's say it's attitudes about transgender individuals. The canvasser and respondent then have a nonjudgmental conversation about it. The canvasser doesn't try to persuade the respondent to adopt a new opinion. Instead, the canvasser uses nonthreatening techniques like helping the respondent take the perspective of a transgender person. For example, "Can you tell me about a time when you felt judged negatively because of being different?" The canvasser then helps the respondent see how their own experience might be like that of a trans person. This process encourages deep processing of the ideas by the respondent, rather than a superficial, knee-jerk reaction like "God intended them to be a male when they were born and it's immoral to change that." With the deep processing, the respondent reflects on their own ideas and may realize that they hold contradictory views, leading them to change their mind.

It takes a lot of training and experience to become an effective canvasser, leading a respondent sensitively through an open conversation and not trying to impose your views on them. The interaction should involve a nonjudgmental exchange of narratives between the respondent and canvasser, with the canvasser offering their own narrative that is relevant to the topic. Many folks resist direct argumentation and are more persuaded, and less resistant to, personal stories.[41] The conversation should not threaten the respondent's sense of self. They are not being told "You're a bad person because you think trans people are creepy." Importantly, the canvasser listens attentively and empathically, conveying respect for the respondent. That in turn helps the respondent to acknowledge the canvasser's point of view as reasonable.

Careful scientific evaluations of the effectiveness of this method of deep canvassing show it to be effective in changing people's attitudes and beliefs. Antitransgender prejudice was the issue in the first study and the canvassing occurred in South Florida.[42] Compared to a control group that had a conversation about recycling, those in the group that had deep conversations about transgender issues showed substantially reduced prejudice and increased support for a nondiscrimination law. Impressively, the effects persisted three months later in a follow-up.

In a study tackling immigration policy, the control group received a conversation involving persuasive arguments. The deep canvassing group experienced a nonjudgmental exchange of narratives with the canvasser; that group showed a reduction in commitment to excluding immigrants, even four months after the conversation.[43]

A successor study is even more relevant to the question of how to reach Christian Evangelicals about their love of guns. This time researchers used deep canvassing but added an additional component: moral reframing.[44] The topic was abortion attitudes and the canvassers were volunteers with Planned Parenthood of Northern New England. During the conversations, the canvasser might ask if the respondent knew someone who had an abortion or an unplanned pregnancy and listened for the respondent's moral values as expressed in their story. There's a standard list of moral values: care (vs. harm), fairness (vs. cheating), loyalty (vs. betrayal), authority (vs. subversion), and sanctity (vs. degradation), and the canvassers had been trained to identify them. Canvassers shared their own views on abortion and pointed out how they held a moral value that was similar to the respondent's. The canvasser then made the argument that abortion should be safe and legal and framed the argument in terms of the respondent's moral values, a technique called *personalized moral reframing*. These conversations not only improved respondents' attitudes toward Planned Parenthood, but they also increased interest in taking proabortion actions such as writing to members of Congress.

Researchers from a different lab have independently obtained results that support the principles underlying deep canvassing. They have found that when a moral divide separates groups, speaking about personal experiences is more persuasive than scientific facts.[45] This finding pains me because I wish that everyone based their decisions on rationality and the best available scientific evidence. But that's just not how many humans work, or at least not all the time. There is a moral divide—chasm, really—between Evangelical Christians' beliefs that gun ownership and use are morally upright and approved by God, versus mainline Christians' moral objections to guns based on all the deaths and injuries they cause. The research shows that if mainline Christians conveyed their personal experiences, especially experiences involving harm, Evangelicals might listen, especially if they felt respected by the speaker. The mainliners, for example, might talk about how hard it is on their children to endure active shooter drills in the schools. Or they might speak of how, following the mass shooting in Highland Park, they skipped the Fourth of July parade this year for fear that a shooter might materialize.

The technique of deep canvassing has great potential for changing the minds of those who oppose commonsense gun legislation, even those for whom guns are bound up with their religious beliefs.

> **GOOD NEWS**
>
> The evidence-based technique of deep canvassing has the potential to change the minds of those who oppose commonsense gun regulations.

Promoting Christian Nonviolence

Despite all the embrace of guns among Evangelical Christians, a strong tradition of nonviolence runs through Christianity as well as Judaism, which represent the dominant religious traditions of the United States.[46] The teaching of nonviolence is found in other religions as well, such as Buddhism and Islam.[47] But I focus on Christian nonviolence here because we need an antidote to Evangelical Christians' belief that they are authorized by God to own firearms and use them.

The Christian tradition of nonviolence not only has theological warrant, but has been quite effective politically. Three examples are abolitionist nonviolence before the Civil War, and during the civil rights movement, the work of Martin Luther King Jr. and Fannie Lou Hamer.

In the first half of the 1800s, the cause of abolitionism was gaining traction in America, especially in the North, and nonviolence was at its core.[48] The Second Great Awakening, a religious revival movement, had swept the country, spawning Christian reform movements on many issues, including slavery. The major driving force was the Evangelicals, although they were not the same as today's Evangelicals. Emerging out of these reform movements were the abolitionists, who believed that slavery was morally wrong and had to be abolished, because no human could be the lord over another human. Only God was Lord. As one abolitionist leader, Henry C. Wright, put it, "A desire to hold dominion over man is rebellion against God."[49]

William Lloyd Garrison was the most famous of the abolitionists. A writer and orator, he founded the journal *The Liberator*. Garrison and his followers in one faction of the movement were profoundly committed to nonviolence, believing that the violence of slavery could not be cured with more violence. Others believed that violence would be necessary. Garrison faced a serious dilemma. How could one eradicate slavery without resorting to violence? He settled on transforming the moral conscience of individuals, including government officials, through magazines, speeches, and sermons. Proslavery forces were violently opposed to him; at various times he was burned in effigy, had a price on his head, and was captured by an angry mob that intended to tar and feather him. Fortunately, the mayor of Boston intervened in the tar-and-feather case. There can be no doubt that, using Christian principles of nonviolence, William Lloyd Garrison effectively played a major role in promoting the idea that slavery must be abolished.

You know the story of Dr. Martin Luther King Jr., minister at Ebenezer Baptist Church in Atlanta, who led the civil rights movement of the 1960s using nonviolence based on his Christian convictions. You may not be as familiar with Fannie Lou Hamer, so I will tell her story instead.

Fannie Lou Hamer was born in Mississippi in 1917 to sharecropper parents.[50] Sharecropping was a not-that-distant cousin of slavery. She attended a one-room school for children of sharecroppers during the non-cotton-picking season, and she excelled. At age 12, though, she had to leave school to support her aging parents (she was the last of 20 children), which she did by picking cotton. The poverty and racism were cruel and endless. Her father was a Baptist preacher and she continued to develop her reading skills during Bible study at her church. Her mother was a person of great faith, courage, and resourcefulness and was an inspiration to Fannie Lou. There's a great story about her mother fighting with the White boss of the plantation when he struck one of her sons— and winning! It's not quite a story of nonviolence, but it was a great model for Fannie Lou of standing up against injustice.

She married Perry "Pap" Hamer in 1945. They wanted children, but none came, or there might have been miscarriages. In 1961, a White doctor, in the process of removing a tumor, also performed a hysterectomy on Fannie Lou, in an involuntary sterilization practice that was all too common. Black people called these procedures the Mississippi appendectomy. Afterward, Fannie Lou Hamer returned to the cotton fields while thinking there had to be a way to change things.

In 1962, Hamer became involved with the Student Nonviolent Coordinating Committee, or SNCC. Notice the "Nonviolent" in the name. SNCC, partnering with the Southern Christian Leadership Conference (SCLC), was spearheading a voter registration campaign in Georgia, Alabama, and Mississippi, where it was difficult if not impossible for Black citizens to vote. Hamer bravely volunteered to be one of the Black people who went to the courthouse to register to vote and emerged as a leader of the group. But in order to register, she first had to pass a literacy test as required by law in Mississippi. She failed, which made no sense because she had excelled at reading in school. On the third try, she passed and registered. But that made the White racists very angry. Her boss fired her and she was shot at by drive-by shooters. Returning from an SCLC meeting, she and others were arrested on trumped-up charges and beaten. She nearly died and never fully recovered from the injuries, which included a damaged kidney. But she went back to Mississippi and continued to register voters.

Despite her lack of formal education, Fannie Lou Hamer was a powerful orator, and she delivered speeches at colleges and universities across the country. Many people underestimated her because she spoke in Southern Black vernacular, but she was compelling and connected with audiences. She moved them to action. Many have attributed the power of her speaking—both in style and content—to her lifetime of experiences in the Black church. One of her most famous sayings was "I'm sick and tired of being sick and tired."

Fannie Lou Hamer died in 1977 at age 59 from complications of hypertension and breast cancer, not to mention the beatings she had sustained.

If anyone had a right to be angry and to use violence against the oppressors, it was Fannie Lou Hamer. Oh, and I haven't mentioned that her grandmother, who had been enslaved, had been raped repeatedly as she was passed from one White man to another. Her grandmother told this story as Fannie Lou was growing up. But Hamer did not resort to violence and instead stayed true to her Christian beliefs and practiced nonviolence alongside Dr. Martin Luther King Jr. In the end, she was a major contributor to the civil rights movement of the 1960s, which succeeded, among other things, in passing the Voting Rights Act of 1965. That movement and its Christian-based nonviolent approach moved mountains in the United States and won freedom for millions.

Could White Christian Evangelicals be inspired to adopt the nonviolent approach of William Lloyd Garrison, Fannie Lou Hamer, and Dr. Martin Luther King Jr., which would involve voluntarily getting rid of their guns? I would like to think that they can.[51]

The words of Dr. Martin Luther King Jr. are especially meaningful in the current context of gun violence. "The ultimate weakness of violence is that it is a descending spiral begetting the very thing it seeks to destroy. Instead of diminishing evil, it multiplies it. . . . Returning violence for violence multiplies violence, adding deeper darkness to a night already devoid of stars. Darkness cannot drive out darkness; only light can do that."

CHAPTER SIX

A Highly Effective Method for Suicide

LUC-JOHN WAS A DYNAMIC, GIFTED, AND TALENTED YOUNG MAN WHO HAD EVERYTHING: girlfriends, a beautiful home, a BMW, a phenomenal six-figure job, and quite an athletic, well-toned, handsome body.

No one asked his mamma if he should have a legal weapon.

Why? He lived five minutes from the local police department. Luc lived in a safe neighborhood. Luc had a very safe job. Luc was not a hunter nor was he a recreational shooter.

No one asked his mamma if he should possess a legal weapon.

Her answer would have been an unequivocal "No!"

Luc was different. He masked his sensitivities. Over-accomplished, he must have suffered terribly within, as he always had dreams of achieving so much. Nonetheless, guns were a very big part of his local environment. His town had two shooting ranges.

Luc was a macho young man. He kept his secrets to himself. He loved his mother and would often take her out to dinner. However, he never confided anything to her.

Luc just broke up with his girlfriend. His sister just had a baby.
After family feuding, Luc killed himself.[1]

THE NUMBERS

Across the 20th century in the United States, we saw declines in mortality from major causes such as heart disease and cancer. According to data from the Centers for Disease Control, however, the three causes of death that have risen the most since 1999 are accidental poisoning (almost all are cases of drug overdoses), suicides, and alcoholic liver diseases.[2] Many of the accidental overdoses may

99

actually have been suicides. All of these are the result of psychological afflictions that kill people.

Although much of the conversation about firearm deaths focuses on homicides, the majority—roughly 60 percent—of firearm deaths in the United States are suicides.[3] They account for the deaths of 25,000 Americans every year. That's 65 deaths every day.

Guns are a uniquely lethal method for suicide. Among suicide attempts using a firearm, 90 percent result in death.[4] Other methods have much lower death rates—for example, drugs/poisoning (2%) or hanging (53%).[5] But won't those folks who survived an attempted suicide just go on to try again and eventually die by suicide? The data say no. Among those who make a nonfatal suicide attempt, only 7 percent die by suicide within the next 10 years.[6] The great majority of people who survive a suicide attempt do not eventually die by suicide. Often the attempt is made in a rash, impulsive moment, and afterward the person realizes how close they came to death and makes no further attempts. If a person uses a gun, however, they don't get a second chance.

A PSYCHOLOGICAL UNDERSTANDING OF SUICIDE

What is going on in the mind of someone who attempts suicide? Who dies by suicide? First, some terminology.

Suicidal ideation is the technical term for having thoughts about killing oneself. Most people who experience suicidal ideation do not go on to make an attempt, but suicidal ideation is definitely a risk factor for making an attempt. *Suicide attempts* are behaviors in which the person tries to kill themselves. In contrast, *completed suicides* or *deaths by suicide* are cases in which the person makes an attempt that results in death. The term *suicide spectrum* is used to capture this range from ideation to attempted to completed suicide. Women make up the majority of suicide attempts, and men make up the majority of completed suicides.

People become suicidal for many reasons, so we can't point to just one factor, and instead we have to consider multiple risk factors.

- *Psychological disorders:* Individuals with major depressive disorder (MDD), bipolar disorder, schizophrenia, impulse control disorders such as ADHD, or PTSD all have higher rates of suicide than people from the general population.[7]

- *Psychological pain:* It is common for individuals who attempt suicide to report experiencing severe psychological pain, sometimes called "psychache."[8] The feelings of unbearable pain may result from any number of sources, such as physical pain or the death of a loved one. Pair that psychological pain with feelings of *hopelessness*—things aren't going to get better and I can't do anything about it—and you have a recipe for suicidal ideation and even a suicide attempt.[9]

- *Serious physical health issues:* In one study, this represented the largest category (32%) of suicide decedents.[10] Folks in this category are less likely to disclose suicidal intent, making it difficult to intervene with them. My own mother-in-law, following months of severe abdominal pain and believing that she had widespread cancer, took her own life using pills. No one expected it.

- *Perceived burdensomeness:* It is common for suicidal individuals to believe they are nothing but a burden to others.[11] They make a mental calculation—an incorrect one—that they are such a burden that their loved ones would be better off without them. If you hear someone making comments like this, be on the alert! This person likely is experiencing suicidal ideation and an intervention is needed.

- *Social influences:* Several social factors can increase the risk of suicidal behaviors. Among adolescents, experiences of being bullied, as well as lack of support from parents, predict suicidal behaviors.[12] Social isolation and feelings of loneliness are major contributors across age groups.[13] Conversely, people who are positively connected to others socially—such as being married, or adolescents who have a positive relationship with parents, or having a social role that provides a sense of purpose—have lower rates of suicidal behaviors.[14] Importantly, interventions that provide increased social support are effective at decreasing suicide rates.[15]

- *Media coverage:* Media coverage of a suicide or cluster of suicides, and the content of the coverage, can have an impact.[16] Spikes in suicide rates often occur following media stories about a celebrity suicide. Local media reporting of one youth's death by suicide may lead to a cluster of adolescent suicides. One study examined a community that had a history of adolescent suicides.[17] The media coverage emphasized intense academic pressure as the cause while ignoring other possible factors. In so doing, the media may have conveyed to teens in the community that academic pressure was a legitimate reason for suicide. Journalists need to be responsible in reporting about such life-and-death topics.

Overall, then, a person who is having suicidal thoughts is likely to be experiencing great psychological pain, perhaps from one specific event such as a breakup with a boyfriend or girlfriend, or chronic issues such as poverty. They feel hopeless, thinking that their life will never improve and they are helpless to do anything about it. The person feels lonely and isolated, and if they lack strong social support—even one individual could help—the suicidal ideation can turn into a suicide attempt. But not all who contemplate suicide are alike, and below I expand on some groups who are particularly vulnerable to suicidality.

ADOLESCENT SUICIDE

According to a report from the Centers for Disease Control (CDC), in 2021, 10 percent of high schoolers made a suicide attempt and 22 percent seriously considered attempting suicide.[18] Even more worrisome is the finding that 42 percent of high school youth in 2021 experienced persistent feelings of sadness or hopelessness, and that's up dramatically from 28 percent in 2011. Persistent feelings of sadness or hopelessness are symptoms of depression, as well as risk factors for suicidal thoughts and behaviors. Experts believe that we should be very concerned about the mental health of American teens. The caveat here is that 2021 was in the midst of the Covid pandemic and a lot of typically happy people were feeling miserable. Just as I was completing this book, data from 2023 became available, slightly after the pandemic.[19] Those findings indicate that the rate of attempted suicide was down to 9 percent, equal to the prepandemic level of 2019 and even 2015. That rate is still too high, but I am less worried about an accelerating trend over time.

Certain subgroups are particularly at risk. For example, nearly 70 percent of LGBQ+ youth report persistent feelings of sadness or hopelessness.[20] And 45 percent of LGBQ+ youth have seriously considered attempting suicide.

For adolescents between 14 and 18, firearms are the most frequent method among cases of completed suicide.[21] Parents with adolescents in the home definitely need to consider whether they should keep any firearms in their home or car. Consider storage outside the home, and if you must keep a firearm in the home, keep it securely stored in a gun safe. A biometric safe is recommended because it can respond just to the parent's fingerprint, so no one else can open it. Adolescents can be clever about finding keys or figuring out combinations to other kinds of locks.

Help for adolescents can come from a number of sources, including schools. The CDC report offered a set of actions that schools can take to improve adolescents' well-being and reduce the risk of suicidal thoughts and behaviors.

- *Improve school connectedness:* We have seen how important social connections are for supporting mental health and reducing suicide risk, across the age span. Teens spend the greater part of their waking hours in school, so feeling connected to the school and the people in it (peers, teachers, coaches) boosts mental health, as shown in numerous studies. LGBT youth can feel less connected to school, and it is important for schools to have programs for this group such as GSAs (gay/straight alliances, or genders and sexualities alliances).

- *Increase access to school-based mental health services:* It is crucial that teens be able to access mental health services through their school, whether the school provides the services or makes referrals to mental health care providers.

- *Implement high-quality health education across all grades:* Health education should be medically accurate and developmentally appropriate, as well as culturally and LGBT-inclusive. The education should be about health defined broadly, and particularly about mental health and healthy emotions.

Schools can play a major role in addressing the mental health issues facing American youth, and specifically in reducing suicidality. Put the teen mental health crisis together with the easy availability of guns and, with no intervention, you have an epidemic of deaths that could have been prevented.

MEN, MASCULINITY, AND SUICIDE

Around the world, male completed suicides outnumber female completed suicides.[22] In 2022 in the United States, 39,255 males died by suicide compared to 10,194 females.[23] That means men accounted for 79 percent of the deaths by suicide. How can we understand this striking gender effect?

It starts, again, with psychological pain, which may come from any of multiple sources. Sometimes the pain has its origins as early as childhood; for example, if a parent is emotionally abusive. In other cases, it's something that happened in the last week, such as the breakup of a marriage or being fired from work. Both women and men experience psychological pain, of course, but regulating and dealing with this pain are especially difficult for men because of cultural norms that teach men to suppress their emotions.[24] They just don't have much practice at identifying, understanding, and regulating their emotions, so their psychological pain can easily get out of control. Sadness especially is an emotion that men are taught not to recognize in themselves or express, much less seek help for. One young man, interviewed within 24 hours of a suicide attempt, said "I'm miserable and I don't know why. You don't know why you are that way; you don't know what's wrong with you."[25] He is clueless about his emotions. Men's lack of emotional expression also makes it difficult for those close to them to recognize there's a problem.

While emotions may be alien territory for men, firearms are not. Real men are gunslingers, not weaklings who are in touch with their emotions. When faced with great psychological pain, some men may most readily turn to a gun for a solution.

In addition, men have to deal with cultural standards that insist that a real man must be successful at work. Of course, not all men can be successful, and those who fail to live up to that masculinity standard can easily feel defeated and hopeless.[26]

Another factor is that social connections such as friendship and talking with friends are emphasized for women but not men. It's an old saying that if a man feels sad or upset, he goes and plays basketball with the guys. If a woman feels sad or upset, she talks with her friends about it. There's something to be said for physical activity like playing basketball, but it doesn't help you focus on the emotional problem to figure out how to solve it. And some men's responses to feeling upset—gambling, drinking, or using drugs—can quickly become unhealthy.[27] Men are supposed to be independent and self-reliant, which cuts off social support and creates feelings of isolation and loneliness.

There are solutions to these problems, though. Experts have proposed the 3R Model of Male Suicide Recovery.[28] As shown in figure 6.1, the 3Rs are emotional recognition, regulation, and reconnection.

According to the 3R Model, for men and boys to recover from suicidality—and stay alive—the key is regulation of psychological pain. To accomplish that, males must learn to recognize their emotions and reconnect with those emotions. Because of male role requirements, they have distanced themselves from their emotions; but they need to get in touch with them because you can't solve emotional problems unless you recognize those emotions. Having done that, they can learn to regulate their emotions, especially those that tilt toward suicidality. One benefit of learning to recognizing their emotions is that men can then accurately communicate them to others, whether a spouse or friend or helping professional, and that will boost social connections and support. Without this kind of emotional intelligence, a distressed man may look to a gun as the solution to his problems.

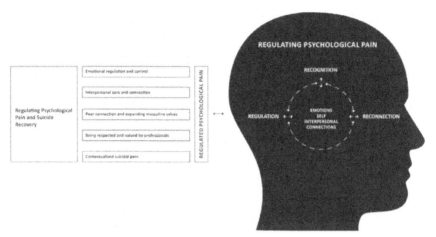

Figure 6.1.   The 3R Model of Male Suicide Recovery.

More broadly, psychologists are developing approaches to therapy that recognize the specific and harmful effects of male socialization so that the therapist and client can address them together.[29] Elements of this kind of approach include recognizing the connections between masculinity norms and men's mental health or lack thereof; assisting men who have difficulty identifying their emotions; understanding that depression in men may include anger and irritability; and identifying the connections between male socialization and suicide. This kind of therapy tailored to men's special needs is an important development.

DEATHS OF DESPAIR

That's what they call them—deaths of despair, the deaths from suicide usually by gun, but also by drug overdoses and alcoholic liver disease, that disproportionately kill middle-aged White men (and, to a lesser extent, women) who do not have a college degree. The term was coined by Princeton economists Anne Case and Angus Deaton,[30] Deaton being a Nobel Prize winner. They set out to determine why the mortality rates of Americans, which had declined steadily during the 20th century, leveled off and even began to increase in the 21st century. As it turned out, the increase in mortality was mainly among Whites without a college degree. It did not occur among those with a college degree, nor did it occur among Black people.

The year 2017 saw 158,000 of these deaths of despair. One of the alarming findings is that among White Americans born in 1980, those who do not have a college degree are four times more likely to die by suicide than their peers with a bachelor's degree.[31] Periodically I see an opinion column that questions the cost-effectiveness of a college education. The columnists never take into account these deaths of despair.

According to the analysis by Case and Deaton, the lives of working-class Whites have worsened over the past 50 years due to multiple forces.

- The economy has created an abundance of new jobs, but the great majority are for those with a college degree. The unemployment rate is substantially higher for workers without a college degree.

- Adjusted for inflation, the wages of working-class Whites have declined. A little more money can relieve a lot of stress. Less money equals more stress.

- Religious membership has declined, and religious organizations provide enriching social interactions as well as beliefs in a higher purpose.

- Union membership has declined, and unions provide both higher wages and a social network.

- With the decline in manufacturing in America, blue-collar jobs became less meaningful. You could feel pride if you put together high-quality clocks, as some of my ancestors did in LaSalle, Illinois. Now the clocks are made in China, and the blue-collar worker is a janitor in an airport, which is much less meaningful.

- Today, those without a college degree are less likely to marry and, overall, marriage is good for mental health.

All of these factors combine to create the feelings of despair, depression, and hopelessness that lead to deaths, whether suicide by guns or more slowly, by drugs or alcohol. Opioid addiction has only exacerbated this crisis.

Middle-aged, White Americans with no college degree are a substantial portion of our population and we are failing them. Add to the mix the easy availability of guns and you have a death rate that is spiking. A similar increase in deaths of middle-aged, blue-collar workers has not occurred in European nations.[32] Several factors account for the mortality differences between the United States and Europe, but a major one is the overabundance of guns in America.

There's a postscript to this story. New analyses show that middle-aged Black Americans' rates of deaths of despair rose sharply starting in 2014, so that by

2022, they equaled those of Whites.[33] This is not what is meant by closing race gaps. The causes of death are somewhat different, with Whites more often using guns and Black people more often dying from drug overdoses, due in large part to the increasing lethality of the illicit drug supply. But overall, Black Americans' rates of death by suicide are approaching those of White Americans. We can't ignore Black Americans and their suicide risk.

Suicide Among Military Veterans

In the United States, 4,600 veterans die by firearm suicide every year.[34] That's more than the terrorist attacks of September 11, 2001, which killed 2,977. And veterans' deaths by gun suicide happen again every year. Can we summon the national will to tackle this problem in the same way that we were galvanized following 9/11?

Veterans are three times more likely to die by gun suicide compared with nonveterans.[35] And from 2002 to 2021, veterans' deaths by gun suicide were 16 times the number of service members killed in action during that same period.

Why do veterans have a much higher rate of gun suicide compared with nonveterans? A major part of the answer is that veterans are more likely to own firearms than nonveterans—a 50 percent ownership rate for veterans compared with just 20 percent for nonveterans.[36] And the average gun-owning veteran has six guns. In 2021, 72 percent of the veteran suicides were by gun.

It's tempting to think that the extraordinary rate of gun suicide among veterans is due to the trauma of combat, with bullets whizzing past and the possibility of stepping on an improvised explosive device (IED) at any moment. Certainly, trauma during war is part of the picture, but data from the period of the wars in Iraq and Afghanistan show that those who were *not* deployed have a higher suicide risk than those who were.[37]

How can we address this national disgrace, which most certainly does not honor those who served? One piece of the puzzle is Red Flag laws, discussed in the Solutions section at the end of this chapter. Beyond that, the overall strategy is to put *time and distance* between high-risk veterans and their guns. The military, friends, and loved ones should insist on secure storage of firearms. One low-cost strategy is for the veteran to give the keys to the gun storage cabinet to a trusted friend. That puts both time and distance between the veteran and the highly lethal means. Some states, including Colorado, Maryland, and New York, have created firearm storage maps so that a person can easily find a place to store their firearm outside their home and vehicle. Again, third-party storage puts time and distance between a high-risk individual and a lethal gun.

In 2021, the Biden administration released a report titled *Reducing Military and Veteran Suicide: Advancing a Comprehensive, Cross-Sector, Evidence-Informed Public Health Strategy*.[38] Of course, I love the emphasis on an evidence-based public health approach! Among the five priority goals in the report, priority goal no. 1 is Improve Lethal Means Safety and the report notes that suicide crises are often brief, so if we can put time and distance between the person and the lethal means—most often guns, but also drugs—we can prevent a death by suicide. Another one of the priority goals is to improve crisis health care and mental health care for veterans and active-duty military. There are clear solutions to this problem.

Treating Suicidality

The good news is that we have a number of psychotherapies that are effective against suicidality,[39] and medication treatment for depression is available, too. Psychoanalysis is not much of a player in today's treatments, so strike that one from the mental list you're making. Here we'll focus on cognitive behavioral therapy (CBT), dialectical behavior therapy (DBT), and Collaborative Assessment and Management of Suicidality (CAMS). Randomized controlled trials (RCTs) indicate that both CBT and DBT are effective in treating suicidality in adolescents, especially when combined with sessions for parents.[40] CBT and DBT are also effective with suicidal adults.[41] CAMS, too, has been tested in RCTs and found to be effective in reducing suicidality.[42]

> **GOOD NEWS**
>
> A number of psychotherapies are effective against suicidality.

Before going any farther, I should call your attention to the fact that therapists who treat suicidal patients are in an extraordinarily precarious situation. If they make even a slight miscalculation, the patient could die. And it is difficult if not impossible to predict precisely whether a given individual will make a suicide attempt, much less when they will do it.[43] The therapist must tread carefully while at the same time trying to produce results quickly. It's not an easy task.

Cognitive Behavioral Therapy

As its name implies, cognitive behavioral therapy focuses on the individual's maladaptive behaviors as well as maladaptive thought patterns and how to change them so that the person is functioning well again. An underlying assumption is that maladaptive thoughts and behaviors have been learned and therefore can be unlearned.

When CBT is applied to suicidality, the problem behavior is attempting suicide. The problematic thought patterns include suicidal ideation, hopelessness, and burdensomeness, which in turn lead to overwhelming negative emotions and the behavior of suicide attempts. Therapy sessions involve identifying and challenging the problematic thoughts as well as learning new behaviors and skills, such as social and interpersonal skills, communication skills, and skills for emotion regulation and impulse control.[44] The therapist challenges negative thought patterns such as the client's belief that they are a burden to those around them and helps the client with *cognitive restructuring*, in which negative, irrational thoughts ("I am a terrible burden to my family and they would be better off if I were dead") are replaced with positive, constructive ones ("I can contribute a lot to my family, such as ____"). The therapist helps motivate the individual to make a commitment to safety, in which no type of self-harm is an acceptable way to deal with stress. Enhanced interpersonal and communication skills should help the individual build relationships with others, feel more socially connected, and gain more social support. Emotion regulation skills strengthen the individual's capacity to tolerate and manage intense negative emotions in healthy ways, not by making a suicide attempt.

With suicidality in adolescents, an important additional element in the treatment plan is parallel sessions for the parents or other caregivers.[45] In those sessions, crucial principles include

- *Safety planning:* If the youth experiences a suicidal crisis, how can they cope successfully and how can the parents support that coping?

- *Means safety:* How can parents ensure they have removed lethal means or restricted access to them? Parents receive education about safety, including, especially, firearm safety.

- *Communication skills for parents:* Parents learn how to communicate more clearly and effectively with their child. Just saying "Don't do it" is not effective communication.

- *Behavioral skills for parents:* Techniques that parents can use to reinforce positive, safe behaviors, such as praising the adolescent for making progress.

- *Cognitive restructuring:* Parents can support the adolescent's new cognitive restructuring skills, focusing on helpful ways to think about stressors.

- *Emotion regulation:* Parents may need to learn emotion regulation skills themselves, especially if emotions are running high with a suicidal adolescent.[46] Parents, too, can become models of emotion regulation.

Parents are trained to be in-home coaches in their adolescent's recovery, thereby magnifying the benefits of once-weekly therapy sessions.

CBT is also effective in treating another high-risk group, military personnel.[47] The basic principles are much the same.

Dialectical Behavior Therapy

Originally developed by Dr. Marsha Linehan of the University of Washington for treating suicidal patients, dialectical behavior therapy (DBT) is now used for other disorders as well, and especially for those who are diagnosed with borderline personality disorder (BPD) paired with suicidality. *Borderline personality disorder* is a mental illness characterized by intense and unstable moods, and likewise intense and unstable relationships with family and friends, as well as impulsive and sometimes dangerous behaviors, suicide being one of them. Intense fears of abandonment are also common in BPD. The "borderline" in the name came from the original recognition of the disorder in which it seemed to be on the borderline between neuroses (depression, anxiety) and psychoses (e.g., schizophrenia). BPD is notoriously difficult to treat.

DBT builds on CBT by adding elements from Zen contemplative practices, especially acceptance and mindfulness.[48] DBT also includes a broader range of emotion regulation strategies to promote distress tolerance, recognizing that some of life's challenges must simply be endured with skill and grace. Linehan has said that the overall goal in DBT is to *build a life worth living.* Amen to that.

With mindfulness skills training, the person learns to focus their attention on their own interior, psychological states. They are encouraged to accept their feelings, as well as events outside their control such as childhood traumas. The therapist validates the client's emotions and helps the client find ways to regulate their emotions. Commitment is a key part of the process, too—the client must commit to implementing solutions.

In treating suicidality, family training sessions, with the elements described above for CBT, can and should be added to treatment of the suicidal individual.[49]

Collaborative Assessment and Management of Suicidality (CAMS)

Developed by Dr. David Jobes, CAMS emphasizes a collaboration between the suicidal patient and the clinician treating them.[50] Patient motivation is crucial with any kind of psychotherapy, and the collaborative aspect of CAMS is intended to increase suicidal patients' motivation for recovery.

Suicidal patients need to feel they are understood, and the assessment component of CAMS aims to meet that goal. The patient and clinician together complete an assessment, the Suicide Status Form. The patient rates themselves on six scales: Psychological Pain, Stress, Agitation, Hopelessness, Self-Hate, and Overall Risk of Suicide. The patient completes these scales again at each succeeding therapy session until their self-ratings indicate they are no longer at risk of using suicide as a coping method. In addition, the suicidal individual completes a list of five reasons for dying and five reasons for living, and the patient and therapist engage in treatment planning. Completion of the form promotes both self-understanding in the patient, and a deep understanding of the patient by the clinician, enabling the clinician to be deeply empathic. Ultimately, the therapy is designed to improve coping with life's challenges by constructive means, not suicide, and—echoing the theme of DBT—creating a life worth living.

Treatment with Medications

Another approach to managing suicidality is to treat the person's underlying psychological disorder—such as depression or bipolar disorder—with medications that target the disorder. In managing the underlying disorder, often the accompanying suicidality recedes as well.

Today we have highly effective antidepressants, most notably the selective serotonin reuptake inhibitors (SSRIs). Clinical trials indicate that antidepressants reduce suicidal ideation and suicidal behaviors across a wide range of ages.[51] In the context of treating depression plus suicide, the catch is that SSRIs generally take several weeks to reach full effectiveness and in a crisis that may be too long. Also, they don't work for everyone, such as those who display treatment-resistant depression.

Therefore, clinicians have been interested in finding alternative drugs to treat the combination of suicidality and depression. One that seems promising but hasn't been fully evaluated yet is ketamine.[52] The advantage of ketamine is that it produces results quickly, within a few hours, in contrast to the SSRIs. Stay tuned on this one.

Approximately 15 to 20 percent of people with bipolar disorder go on to die by suicide.[53] Bipolar disorder is often treated with mood stabilizers such as lithium, but many individuals with this diagnosis are not great at adhering to the treatment, making it difficult to achieve the best results for them.

There are no known effective drug treatments for borderline personality disorder.[54] Dialectical behavior therapy and cognitive behavioral therapy are the best bets for BPD.

The bottom line is that some of the disorders associated with suicidality—especially depression—can be helped with medications, but to achieve the best, lasting results, CBT, DBT, or CAMS are essential.[55] We Americans like to pop a pill and fix ourselves up instantly, but with suicidality, the hard work of talk therapy over a period of months is necessary.

Culturally Tailored Approaches

Let's face it, these treatment and prevention methods were designed by White people and reflect the lived experiences of Whites. Meanwhile, suicide rates are rising in Black and Brown communities. There are some special challenges in addressing suicide with this population. One is that stigma about mental health issues and therapy is especially strong in Black and Brown communities.[56] A stereotype holds that depression is a White problem.

Psychologists of color are working on culturally tailored techniques for working with people of color.[57] And the American Foundation for Suicide Prevention has developed an initiative called LETS (Listen, Empathy, Trust, Support) specifically for Black communities.

One important resource in prevention is the Black church, which has close ties in the Black community.[58] It can help shape cultural norms about mental health as well as help seeking.[59] With mental health problems, Black Americans are actually more likely to seek help from a pastor than from a psychologist. It has even been said that in the Black community attending a church service is just as therapeutic as attending a group therapy session.[60] And religiousness is a protective factor against suicidality. The Black church can also play a pivotal role in encouraging gun safety practices.

PREVENTING DEATHS BY SUICIDE

To prevent a death by suicide, two things must happen: (1) address the suicidality as explained above; and (2) remove all access to "lethal means," and at the top of that list of lethal means are firearms.[61]

There is simply no doubt that access to guns contributes to deaths by suicide, especially in the United States.[62] Several lines of evidence point to this conclusion. An analysis across 194 nations correlated firearm availability with suicide rates and found a positive correlation.[63] The higher the number of firearms per 100 people in a nation, the higher the firearm suicide rate. Firearm availability, however, does not correlate with the nonfirearm suicide rate. This latter finding counters the notion that if someone wants to kill themselves and doesn't have access to a gun, they will find some other method. If that were true, then we would expect a negative correlation between firearm availability and nonfirearm suicide rates. That is, fewer firearms would be associated with more nonfirearm suicides. But there was no correlation. It's the firearms.

Another analysis compared the United States with just 20 other Western countries, considering trends in the 21st century.[64] The United States has three times the firearm ownership rate of the next-highest Western country, Canada. Across the other Western nations, suicide death rates dropped from 2000 to 2016, whereas the rate increased by 27 percent in the United States. In the year 2000, the United States was 14th among the 20 Western nations in its suicide rate. We did not have a comparatively high suicide rate. But by 2016, the United States had risen to second among the 20 countries in its suicide rate, a dubious distinction (the highest rate was in Belgium). Over that same period of increased suicide rates in the United States from 2000 to 2016, firearm ownership in the United States skyrocketed. It's not a coincidence.

If we look at suicide rates just for those who are age 19 or younger, the United States has an astronomically higher rate than comparable countries, as shown in figure 6.2.[65]

Firearm ownership rates also vary across US states, as do suicide rates. Do firearm ownership rates correlate with firearm suicide rates across the 50 states? The answer is yes.[66] For those who have some background in statistics, in this study the correlation, r, was .67, which is substantial! The states with the highest rates of gun ownership have the highest rates of firearm suicide. And, again, there was no correlation between firearm ownership rates and nonfirearm suicides.

What are we to do in the United States with all those guns available? A major part of the answer is Red Flag laws, also called Extreme Risk Protection Orders or ERPO laws. These are described in the Solutions section that follows. Among men who die by gun suicide, fully 88 percent used their own gun.[67] Even a man who locks up his own gun but keeps the keys or combination still has access to it, which can be deadly. That makes Red Flag laws all the more important.

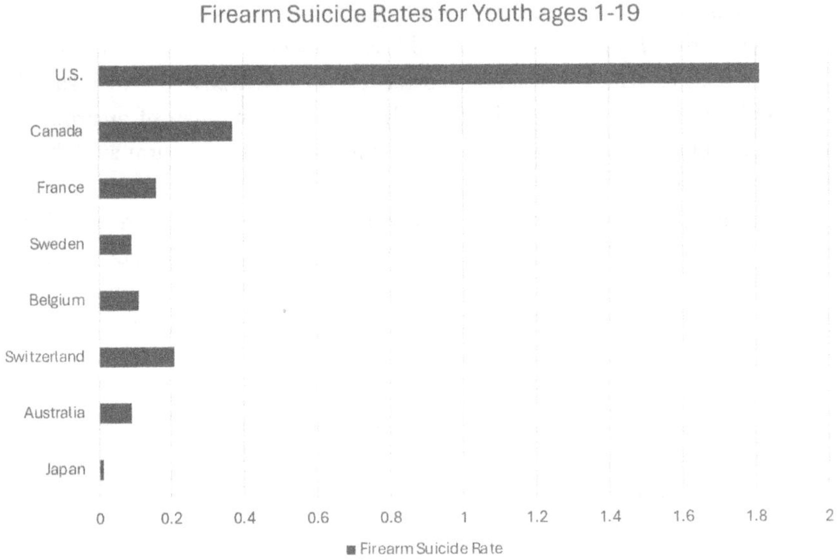

Firearm Suicide Rates for Youth ages 1-19

Figure 6.2. Firearm suicide rates in the US and other nations per 100,000 population for youth ages 1–19.
DATA FROM MCGOUGH ET AL. 2023; GRAPH BY JANET HYDE

Some states now have Voluntary Do Not Buy lists, so that a person who worries about impulsively attempting suicide can put themselves on a list that bars them from purchasing a firearm. This legislation is sometimes called Donna's Law after Donna Nathan, who had bipolar disorder and, in 2018, searched online for "gun stores New Orleans" and immediately followed her GPS to the nearest one. Within minutes, she had purchased a Smith & Wesson .38. She drove to a local park and fatally shot herself. Her daughter, Katrina Brees, has led the charge toward passage of state laws enacting Do Not Buy lists. If someone places themselves on the list and later, in a sound state of mind, decides to purchase a firearm, they can file a request to have their name removed from the Do Not Buy list, with a 21-day waiting period. Time and distance.

The case of Donna Nathan highlights how impulsivity is key to a large number of suicide attempts.[68] In one study, researchers from the US Centers for Disease Control identified 153 people in the Houston area who had committed nearly fatal suicides but had survived and therefore could be interviewed.[69] Fully 24 percent reported that less than 5 minutes elapsed between their decision to attempt suicide and the actual attempt, and an additional 24 percent said 5–19 minutes. That's impulsive! And it shows how important it is to keep lethal means away from someone so they can survive their suicidal moment.

Solutions

The Society for Research in Child Development (SRCD) is the top organization for scientists who conduct research on child and adolescent development. The greatest number of members are from psychology, but many other disciplines are represented as well, including social work, education, child and family studies, and public health. In 2023 SRCD issued one of its official policy reports, titled *Preventing Adolescent Suicide: Recommendations for Policymakers, Practitioners, Program Developers, and Researchers*.[70] That report provides the blueprint for the solutions that follow, all of which are evidence-based and were evaluated carefully by the team that wrote the report. I include solutions that go beyond firearm policy because all of us need to be aware of the multiple approaches that are needed to get the epidemic of adolescent suicide under control.

GOOD NEWS

We can help prevent adolescent suicide by restricting access to lethal means, especially guns, and requiring secure storage. Pediatricians can emphasize this to parents.

Restrict Access to Lethal Means

At the top of the list of prevention strategies is restricting adolescents' access to lethal means, and the major culprit in that category is firearms. The report recommends that policymakers pass regulations limiting adolescents' access to firearms. It also advocates for programs that encourage safe storage of firearms. These programs can be implemented in a variety of ways, including legislation requiring safe storage and information provided at visits to pediatricians. The report also recommends building barriers on bridges so that a person cannot jump off, and having healthcare providers distribute free lockboxes for medications.

Foster LGBT-Affirming Environments

LGBT youth are at heightened risk of dying by suicide, and much of that increased risk is due to the stress of anti-LGBT messages in many segments of American culture. Schools in particular need to develop policies that affirm LGBT youths' identities. Lawmakers, for their part, should refrain from passing anti-LGBT laws, such as "bathroom" laws that restrict trans adolescents to using the bathroom of their birth-assigned gender. These laws only add to the daunting pile of stresses on LGBT youth.

Universal Suicide Risk Screening for Adolescents

This screening can be implemented by healthcare providers during regular visits. "Universal" means screening all adolescents, including those who don't appear to be at risk. Research shows that people who die by suicide have typically visited a healthcare provider within a few months of their death,[71] so not screening is a tragic missed opportunity to prevent suicide. It takes only about 30 seconds to ask the four crucial questions: In the past few weeks, have you ever wished you were dead? In the past few weeks, have you ever felt that you or your family would be better off if you were dead? In the past week, have you been having thoughts of killing yourself? Have you ever tried to kill yourself? (See the website of the American Academy of Pediatrics for all of the recommendations.)

Engage Peer Leaders

Peer leaders can be tremendously effective in changing peer culture and spreading health messages. Importantly, they can make help-seeking normative in schools and on social media. Part of the problem with adolescents who are having suicidal thoughts is they do not seek help and instead hide their problem. And peers are often the first ones to know about an adolescent's suicidal thoughts. A number of programs have been developed to train peers and give them the skills they need.[72]

Provide Rapid and Remote Access to Help

The national suicide hotline (988), instituted in 2020, is a huge step in the right direction. Remote access is especially crucial for youth in rural areas, where in-person care may be nonexistent or require long travel. You don't have to be feeling suicidal yourself to use the 988 number. You can use it, for example, if you are concerned about a friend. Everyone should have 988 memorized in the same way they do 911.

What About Adults?

Although the SRCD report addressed prevention of adolescent suicide, most of the recommendations apply to the prevention of suicide in adults. Restricting access to lethal means—especially guns—is crucial, and the 988 number can help everyone.

Red Flag Laws

Red Flag laws are also known as ERPO (Extreme Risk Protection Order) laws. According to a 2022 Gallup poll, 81 percent of Americans agree with allowing courts to order the removal of guns from a person who has been determined to be a danger to themselves or others.[73] There is broad consensus about this one. Can we get Congress to pass it? If not that, does your state have a Red Flag law?

In encouraging states to pass ERPO laws, the media can be the good guys. Researchers analyzed newspaper coverage about ERPO laws in three states that passed the legislation (Florida, Vermont, and Rhode Island) and three states that did not pass it (Pennsylvania, Ohio, and Colorado).[74] Articles in the ERPO-passing states were more likely to frame gun violence as preventable and to mention scientific research on ERPOs. Reporters can play a key role in reducing gun suicides and homicides by the way they write stories on gun violence.

Collaborations with Progun Advocates

An unlikely alliance has come together to prevent firearm suicide: progun advocates, government agencies, suicide prevention organizations, health care providers, and psychology researchers.[75]

One of the accomplishments of the alliance is the development of safety counseling about highly lethal means (guns) that is consistent with firearm owners' values. So much of the effort in suicide prevention has focused on mental health, as it should, but it has ignored the critical role that firearms play in suicide attempts that are lethal. The safety counseling may come from pediatricians, psychologists, and any number of other health care providers who see people who are at risk or are the parents or other relatives of someone who is at risk.

A second accomplishment is the launch of public education campaigns led by progun advocates to promote extra-secure storage practices among high-risk individuals. With these programs, gun owners at risk for suicide can voluntarily store their weapons away from home, in a facility where they can't get at them quickly in an impulsive moment. For example, Hold My Guns is a "liberty-based non-profit" that connects firearm owners with federal firearm licensees (gun sellers) who can provide safe storage. Notice the term "liberty" in the description, which is consistent with the values of progun advocates.

These initiatives rest on a key insight: most progun advocates know someone who has died by gun suicide. That creates a psychological opening to engage them in constructive work to prevent firearm suicide. The initiatives also rest on an assumption that progun advocates can become allies in efforts to reduce the number of suicides.

A major strength of these initiatives is they don't require anything like overturning the Second Amendment, or even passing legislation at the state level. These are great, evidence-based practices. Let's spread them more widely across the country!

CHAPTER SEVEN

How the Gun Lobby Uses Psychology for Profit and Power

WHEN WE THINK OF SECOND AMENDMENT ISSUES AND ACTIVISTS WHO BLOCK commonsense gun regulations, the NRA (National Rifle Association) first comes to mind, but the Gun Lobby extends well beyond the NRA and includes other gun organizations such as the Gun Owners of America (GOA), as well as gun sellers and gun manufacturers. Each of these troupes of actors plays a role in ensuring that more and more Americans buy more and more guns, and that the Second Amendment remains untouchable. And each of these troupes of actors use powerful psychological techniques to achieve those goals, probably without realizing their debt to psychology.

THE NRA

The NRA was not always the crushing political force that it is now. Founded in 1871, its original purpose was to improve marksmanship, which was thought to be urgent after the Civil War had demonstrated that so many American men were terrible shots.

Since then, the fortunes of the organization have ebbed and flowed until, beginning in 1977, the NRA pursued a continuous path to ascendancy. In 1921 it had only 3,500 members, but by 1960 it had 325,000 and currently claims that it has five million members.[1]

A turning point occurred at the annual meeting in 1977, held in Cincinnati, in what is called the Revolt at Cincinnati. In the years before that, two factions had emerged within the NRA: the traditionalists, who wanted to continue the long tradition of NRA cultivation of marksmanship and shooting sports, and the insurgents, who wanted to take a hard line in support of the Second

Amendment and in opposition to any gun control legislation.[2] The insurgents won the election for NRA leadership and they charted a course that continues to the present. In addition, whereas before 1977, the NRA had been relatively nonpartisan, beginning in 1977 it aligned itself with the Republican Party. Both organizations helped grow each other's power.

An analysis by political scientist Matthew Lacombe shows that the NRA has achieved its goals of influence and power in two ways: by systematically promoting gun ownership as an *identity*, and by fostering *gun-centric beliefs*.[3] To obtain data on these questions, Lacombe analyzed NRA editorials. An editorial appears in each issue of the *American Rifleman*, the official magazine of the NRA, and a subscription to it is included in membership. The editorial is typically written by the president of the NRA, so the editorials provide a window into what the leadership of the NRA is promoting.

The NRA, over decades, has fostered a gun-owner identity in a number of ways; one of those is a psychological technique that involves favorable portrayals of the in-group (other gun owners) and unfavorable portrayals of the out-group (those who favor gun regulations). Computerized analysis of the language used in editorials from 1930 to 2008 shows that gun owners are consistently portrayed as courageous, law-abiding, patriotic citizens who love freedom.[4] Supporters of gun control are described in negative terms such as in the following excerpt, which addressed a gun-control proposal during the Clinton administration, in response to the 1999 deadly shootings at Columbine High School: "[The proposal is] a hateful and bigoted war . . . against American firearms owners. [President Clinton is pursuing] what can only be called a "cultural cleansing"— specifically targeting the bedrock Second Amendment beliefs of firearm owners for extinction."[5]

Pretty extreme words! You can also see in this excerpt the striking ways in which the NRA cultivates the emotion of fear to promote in-group cohesion. Gun owners must stand together in the face of imminent threat.

To get at whether this heated rhetoric actually affects NRA members, Lacombe analyzed the language used in letters to the editor of four major American newspapers (the *New York Times, Arizona Republic, Atlanta Journal-Constitution*, and *Chicago Tribune*) about gun regulations. These letters offer a window into the thinking of average gun owners, not the NRA leadership. Lacombe compared the letters from progun writers with those from antigun writers. The progun writers' letters did indeed reflect a gun owners' identity and—this is the concerning part—used language from NRA editorials that appeared a few months earlier. The NRA has been extremely successful at shaping the identities and thinking of its members.

The NRA has further embellished the gun-owner identity by linking it to actual American soldiers' sacrifice to the nation in Vietnam and other wars.[6] In this New War culture, honors fit for soldiers are extended to nonmilitary men armed to defend their families in a dangerous world.

Beyond identity, the NRA has also promoted a gun-centric set of beliefs.[7] For example, in recent decades it has declared that the Second Amendment is "America's First Freedom"—that is, the right to guns is necessary to protect all other rights and is more important than all other rights. Never mind that a major force in its inclusion in the Bill of Rights was the demand from Southern slave owners, who had to have guns to put down slave rebellions, as you may remember from chapter 4. Guns most definitely did not mean freedom for a large segment of Americans in 1789.

If you asked constitutional law scholars whether the right to bear arms is America's first freedom, I doubt they would agree. But that's not what the NRA is about, well-thought-out legal principles. "America's First Freedom" is a snappy slogan that rallies believers, and that's all that counts.

The NRA also promotes a broader set of beliefs by linking gun rights to other issues, such as control of crime, liberty, and limited government. The result is a gun-centric worldview in which gun rights are the central focus, and a natural alliance with the Republican Party.

In their book *Guns, Democracy, and the Insurrectionist Idea*, legal scholars Joshua Horwitz and Casey Anderson make the case that the NRA has also sold a closely related belief, that widespread private ownership of guns is essential to ensure freedom and prevent a tyrannical US government from taking over and wiping out our freedoms.[8] But that's not all. According to this view, armed insurrection by American citizens may be needed and can be justified. The consequence? A sizable segment of gun owners believe they have a right to engage in insurrection if they don't like the direction the government is taking. The eerie thing is that this book was published in 2009, 12 years before the January 6, 2021, insurrection at the US Capitol attempting to overturn the results of the 2020 presidential election. Clearly the authors' arguments were validated, and in a deeply troubling way.

In recent years, the NRA has promoted the gun-owner identity and gun-centric beliefs not only through the *American Rifleman*, but also through its concealed carry training programs in most states, as described in a later section.

It is worth noting that, in the *American Rifleman*, the NRA promotes two ideas that are logically inconsistent: government overreach and government underreach.[9] That is, it seeds the belief that the government could take away your firearms at any moment (government overreach) while simultaneously claiming that the government is too weak to protect you (government underreach).

In 2024, there were signs that the NRA was in decline, at least somewhat. Membership was down to 4.2 million from 6 million just five years before, and revenue was down substantially.[10] The organization had, strategically, filed for bankruptcy in 2021, although the request was denied by a judge. Wayne LaPierre, the longtime leader of the NRA, resigned in January 2024 and was convicted, along with other leaders, of financial misconduct and corruption in the organization.[11] Even if the NRA were to implode tomorrow, though, it would still leave behind legions of those whom it has persuaded to adopt a gun-owner identity and a gun-centric set of beliefs.

GRASSROOTS ACTIVISTS: GUN SELLERS

Merchants of the Right. That's what sociologist Jennifer Carlson calls them, based on her extensive interviews with gun sellers and analysis of their websites.[12] As it turns out, your local gun sellers in brick-and-mortar stores do a lot more than sell guns. They also spread a gospel—or in psychological terms, socialize their customers into a culture of gun ownership and politics. They constitute an enormous informal network of grassroots gun activists across the country. To get an idea of the magnitude of this network, there are 78,000 licensed gun dealers in the United States—more than all the McDonald's, Burger King, Subway, and Wendy's stores combined.[13]

According to Carlson, gun sellers promote three bedrock principles: armed individualism, conspiracy theorizing, and partisanship.[14] *Armed individualism* capitalizes on the American spirit of individualism, in which individuals are expected to take care of themselves and solve their own problems. To take care of yourself today, says the Gun Lobby, you need firearms because the police and government will not take care of you, and civil society might collapse at any moment. You need a gun to survive.

Conspiracy theorizing encourages people to be skeptical of experts and the government. This skepticism was on full display during the Covid-19 pandemic beginning in 2020, when a segment of the population thought that the government was trying to seize power by encouraging the wearing of face masks and ordering the closure of some businesses. That same segment of the population didn't believe that scientists could produce a vaccine against Covid, much less as quickly as they did. Amid this conspiracy theorizing, the solution was to arm yourself against the government takeover.

Partisanship is the third bedrock principle conveyed by gun sellers. Following this principle, the Republican Party is the only one that can be trusted to uphold the Second Amendment and your right to guns. The Democratic Party and its members are viewed contemptuously. They are the enemy and no negotiation, no compromise, is possible. It's tough for a democracy to function in the absence of a spirit of compromise. And yet the Gun Lobby's stance has been "No compromise. No gun legislation."

By promoting these three principles, the Gun Lobby and your local gun seller have bulldozed their way through American government. This was most stunningly displayed on January 6, 2021, when a mob attacked the US Capitol, attempting to overturn the results of the 2020 presidential election. As armed individualists, the insurrectionists thought they needed to solve the election problem themselves because the government wouldn't do it. Conspiracy theories—the election had been stolen—spread like wildfire, and the election of a Democrat, Joe Biden, would spell the end of their gun rights and, more broadly, the end of society as they knew it. The formation of such a large mass of like-minded people occurred partly on the internet, but it also was the fruit of hundreds of thousands of one-on-one, face-to-face interactions between gun sellers and their customers.

Based on my conversations with gun sellers, I have to say that I am impressed with their sincerity. They seem to truly want to help people who want to protect themselves, and their solution is guns. I accept their sincerity and good intentions, but that does not negate the fact that their efforts rest on a set of false assumptions, notably that having a gun in your home or your handbag will keep you safer, when the data show just the opposite. It's also true that the men I spoke with are licensed sellers. They may well be a more virtuous group than online sellers and various illegal sellers.

The year 2020 saw a particularly combustible combination of three crises: the Covid-19 pandemic, the murder of George Floyd by Minneapolis police and resulting race demonstrations, and the presidential election. "Panic buyers"—folks who previously were antigun but now wanted one—appeared at gun stores. One gun seller, reflecting on the new types of individuals who were gun buyers in 2020, said,

> *They are the people—all the people that [people] say shouldn't have guns, they are the ones coming in to buy guns! Everybody else already had their gun. I*

hate to say it so plainly like that, but I had a kid walk into my store with a Bernie Sanders shirt on. I got a Trump 2020 poster here, I got all kinds of shit here! This kid says, "Oh I need a gun! I want to use the gun show loophole!" I had to stop him—he left out of here almost crying. I am very confident that I converted him to grow up in the little time I had him, and he actually left here thanking me for Trump.[15]

In social psychological terms, gun sellers engage in persuasion, and the power of that persuasion is enormous.

Another gun seller, reflecting on the surge of buying associated with racial protests, said,

You are on your own. The riots proved to everyone, regardless of political agenda or political affiliation, that they cannot protect you. People were getting drugs out of their cars, places of business were being burnt to the ground, people were being killed, people were being attacked, and the police could not do anything. And the general theme was: I always just thought I was safe. I didn't realize that when it hits the fan, there's no one to protect you but yourself.[16]

In this context and with this set of beliefs, the story of Kyle Rittenhouse makes some sense. Kyle, a White 17-year-old, was from Illinois. In August 2020, he traveled to Kenosha, Wisconsin, to do something about Black Lives Matter protests that were being held there. Ostensibly, his goal was to protect businesses. The protests had been triggered by the police shooting of Jacob Blake, a Black man, in Kenosha. Rittenhouse carried an AR-15 into the midst of the protesters. What followed is disputed, but the bottom line is that Rittenhouse shot three people, two of them fatally. He was later acquitted of the murders, claiming self-defense, despite lack of evidence for the claim. Rittenhouse became a hero in conservative media. Tucker Carlson recorded a long interview with him for Fox News, and his image was used widely in spaces such as a gun sale and a video game.

Beliefs in armed individualism help us understand his actions. How else would it make sense for a 17-year-old from another state to think that it was his job to travel to Wisconsin and solve the "problem" of protests, armed with his AR-15? (For a list of gun terms, see table 7.1.)

Table 7.1 Gun Terminology

AK-47	A Soviet semiautomatic rifle derived from a German design at the end of World War II. The Soviet developer was Kalashnikov.
AR-15	A semiautomatic rifle designed by Eugene Stoner at the ArmaLite company, USA.
Automatic rifle	Fires a stream of bullets when the shooter holds down the trigger.
Bump stock	A part that replaces a rifle's standard stock, the part against the shoulder, harnessing kickback energy so that the rifle fires nearly as rapidly as a machine gun.
Caliber	The caliber of a bullet is its diameter. The caliber of a gun is the internal diameter of the barrel.
Cartridge	A bullet in a metal casing that includes propellant.
Ghost gun	Untraceable gun with no serial number, which can be assembled at home from purchased parts or an individual milling machine.
Glock switch	A quarter-size device that changes a Glock pistol so that it can fire 1,200 rounds per minute.
M16	The US military's version of the AR-15.
Machine gun	A fully automatic firearm, usually mounted on a tripod, that fires rapidly from a single trigger pull.
Round	Another term for cartridge.
Semiautomatic rifle	Fires one shot per trigger pull and automatically loads the next round so the shooter can immediately pull the trigger again, thus firing rapidly.

Source: Janet Hyde.

The AR-15

So many mass shootings have been committed with AR-15s that it is impossible to number them, but here is a partial list: Aurora, Colorado, movie theater shooting (2012); Sandy Hook Elementary School, Newtown, Connecticut (2012); Las Vegas music festival (2017); Marjory Stoneman Douglas High School, Parkland, Florida (2018); Buffalo, New York, grocery store shooting (2022); Robb Elementary School, Uvalde, Texas (2022); Louisville, Kentucky, bank shooting (2023); Allen, Texas, mall shooting (2023); and Jacksonville, Florida, Dollar General Store (2023), not to mention the attempted assassination of Donald Trump (2024). How did this weapon that is so effective for mass shootings come into being? And how did it get into the hands of so many civilians?

It all began with an amateur engineer/inventor, Eugene Stoner, born in 1922 in Southern California.[17] His father took him hunting, a common father-son activity at the time. Even as a 10-year-old, Gene built small rockets. As I read Gene's story, I don't see anything that sounds like he was a little pre-psychopath or anything even close. He was just a kid who loved to tinker with mechanical things and figure out how to make them work better. He was a genius at that kind of thing.

Stoner didn't have the money to go to college, so he went straight from high school to working at Vega Aircraft Corporation, work that involved installing machine guns on war planes, and soon World War II was in high gear. When Stoner enlisted in the Marine Corps, they wisely took note of his experience and assigned him to work on machine guns on their planes. All along the way, he was learning more and more about guns and how they functioned best.

After the war, he worked for a company that manufactured aircraft parts. His performance in the machine shop was so excellent that the head of the engineering department, Bob Wilson, invited him to work with them, despite his lack of a college degree.[18] Wilson mentored Stoner in engineering and soon they formed their own consulting business.

Then the Korean War started. American soldiers were using the semiautomatic rifle of World War II, the M1 Garand, which weighed nearly 10 lbs. without ammunition. After one stunning defeat, the American military realized their equipment was inadequate and, in particular, they needed a new model for a rifle.

As a sidebar, but an important one, toward the end of World War II, German engineers had developed a new rifle, the name of which Americans translated as "assault rifle," which is the origin of that term. Germany was defeated so quickly at that point that Germans never got to use the rifle. But Russians captured many of those rifles and took them back to the motherland, where they were studied and developed into semiautomatic AK-47s. In the Korean War, the North Koreans had AK-47s kindly supplied by Russia, which overwhelmed the Americans' old M1 Garands. The race was on to develop a better American semiautomatic rifle, and Gene Stoner was just the man for the task.

Stoner realized the immense potential of aluminum for manufacturing guns because it weighs a fraction of what steel does. He also had major insights about how to improve the insides of a gun, but I won't drag you into that. His new gun weighed less than 7 lbs. and had little kickback to the shoulder compared with the M1 Garand. Eventually he and others formed a company called ArmaLite, and it is the source of the "AR" in AR-15 (not "assault rifle" as some mistakenly think).[19]

One problem with this lighter rifle was that it wasn't as accurate as the old-style rifle, but then the developers figured out that with a semiautomatic if you just fire a lot of bullets, you're bound to hit what you want. That's what the Soviet AK-47 did.

Stoner's rifle went through rounds of engineering improvements but the American military tried to block it at every stage. They didn't like innovation. Stoner also had the insight that smaller bullets would be better—troops could carry more ammunition—so he used .223 caliber bullets.

The military worried that such a small bullet wouldn't do enough damage.[20] I can't bear to tell you all the details about how they tested it on a herd of pigs and later a herd of goats. The upshot was that, because the bullet was light, once it entered the body, it started to spiral around and do much more damage to the body than a larger, heavier bullet would. The AR-15's bullet rips up flesh, and does so to this very day. Stoner believed that he was building something that would help the United States defeat communist insurgents around the world. It was designed strictly for military use.

One US general championed the AR-15 and convinced the military to adopt it, but then a committee within the military decided to make modifications to it and its ammunition. None of them were engineers and the modifications were a disaster, as you might expect for gun design by committee. No one thought to consult Stoner. As a result, the AR-15, called the M16 by the military and now manufactured by Colt, performed horribly for soldiers in Vietnam. Countless American soldiers died because of the modifications by committee, and the M16 gained a reputation as a terrible firearm.

In the 1960s, a watershed moment occurred when Colt decided to sell a modified version of the AR-15, which they called the Sporter, to civilians. What a great way to generate more profits! Colt marketed the Sporter as a semiautomatic version of the automatic rifle that the armed forces purchased and used, but it didn't catch on at the time, partly because things were going badly in Vietnam. However, by the late 1970s, White nationalism was gaining strength in the United States and its devotees loved the AR-15.[21] In the 1980s, AR-15s became more common and were marketed widely as assault rifles. Other companies besides Colt, such as Bushmaster, began manufacturing and marketing them, generating record profits, in a business plan that persists to the present day.

Meanwhile, the NRA had transformed from an organization for hunters into a powerful political force that opposed any kind of gun safety regulations. Mass shootings with the AR-15 occurred, the public demanded gun regulation, some politicians tried to propose meaningful legislation, and the NRA shot it down every time. This pattern repeated itself in countless cycles over the years.

And that, my friends, is how we got here today, with semiautomatic AR-15s designed for the military to do maximum damage to the enemy, readily available to the general public and unregulated. That brings us to the psychology of the strategies to market the AR-15 and other firearms to civilians.

The Gun Lobby's Marketing Strategy I: Fear

The frightening terrorist attacks of September 11, 2001, thrust the AR-15 into prominence. Members of the armed services, deployed everywhere including US airports, carried their AR-15s openly, incidentally providing free advertising.[22] The gun was patriotic, a defense against the overwhelming assault of terrorism. Sales to civilians soared. The Gun Lobby capitalized on the fear ignited by the terrorist attacks to sell their products, and especially the AR-15.

Research shows that the Gun Lobby systematically stokes Americans' fears to get them to buy guns.[23] In 2008, Barack Obama was the Democratic candidate for president and the next chapter of fear-based marketing unfolded. On the campaign trail, Obama did his best to maintain a moderate position on guns, saying that he supported the right of individuals to own guns and also supported some gun regulations.[24] He had to be cautious because Democrats had already been defeated by Gun Lobby forces on numerous occasions over the past 15 years. But even with that moderate approach, the NRA took aim against him, while supporting John McCain, the Republican candidate.

The NRA used just the prospect of Obama's election to sell guns, and they didn't feel the need to constrain themselves to telling the truth. The NRA told its members, "Never in NRA's history have we faced a presidential candidate . . . with such a deep-rooted hatred of firearm freedoms."[25] No doubt the fact that President Obama is Black activated some implicit associations with threat, too.

In the three months before the election, Smith & Wesson sold three times as many AR-15s as they had in those same three months the year before. Americans had to stock up before the Obama-imposed drought that was forecast. After the election, with Obama in office, AR-15 sales soared even more, fueled by the fears that had been seeded by the Gun Lobby. Despite the global recession that began in 2008, gun manufacturers and sellers prospered.

In 2019, in an event emblematic of the current pattern, a man with an AR-15 and a 100-round drum started firing in a bar in Dayton, Ohio.[26] Police were right there and fatally shot him just 30 seconds after he opened fire. You couldn't ask for a faster police response. But in that time, he had pulled the trigger 41 times and had killed nine people while wounding 14. The semiautomatic capabilities of the AR-15, so effective in war, now enabled a war on civilians in the United States. In response to incidents like the Dayton shooting, the NRA promotes the idea that the solution is an "armed citizenry," who can act before police can. Once again, the NRA uses the strategy of evoking fear to drive people to buy more guns. The Dayton case exposes the faulty logic in the armed citizenry argument. The police response was swift and they got the bad guy. The problem was not the police response, it was the lightning-speed lethality of the AR-15.

Analyses of gun manufacturers' communications show that they attempt to encourage fear about personal safety,[27] never mind that the rate of violent crime has declined since the 1990s. The manufacturers' communications also seek to undermine scientific evidence and minimize the harm inflicted by guns, all in the interest of profits.

THE GUN LOBBY'S MARKETING STRATEGY II: MASCULINITY
As discussed in chapter 3, owning and carrying a gun have long been ways for a man to project an aura of masculinity. Guns help men "perform" masculinity, and gun manufacturers and sellers use this capability to sell their wares. The NRA portrays the ideal gun owner using iconic images of masculinity linked to American virtue.[28]

In addition, some have suggested that guns are Barbies for men.[29] Owning a gun projects masculinity, but you can still play with them. You can even buy accessories for firearms. And, just as some girls feel the need for 10 or 20 Barbies, some men feel the need for 10 or 20 guns. Meanwhile, profits soar for the gun manufacturers and sellers.

THE GUN LOBBY'S MARKETING STRATEGY III: NEW MARKETS

In 2023 I was relaxing, watching an episode of the new series *NCIS: Sydney*. During a break, a commercial appeared on the screen, although it took me a moment to figure out what it was about. It featured an attractive, blonde, twenty-something woman. First, she saddled up her horse and herded a few cattle in an unsystematic way. Next she appeared in camo gear in a forest with high-tech bow hunting equipment. Then she was in exercise clothes, jogging down a highway. In each segment, a little rectangle appeared, pointing to something at her waist, with the word "Glock." In the next screen, the message was "Confidence fits any lifestyle." She continued running and the words "Glock Strong" appeared. The finale showed a black screen with GLOCK.COM in stark block letters. Having exhausted the market for guns as masculinity boosters for men, the gun manufacturers needed a new market and conceived a major innovation, marketing to women.

On the NRA website, there's a section called "Women's Interests." It features programs such as Women on Target® Instructional Shooting Clinics, and Refuse to be a Victim®. All photos show White women, most of them blonde. The advertising and training foster the image of "a good woman with a gun."[30] The NRA has also produced videos intended to boost sales to women. Analysis of the language used in the videos indicates they imply the solution to the problem of violence against women is for women to own guns—instead of men ceasing to engage in violence.[31]

Next, the Gun Lobby got the idea to not limit themselves to adult purchasers and extend their reach to children. The result? The JR-15, a child-size AR-15. If you don't believe me, go to AmmoLand.com and you can see videos. Figure 7.1 shows one of the advertising photos for the JR-15, with a father kindly helping his daughter—who looks like she's about six years old—to peer down the sight of her JR-15. When these ads were released in January 2023, a public outcry ensued, but I did a screen capture before the photo was taken down.

When it comes to increasing markets, the Gun Lobby knows no bounds.

An association supports all these marketing efforts. The National Shooting Sports Foundation is the gun industry's trade association, that is, marketing group. It sponsors SHOT Show annually, during which you, as a retailer, can take courses from SHOT University. For 2024, sessions included "Improve Profits NOW!: Ten actions to improve profits in 2024!" and "The FFLs Guide to an ATF Audit & How to Prevent a NOR." Just so you know, FFL refers to federal firearm licensees, that is, licensed gun sellers. ATF is the federal Bureau of Alcohol, Tobacco, and Firearms, and NOR is a Notice of Revocation—losing

Figure 7.1.   Advertising the JR-15 for children, 2023.
WEE 1 TACTICAL

your license. Oh, and SHOT is an acronym for Shooting, Hunting, and Outdoor Trade Show. Through the National Shooting Sports Foundation, sellers gain immense resources for managing their business and selling more guns.

THE CONCEALED CARRY TRAINING PROGRAM

The majority of states allow concealed carry, which refers to an individual carrying a pistol under their jacket, in a backpack, or in some other concealed way, outside their home. Although a few states just let people do it with no need for a license, most of the states require some training in order to obtain a license. What a great idea! Making sure that anyone who will be carrying a gun routinely has some training in gun safety, marksmanship, and so on.

Not so fast. Sociologist Jennifer Carlson (winner of a MacArthur "genius" Award for her superb research on Gun Culture) conducted an in-depth study of the culture of concealed carrying and licensing in the state of Michigan.[32] As it turns out, the NRA has a near-monopoly on training the instructors for these courses, who become NRA-certified instructors. Many of them go out to open their own training programs, all based on the same model and using NRA training materials. In this part of its operation, the NRA portrays itself as a service organization, but from a psychological point of view, it has taken on the role of a massive agent of socialization, inculcating a particular point of view.

A typical course takes place in a single, eight-hour day.[33] Only a small portion of it—perhaps two to three hours—is devoted to marksmanship training, that is, shooting to accurately hit a target. The majority of the day is classroom time, during which the approach is ostensibly to cultivate responsible, safety-conscious, gun-carrying citizens. Let's unpack the psychology of what goes on.

As the class gets underway, the NRA-certified instructor asks whether you are the rare kind of citizen who is willing to use a gun to protect innocent life.[34] Are you capable of using deadly force? Psychologically, if you're asked if you are that rare kind of citizen, of course you want to be in that elite group. It's a challenge and you want to rise to it. The use of euphemisms is also meaningful. "Are you capable of using deadly force?" actually means, "Are you capable of murdering another human being?" Deadly force is so much more palatable, and "force" itself conjures up masculine strength rather than murder.

In its training materials, the NRA says, "Those who include a firearm in their personal protection plans are affirming the value of their own lives and those of their family members. The ethical person does not ever want to use deadly force, but recognizes that there are times when it may be the only option to protect innocent lives."[35] These two sentences reframe a gun owner's cognitions so that they come to think of the use of deadly force (killing) as ethical.

The concealed carry course uses the technique of visualization, borrowed from psychology. Students are told to visualize imagined threats and how they would respond to them to defend themselves and others. One instructor joked that he visualizes crime scenarios so habitually that "I've already killed about a dozen guys since we've been sitting right here."[36] Let's unpack that juicy one.

Humans have *attentional biases*. We selectively pay attention to some things in our environment and ignore—pay no attention to—others. According to one theory, humans are predisposed to direct their attention to stimuli, such as snakes, that were threatening as we evolved.[37] It was a matter of survival, and it was adaptive to quickly detect such stimuli and feel fearful when we detected them so that we ran away. Research also shows that we pay extra attention to modern threat stimuli such as knives and guns.[38] They weren't present in early human evolution so why do they grab our attention? The answer is learning. That is, we have learned that knives and guns pose threats. It's not only about evolution; it's also about conditioning. Even three-year-olds show an attentional bias toward syringes.[39] They have learned to associate a syringe with a poke in the arm. In laboratory studies, their little eyes go right to the photo of the syringe and not to the photo of a neutral object.

Back to the NRA-certified instructor who constantly visualizes crime scenarios and killing the bad guy. He is conditioning himself, over and over again, in two ways: (1) to detect threatening stimuli in his environment; and (2) to shoot to kill when he detects one. All this visualized practice will be quite useful if he is suddenly confronted with a terrorist armed with an AR-15. This has never actually happened to me, but perhaps it would happen to him.

The catch is that there is an error rate in detecting threatening stimuli.[40] Two kinds of errors may occur. One is to miss the threatening stimulus. The instructor doesn't see the terrorist and is mowed down by the AR-15. That is highly unlikely to happen because the instructor has conditioned himself so thoroughly to detect threats in his environment, and also because the probability of a terrorist springing out of the bushes is very low. The other kind of error is the more concerning: he thinks he sees a threat and fires his weapon, but there was actually no threat. He has killed an innocent person. He has conditioned himself so strenuously to avoid the first kind of error that he has vastly increased his chances of making the second kind of error—perceiving a threat that isn't there. And that mistake could lead not to the protection, but to the loss of innocent life.

The NRA training materials provide no instruction on perceiving the difference between a real threat and a nonthreat.[41] The training is all about detecting threats in a situation and completely neglects recognition of situations that are just fine. It therefore seriously biases students' attention toward seeing threats everywhere.

Jennifer Carlson tells the story of Aaron, one of the gun carriers she interviewed.[42] Aaron, who is African American, was driving home with his kids in the car when he decided to stop at a gas station to buy some lottery tickets. He carried because he wanted to be able to protect his children, and he was an NRA-certified instructor. A woman had her car at one of the pumps and Aaron left space for her. As he entered the gas station, she accosted him, angrily swearing and saying that he had blocked her in. She threatened to damage his car and he knew his kids were in it. He rushed out of the gas station to see her driving her truck toward his car. Aaron drew his weapon and told her to stop. She pulled out her cell phone, but Aaron couldn't tell whether it was a gun. She dialed 911. No shots were fired. The police arrived in response to the 911 call from the woman, and Aaron was arrested, in front of his children, for brandishing a deadly weapon toward an unarmed woman. Aaron had started out the day as a responsible citizen protector, but due to his conditioning to perceive threats and to respond by pulling out his gun, he ended the day having committed a felony.

POLICE TRAINING

Crucial elements of police academy cadet training bear a striking resemblance to the NRA-managed training of civilians. Sociologist Samantha J. Simon spent nearly a year embedded in four police training academies.[43] Principles of research ethics require her to keep the academies and the individuals anonymous. She describes them only as being in a Southern state.

Cadets are repeatedly warned that their lives are on the line every day in police work, and they must be ready to shoot and kill if they want to make it home alive. Across academies, cadets are shown a photo of the aftermath of the 2017 ambush murder of Clinton Greenwood, a police constable, with blood spattered across the side of his car. One can't help wondering if there are many of these ambushes because there seems to be only one photo of one incident to show. Cadets watch videos of police being beaten and killed while on duty. In short, they are conditioned to perceive threats everywhere.

All the emphasis is on the suspect who has a gun and fires at an officer who made a mistake and didn't detect the gun. Only lip service is paid to the opposite error: believing that an unarmed citizen has a gun and shooting to kill that person. We won't stop police shootings of innocent people until we correct this and other aspects of police training.

I am not denying that police officers encounter dangers in their work and must be ready to defend themselves. But a large part of the problem is all the guns in the hands of US civilians, some of whom really are bad guys. If firearms were not so easily available, the police would have less cause to worry about being shot by criminals and would be less likely to make the fatal error of shooting an unarmed citizen. In support of this idea, research shows that the rate of fatal police shootings is correlated, across states, with the rate of household gun ownership in those states.[44] The 10 states with the highest gun ownership rates (e.g., Alabama, Mississippi, Louisiana) have more than twice the rate of fatal police shootings compared to the five states with the lowest gun ownership rates (e.g., Massachusetts, Hawaii, New Jersey). Across all states, only 56 percent of decedents were armed with a gun.

Overall, then, the good news is that a more balanced approach to training police, emphasizing the detection of both threats and nonthreats, paired with stricter gun laws that reduce the threat to police of armed civilians, should reduce the rate of fatal police shootings. Offering a scientific ray of hope, a recent study

> ## GOOD NEWS
>
> A more balanced approach to police training, including recognition of both threats and nonthreats, should reduce the rate of fatal police shootings.

showed that a well-structured session of visual training to detect a firearm versus neutral object greatly increased the accuracy of subjects' identification of guns versus cell phones in a fast-paced encounter.[45] This exercise could be incorporated into police training easily and cheaply. And just imagine the impact it would have if it were incorporated into all the concealed-carry licensure programs for civilians.

UNWITTING ALLIES: THE MASS MEDIA

The US studios that create television programs and movies are not, to my knowledge, controlled by the Gun Lobby, but their portrayals of guns and gun violence make them unwitting allies.

Researchers from USC's Annenberg School studied 250 episodes from 33 different TV series from the 2019–2020 and 2020–2021 seasons to see how guns and gun safety were portrayed.[46] Here are some of their key findings:

- Guns were everywhere—about 6 in 10 episodes had gun-related content.
- In 30 percent of episodes, a gun was fired.
- Fewer than 10 percent of the episodes included anything about secure gun storage or gun laws. *The Equalizer* stood out, though, for showing secure gun storage in multiple episodes.
- The majority of firearm depictions involved law enforcement officers acting in the role of "good guys."
- Those who were shot were usually "bad guys."
- Only one episode, out of all 250, portrayed the role of guns in domestic violence.

This programming is not doing a thing to address the epidemic of gun violence in America. In fact, it is contributing to Gun Culture. We should demand that the studios develop a code that discourages this normalizing of guns and shooting, just as the studios developed a code about portrayals of smoking.

In 2021, actor Alec Baldwin was filming a movie, a Western titled *Rust*, in New Mexico. Baldwin fired a prop gun that, appallingly, had live ammunition in it, killing one person and wounding another. My concern is not with who was guilty of what. Instead, let's do a cost-benefit analysis. What is the benefit? How much does one more movie about the Wild West contribute to American culture? I would say it's close to zero. What are the costs? Even without the killing, there is a cost to yet another portrayal of the use of guns to resolve disputes. And with the death, the cost is astronomical. Why should a movie like this ever be produced? The Motion Picture Association of America might take up this question.

I have to admit to a fondness for British crime shows. The police cleverly solve the crime and arrest the perp, and no one has a gun. The police rarely carry guns unless they are going into a situation where the perps have guns, but the perps rarely have guns because . . . it's not the United States The shows are no less compelling and entertaining.

Not only could the producers of movies and television eliminate their contributions to Gun Culture, they could actually help to promote gun safety. One study showed a sample of American adults either a clip from *Grey's Anatomy* that addressed an unintentional shooting in a home involving an unsecured gun, or a control clip with no gun content.[47] Afterward, those who had viewed the *Grey's Anatomy* clip showed greater knowledge of gun safety facts. If gun safety content were included in dozens of programs, the impact could be enormous.

Solutions

From an analysis of the Gun Lobby's use of psychology, two strategies emerge for reducing gun deaths: promoting a GunSense Majority identity; and countering the all-too-persuasive messages of the progun forces. It is also imperative that we hold banks accountable for their role in gun sales.

A GunSense Majority Identity

The Gun Lobby's successful psychological approaches can actually provide a road map for those who seek to reduce gun violence in America. The NRA, gun sellers, and gun manufacturers have been brilliantly successful at creating a gun-owner identity and convincing millions of Americans to take on that identity, in many cases as their primary identity, eclipsing other identities such as father or husband. That powerful identity then mobilizes its adherents to vote for certain political candidates to protest even the mildest gun regulations, and so on. Can those who want to reduce gun deaths apply some of these same principles?

An important finding from Lacombe's analysis of letters to the editor is that among the progun letters 64 percent used identity language, whereas among the antigun letters only 39 percent used identity language. Those who advocate for gun safety by and large lack a compelling identity, an identity as strong as that of gun owners.

What should this new identity be called? The NRA calls it antigun, but that's not really what it's about. It's really about applying some common sense about guns—GunSense—to policies, laws, and the way we live our lives. It's about gun death prevention—preventing children's deaths by firearms, preventing adults' deaths, preventing suicide deaths by guns. It's not about striking down the Second Amendment; it's about saving lives, and just using some common sense. And GunSense folks constitute the majority in the United States.

Some organizations have already entered this arena, most notably two linked nonprofits: Everytown for Gun Safety, and Moms Demand Action for Gun Sense in America. Everytown is the central organization, conducting research, leading legal challenges, and receiving donations. Moms is the grassroots activist group, with chapters in all 50 states.

Moms is, in many ways, the gun-safety parallel to the NRA and its members. Moms boasts nearly 10 million supporters, more than the NRA. Does Moms successfully deploy the same strategies that have made the NRA so powerful, especially creating a salient identity and worldview? I have immersed myself in the organization since 2022, not in the sense of conducting systematic research, but in the sense of exploring as many aspects of it as possible. My overall observation is that Moms does many things right, but is sometimes limited in its effectiveness because of its high ethical standards.

- Moms does promote an identity, marked by volunteers wearing red T-shirts that say Moms Demand Action (and, in small letters, For Gun Sense in America). Moms volunteers appear en masse in the red shirts, in places like legislative hearings on gun laws. Monthly local gatherings also foster the Moms identity.

- Moms does not insist that its members put that identity above all others. Although you don't have to be a mom to join—men, grandmas, and so on are welcome—the majority of the membership probably is mothers, who therefore are managing childcare and careers in addition to volunteering with the organization. They have many other important priorities competing for their time, identity, and mental bandwidth. Moms messaging is very kind about these issues. Comments are always supportive and there is never criticism of anyone for failing to take some action or stepping back from a leadership role. So the Moms identity is important, but it doesn't trump all other identities.

- Moms is doggedly fair and nonpartisan, in contrast to the alignment of the NRA with the Republican Party.

- Moms never uses scare tactics, much less lies, to motivate its members. The scare tactics, making members feel like they are constantly threatened, have been highly successful for the NRA. Of course, frequent mass shootings and other gun deaths should help Moms to motivate members, but Moms doesn't use those tragedies to manipulate members or crazy-glue members to the organization.

- Moms does have some training programs, but unlike the NRA's concealed carry trainings, they are not required by the government for any sought-after licensing. One of the programs is Be SMART, which is an educational program about gun safety for parents and others responsible for children. Could that program or one like it become a requirement for certifying teachers for preschools? for other kinds of licensing?

- The NRA grades politicians on a scale from A to F, with the A being intense support for gun rights and opposition to gun regulation. Anyone associated with the NRA knows about this system and takes it to heart when they vote. Moms has a website, gunsensevoter.org, where you can look up a candidate and see if they have an official Gun Sense Candidate designation, which they get by completing a questionnaire and showing they favor commonsense gun regulations. However, this system is not nearly as well known as the NRA's system, and Moms members are probably not single-issue voters in the way that NRA members are.

Overall, we don't need any additional organizations devoted to reducing gun deaths. Many fine ones already exist, especially Moms Demand Action and Students Demand Action, as well as the Giffords Law Center to Prevent Gun Violence and the Sandy Hook Promise. The question is, how can we make these organizations more effective? They need to become more effective not only at producing legislation on gun regulations, but also in promoting a worldview that insists that guns are not necessary for personal safety or public safety and that the solution is fewer guns, not more.

One of the strengths of using the label GunSense Majority is that it emphasizes that those who favor gun regulations are in the majority in America. And those who refrain from gun ownership are also in the majority.

Holding Banks Accountable

If you stay at a Marriott Hotel and put the charges on your credit card, they will show up as being payments to Marriott. If you buy groceries, the charge on your credit card will appear as being at that grocery store. If you use a credit card to buy a gun from a licensed dealer, it won't show up that way. Banks have colluded with the gun industry to mask gun purchases. If a person buys five AR-15s in a month, he's up to no good and ATF should be able to flag those sales, but right now they can't because the charges don't show up as gun purchases. It would be such a simple intervention to require that banks record firearm purchases accurately, just as they do with other charges, but there has been tremendous resistance to the idea.

Go to the website isyourbankloaded.org for information on banks' collaboration with the gun industry, including ratings of banks.

Countering Progun Misinformation

In its 2024 report, the prestigious World Economic Forum ranked misinformation number 1 among global risks, even ahead of climate change![48] Aided and abetted by artificial information (AI), misinformation affects everything from the outcome of elections to whether someone gets vaccinated against a deadly virus.

Social psychologists have developed and tested methods to help people detect misinformation and resist attempts to persuade them to do unhealthy things like smoking cigarettes. How can these insights be used to help folks resist the progun messages of the Gun Lobby and its worldview that guns are the solution to every problem?

Misinformation has been defined as "information that is false or misleading, irrespective of intention or source."[49] That is, the information could be downright false or, more subtly, misleading. And it could be that the source intentionally wanted to put out false information, or it could be that the source thought their information was accurate but it turns out not to be. For example, the slogan "the only thing that stops a bad guy with a gun is a good guy with a gun" is misinformation because the scientific data show it to be false. It is difficult to judge the intentions of those who repeat the slogan—perhaps many truly believe it, so their spread of misinformation is unintentional.

Social psychologists have pioneered an effective set of techniques to battle misinformation based in what is called *inoculation theory*.[50] The idea is that we can create psychological parallels to medical approaches in which people are inoculated or vaccinated against dangerous microbes so that the microbes don't make them sick. Prevention is better, cheaper, and easier than cure. Following the parallel, we can inoculate people against efforts to persuade them to accept harmful, false beliefs. Dozens of experiments have shown that psychological inoculation works![51]

Let's take a deep dive into one of the experiments to see the details. This one tackles conspiracy theories, which have become widespread in the United States, fueled by word of mouth and social networking sites (SNS). People's beliefs in conspiracy theories actually pose a problem for democracy because citizens go to the polls and vote based on misinformation. Some conspiracy theories trigger folks to buy guns to defend themselves against whatever threat is promoted by the conspiracy theory. Researchers asked, can we inoculate people against conspiracy theories?

In phase I of the experiment, researchers first measured subjects' general susceptibility to conspiracy theories by having them rate their agreement or disagreement with statements such as "The government uses people as patsies to hide its involvement in criminal activity," "A small, secret group of people is responsible for making all major world decisions, such as going to war," and "Groups of scientists manipulate, fabricate, or suppress evidence in order to deceive the public."[52] Subjects in the inoculation group then were informed that[53]

- Although "most people are confident that they can spot and resist conspiracy theories, some of these theories are so convincing that they may lead you to harmful perceptions—despite your best efforts to resist them."

- One of the ways that conspiracy theories can lead to harmful misperceptions is by dividing the world strictly into the "evil conspirators" and the "innocent victims."

- Many conspiracy theories claim that the conspiracy "exists in darkness" but is discoverable through secret knowledge.

- Conspiracy theories "argue that nothing happens by accident; nothing is as it seems; and everything is connected."

Those in the control group did not read any of this.

In phase II, five days later, subjects were exposed to a story purportedly from an online news source (Business Insider) or a SNS (Reddit). The headline read "CIA Created Bitcoin; NSA Is Monitoring All Private Venmo Transactions" and continued from there.[54] Would participants who had been inoculated against conspiracy theories buy the story? Would they be more likely to resist it than the control group?

Compared with the control group, those who had been inoculated were significantly more likely to resist the arguments in the message and were more confident in their ability to resist conspiracy theories in the future. The inoculated folks also scored significantly lower, in phase II, on the scale measuring susceptibility to conspiracy theories. The inoculation was successful!

One interesting aspect is that the inoculation was about *generic* conspiracy theories, and it helped people resist a very *specific* conspiracy claim, about the CIA and the NSA. That's a happy result, because it means that you don't have to inoculate people against every specific conspiracy theory. General, broad inoculation should work.

These methods could be used to inoculate people against persuasive conspiracy theories promoted by the NRA. For example, in January 2024, I went to the NRA website and found this juicy news item. "Just in case anyone needed further proof that much of the federal bureaucracy is more interested in serving themselves and left-wing political interests than public service, news broke this week that rogue elements of Bureau of Alcohol, Tobacco, Firearms and Explosives (BATFE) have been conspiring with Joe Biden's transition team to enact gun control by executive fiat." It even uses the word "conspiring"! The item was, in fact, out of date, because Biden's transition team was working three years earlier, in 2021, not in 2024. And we therefore have three years of evidence that President Biden did not enact gun control by fiat. But members of the NRA read that statement and many believed it. How can we help people not fall prey to such inaccurate and harmful conspiracy ideas?

How would you design an intervention based in inoculation theory? Take a few minutes to think out the details.

Numerous possibilities suggest themselves. Here's one. We would want to administer the inoculation to adoles-

> **GOOD NEWS**
>
> Media literacy training in the schools, including critical analysis of conspiracy theories, can produce citizens who are less vulnerable to conspiracy theorizing that promotes gun violence.

cents, before they become adults who could already be enmeshed in conspiracy thinking. High school would be a good time. Many schools provide media literacy training to help students learn to resist unhealthy media messages, such as messages that encourage girls to diet persistently so they can be (too) skinny (see the website of Media Literacy Now for more details). A major component of media literacy programs is helping students learn critical analysis of media texts.[55] Inoculation against conspiracy theories, providing the simple information used in this experiment, would be a natural addition to media literacy training. There is even a *Bad News* video game that can be incorporated (have a look at www.getbadnews.com).[56] Et voilà! We have a new set of young adults who are less vulnerable to conspiracy theories of all kinds, including those that promote gun violence.

One of the goals of education is to produce informed, thoughtful citizens. Detecting false arguments and resisting them is a necessary part of that education.

CHAPTER EIGHT

The Second Amendment Does Not Doom Us

ALL OF THE INFORMATION SO FAR HAS BEEN INTERESTING AND INFORMATIVE, you say, but what about the Second Amendment? Isn't it a rock-solid barrier that stops any efforts at reform of gun laws, leaving the nation stuck with 43,000 or more deaths per year due to guns? In this chapter, I review scholarship on the Second Amendment and how it came into being, because you have to know its origins to comprehend its meaning today. I consider the current state of legislation at the federal and state levels, and what kinds of laws, according to experts, are most needed. Finally, I propose the concept of rights for GunSense citizens and explore what those rights might look like.

This book is devoted to identifying exactly how psychological and public health approaches can help end gun violence in America. Those insights and interventions must operate within the framework of the law, especially the Second Amendment, so it is crucial that we examine it in detail here.

But first, what is the exact wording of the Second Amendment?

WHAT DOES THE SECOND AMENDMENT ACTUALLY SAY?

I was in a meeting with about 10 people, one of whom is a friend and a high-level business executive. I was new to the effort of reducing gun violence and I wanted to begin talking with gun owners to get their point of view. As I looked around the room, I concluded that my friend—let's call him Paul—was the likeliest one to be a gun owner. I'm a psychologist, after all. Shouldn't I be able to predict something like that? So during the lunch break, I told Paul about my new dedication to reducing gun violence and asked if he owned a gun. He responded, "Yes, and no one is going to take away my Second Amendment rights." I was surprised by the response—not that he had a gun, which I had already predicted, but because of how quickly the Second Amendment entered the conversation. Next I asked Paul if he could quote the Second Amendment for me. I'm a professor to the core and I can't stop myself from asking questions like that, to draw out people's thinking on a topic. He replied that it said that no one could take away his right to keep and bear arms. The problem is that's only half of what the Second Amendment says. This man is very smart and highly successful, and yet he could not quote the Second Amendment that is so important to him.

Here's the exact wording of the Second Amendment. *A well regulated Militia being necessary to the security of a free State, the right of the people to keep and bear Arms, shall not be infringed.* That's all, just that one sentence. Most people focus on the second half of the sentence and ignore or are unaware of the first half. Notice that the concept of "well-regulated" is inherent, as is "militia." Would you say that the gun situation in the United States today is well regulated? But I'm getting ahead of myself.

HOW DID THE SECOND AMENDMENT GET INTO THE US CONSTITUTION?

Emory University historian Carol Anderson has conducted powerful research showing that the Second Amendment became part of the Constitution largely to protect the interests of slave owners in the South.[1]

The southern colonies began their arguments even before the framing of the Constitution. In 1776, leaders of the colonies wrote the Declaration of Independence. A shot was heard around the world, with the battles of Lexington and Concord in Massachusetts. Leaders of the colonies quickly realized that it was going to take money to win the War of Independence—to pay soldiers, buy guns and ammunition, and so on. Representatives from Pennsylvania and other northern colonies proposed a wartime tax based on the headcount of people in each of the 13 colonies. The South balked. In South Carolina, for example, more than 50 percent of the population were enslaved people. Would South Carolina citizens (and enslaved people were not considered citizens) have to pay taxes on that whole population? Southern leaders argued that they should not have to pay taxes on the grounds that slaves were property, not people. If the North did not agree, the South would pull out of the confederation of colonies waging war against Britain.

Even before that, from the 1600s, Southern plantation owners lived in constant fear of slave rebellions.[2] As it turned out, the Black people who had been kidnapped from Africa and brought to the colonies didn't much like being enslaved and, given a chance, they would fight for freedom. In Virginia alone, insurrections threatened the social order in 1687, 1709, 1710, 1722, 1723, and 1730. To keep things in check, Black people—including free Blacks—were forbidden from having a gun. Meanwhile, White people formed armed militias—yes, the term that's in the Second Amendment—that were constantly at the ready to put down any slave rebellions that might occur. The whole security system was based on White people having guns and Black people being denied them. In 1774, 77 percent of White land-owning North Carolinians owned firearms.[3]

When the colonies began their own insurrection against the British, it was a Whites-only policy for army volunteers. A few years into the war, however, it became clear that there weren't enough White recruits to win the war. If you're a fan of the musical *Hamilton*, you know the lyrics "outgunned, outmanned, outnumbered, outplanned," and that was exactly the situation. Many more able-bodied men were available, of course, it was just that their skin was Black. Meanwhile, British colonial governors were offering a deal: enslaved people would be freed if they fought for King George III. The Continental Congress reconsidered their race policy, but if they admitted Black men to the army, they would have to arm them, raising the frightening specter of Black men with guns.

Eventually, some colonies took down their color barriers. Connecticut allowed owners to free slaves so they could enlist in the Continental Army. Even Virginia broadened its recruitment criteria to allow free Blacks to enlist. By 1778, the Continental Army was racially integrated. Apparently, necessity is the mother of integration. And it is worth noting that Black people fought bravely in the Revolutionary War, on the right side.

South Carolina was not quite on board, though. The British had just invaded Savannah, and Charleston was next in their sights. South Carolina's legislature could have armed all its able-bodied men, including the enslaved ones, to fight back effectively. Instead, the legislature decided to surrender to the British. The thought of armed Black men was too horrific to even consider. Surrender was preferable.

The 13 colonies won the war and were trying to form the United States of America, but things were not going well. The Articles of Confederation, ratified in 1781, were a failure in large part because they called for a very weak central government. The young country was in disarray.

At that point, James Madison, later to become the fourth president of the United States, emerged as a major force. A slave-owning Virginian, he nonetheless had many fine qualities including wisdom, brilliance, and serious qualms about slavery (as did Jefferson and Washington). His peers in other Southern states did not share those qualms. It was Madison who argued persuasively to give up on the Articles of Confederation and write a real Constitution with a strong central government.[4]

Here's a fascinating bit of trivia. The word "slavery" is never mentioned in the US Constitution. It was the elephant in the room as the Constitution was drafted, always massively present and influential but never spoken of.

Fast-forward to the Constitutional Convention of 1787 in Philadelphia. The delegates from the Deep South had a particular set of goals that were decidedly different from the goals of all the others. The Deep South (at that time, North Carolina, South Carolina, and Georgia) was focused on maintaining slavery and increasing the power of slaveholders. Their whole economy and way of life were based on slavery. The rest of the delegates were doing their best to create a democratic government that would survive. Some delegates from the North, for example, wanted to ban the Atlantic slave trade, but those from the Deep South basically held the Constitution hostage, refusing to sign on if that ban were instituted.

And then we have the three-fifths rule. Representation in the House of Representatives was to be proportional to the population of the state. The South—which previously had refused to categorize enslaved people as humans and instead classified them as property—now insisted they be counted as full members of the human population when apportioning representatives. Some in the North said that if slaves were counted in this way, then they should be made citizens and given the vote. The South wasn't buying it. The compromise: each enslaved person would count as three-fifths of a person. The North didn't like it, but it was the only way to save the Constitution and the nation.

Some Southerners—including Virginian Patrick Henry—still wanted to block the ratification of the Constitution. What if the federal government attempted to abolish slavery? So the South extorted another concession: that a Bill of Rights be immediately added to the Constitution.[5] James Madison was in charge of drafting it. He and others, such as Jefferson, believed there were certain fundamental rights that should be enumerated: trial by jury, freedom of the press, and liberty of conscience. Bearing arms and militias were not on the list. But again, the South was more than willing to take all their marbles and go home if they didn't get their way on arms and militias. So Madison, reluctantly, included the Second Amendment. The states signed on and the Constitution was approved, and that's how the Second Amendment came to be.

To be sure, other forces played a role in inclusion of the Second Amendment, especially the fear of a strong central government and a standing army[6]—having just gotten out from under the thumb of King George III—and the potential need of citizens to protect themselves from such a government. But the insistence of Southern enslavers about their guns and militias pushed the ball into the end zone.

Knowing the origins of the Second Amendment takes off a bit of the luster. The right to keep and bear arms was not considered a fundamental right by the framers of the Constitution. Instead, it was a miserable compromise exacted by Southern men who enslaved people.

When you were studying the Constitution and the founding of the nation in school, did you learn about all this background wrangling? I certainly didn't. My grandchildren know about the three-fifths rule, but not the rest of it. And yet it is imperative that we know this information as we consider what the Second Amendment means and *doesn't* mean today.

The Second Amendment is the cornerstone of Gun Culture in America. That Gun Culture, in turn, has had a profound psychological impact on a large swath of Americans. Gun Culture has socialized many Americans to believe that the right to keep and bear arms is a fundamental human right, one that is constantly threatened and must be maintained at all costs. Gun Culture has also socialized many Americans to believe that nothing can be done about the 43,000 deaths every year due to guns.

Using a psychological approach, we can study people's attitudes toward the Second Amendment. A 2018 poll by *The Economist* asked Americans whether they supported a repeal of the Second Amendment.[7] Fully 21 percent supported a repeal. On another question, 46 percent favored modifying the Second Amendment to allow stricter regulations. A sizable number of Americans do not necessarily think of the Second Amendment as set in stone.

ARE REGULATIONS ON GUNS COMPATIBLE WITH THE SECOND AMENDMENT?

Duke University law professors Joseph Blocher and Darrell Miller have concluded that from colonial times in America the right to keep and bear arms has always been paired with regulations.[8] Gun regulations are as American as the Second Amendment, and the idea of gun safety regulations is not at all a modern invention.[9] Here are some significant examples.

- Colonial cities—even before the Declaration of Independence—regulated the storage and use of firearms within city limits. In Boston, for example, no loaded firearms were allowed in any house, stable, barn, outhouse, store, or other building.[10]
- The colonies passed militia acts requiring all eligible men to report for muster with their own weapon and ammunition. The kinds of guns that were acceptable were clearly specified. Not any old gun passed muster.[11]
- Many of the colonies' proposals for what became the Second Amendment tied the right to keep and bear arms to military service, not to any private use.[12]
- In Massachusetts, a person could carry a gun publicly only under certain narrow circumstances such as when they feared an assault, and a person carrying publicly could be arrested if another person complained about it.[13]
- Even in the South, there was tight regulation of concealed carry; generally, it was forbidden.[14]

Moving beyond colonial times to the twentieth century, gun technology advanced and gun regulations were passed, often in response to out-of-control gun violence. The 1920s were an era of unprecedented mob shootings, exemplified in Chicago by Al Capone and the gang war between the Irish and Italian mobs. Bonnie and Clyde went on their killing spree in the early 1930s. Congress took action and, in 1934, passed the National Firearms Act. It specified that machine guns (the weapon of choice for mobsters) were subject to a $200 tax (the equivalent of $4,400 today) at the time of sale or transfer, and that owners had to register and be fingerprinted.

The 1960s saw a tsunami of assassinations by gun: President John F. Kennedy in 1963, Malcolm X in 1965, Martin Luther King Jr. in 1968, and Senator Robert Kennedy also in 1968. Several commissions in the 1960s noted that 24 million handguns were owned by civilians in the United States and recommended that the number be reduced to 2.4 million, through tough licensing standards.[15]

In response to the assassinations and expert reports, President Lyndon Johnson shepherded the Federal Gun Control Act of 1968 through Congress. Among other things, it required anyone engaged in the business of selling guns to have a federal license and maintain records of all gun sales, including the names and addresses of all purchasers.

The rifle that shot and killed JFK was purchased by mail order from an ad in *American Rifleman,* the NRA's magazine. At hearings on the Federal Gun Control Act, a representative of the NRA, Franklin Orth, supported a ban on mail-order sales, stating, "We do not think that any sane American, who calls himself an American, can object to placing into this bill the instrument which killed the president of the United States."[16] The bill passed in the House by a vote of 305 to 118, and in the Senate by 70 to 17, large majorities that reflected a broad, bipartisan consensus in favor of its regulations.

As you can see, regulations on guns and gun purchases are well established in American history. In the meantime, the mail-order purchases of 1963 have morphed into online purchases today, and they are much more difficult to track and regulate.

ADDITIONAL EDIFICATION FROM THE SUPREME COURT

Questions about the Constitution crop up all the time. What does a certain sentence mean? How broad or narrow is a particular right in the Bill of Rights? The Supreme Court issues decisions about such questions, in response to particular cases that test the meaning of various provisions in the Constitution. Surprisingly, there have been very few Supreme Court decisions on the Second Amendment, in contrast to, for example, the First Amendment and its stated right to freedom of speech. Here I will review the relevant cases—the most important being *District of Columbia v. Heller* (2008)—on gun rights and regulations and their implications for what we can do to end the epidemic of gun violence in America. These Supreme Court decisions play a crazy game of dodgeball with federal legislation and state legislation, which I will cover in later sections.

United States v. Miller (1939)

Jack Miller was a shady character, a member of the O'Malley gang of bank robbers. In 1938 he was arrested in Arkansas on charges of transporting a sawed-off shotgun across state lines and violating the National Firearms Act of 1934, discussed earlier. Miller claimed that he had a Second Amendment right to that sawed-off shotgun. The case is important because it was a test of the constitutionality of the National Firearms Act (NFA).[17] Could Congress regulate firearms as it did with the NFA, or did the NFA violate the Second Amendment?

There are elements of the case that are comical. Miller was actually acquitted in federal court, so the prosecution appealed to the US Supreme Court. But before the case was heard by SCOTUS, Miller vanished, and his lawyer, who was not getting paid, declined to represent him anymore, so neither Miller nor his lawyer were actually there at the Supreme Court to present arguments. And shortly before the decision in his case was handed down, he was found dead near Chelsea, Oklahoma, shot four times with a .38. His .45 was found at the scene, and he had apparently fired three times in self-defense. So much for carrying a gun for "protection." Miller lived by the sword and died by the sword.

The Court's decision was unanimous: it found in favor of the government (not poor Jack Miller, who was already six feet under and probably couldn't care less) and upheld the National Firearms Act. The decision focused on the first clause of the Second Amendment, saying that the right was "restricted to the keeping and bearing of arms by the people collectively for their common defense and security" and the right may not "be utilized for private purposes."

The Court therefore took a *militia-based view of the Second Amendment* in this 1939 case.[18] The right to keep and bear arms exists only in the context of maintaining a militia to protect the nation or the state. In 1989, conservative judicial scholar Robert Bork again articulated this view when he stated about the Second Amendment, "its intent was to guarantee the right of states to form militia, not for individuals to bear arms." The militia-based view stands in contrast to the *individual rights view*, which holds that individuals have a right to keep and bear arms, regardless of any connection to a militia. And that brings us to the game-changing *Heller* case.

District of Columbia v. Heller (2008)

In the decades following the *Miller* decision, the NRA changed dramatically and took a sizable chunk of the country with it, as documented in chapter 7 on the Gun Lobby. The NRA forcefully promoted an individual rights view of the Second Amendment. It was really just a matter of time until another challenge to gun regulations was mounted.

In the 1960s and 1970s, the District of Columbia had a terrible problem with gun homicides, highlighted by a triple murder occurring over the Christmas holidays in 1974. The great majority of these homicides resulted from handguns. DC still has a terrible problem with gun homicides, which kill 144 people on average every year, and the rate of gun deaths increased by 159 percent from 2012 to 2021.[19]

What we are concerned with here, though, is the fearsome problem in the 1970s. The residents of DC demanded that something be done and, in 1976, officials passed a law that banned handguns and required guns to be locked when not in use.

Dick Heller was a special police officer for the Federal Judicial Center in DC. He had the right to carry a handgun while he was at work, but he was also a strong believer in the Second Amendment and wanted to keep a handgun at home for self-defense. His house, after all, had been hit by bullets twice in the 1970s. When he applied for a permit for a handgun, it was denied because of the DC regulation. Heller became the ideal plaintiff in a challenge to the DC law.

Two libertarian nonprofits—the Institute for Justice and the Cato Institute—had been looking for a good case to advance Second Amendment rights, and Dick Heller provided just what they needed. Both organizations have goals of strictly limiting government and expanding individual liberties. They recruited a lawyer, Alan Gura, who is himself a libertarian dedicated to the Second Amendment.

In a surprising development, the NRA opposed the case.[20] Apparently, they did so for two reasons. First, the NRA lawyers thought Heller would lose. The votes just weren't there, and no one likes to lose. Second—and here's the juicy part—the NRA was worried that if the court decided in favor of Heller and individual gun rights, it would sabotage the NRA's method of motivating its members by making them fear that the government would confiscate their weapons. This is a revealing example of how the Gun Lobby uses psychology to advance its goals, as discussed in chapter 7.

In a close 5–4 decision, the Court ruled in favor of Heller and individual rights to own guns, breaking with more than 200 years' understanding of the Second Amendment. The decision established an individual's right to own a gun, presumably for self-defense, and struck down DC's regulations.

Does that mean that all is lost for sensible gun regulations in America? No, because the decision, written by Justice Scalia, simultaneously recognized individual rights to guns and the possibility of reasonable regulations. As Scalia wrote, "the right secured by the Second Amendment is not unlimited." He went on to note historical prohibitions on the carrying of concealed weapons and the carrying of weapons by felons, as well as prohibitions on guns in "sensitive places" such as schools and government buildings. So the *Heller* decision established both an individual right to own firearms and a right to regulate, but was murky about how much gun rights could be regulated, except for giving a few examples.

Just as the majority decision was decisive, so too were the dissenting opinions informative. Justice Breyer noted that if there is an individual right to arms for private purposes, how can courts decide what gun regulations are constitutional? The majority opinion was disturbingly vague on this crucial question.

Breyer also articulated the need to balance private rights to guns with society's interest in promoting public safety.[21]

Historian Dominic Erdozain has conducted research showing that the framers of the Constitution understood that the civil liberties it guarantees were designed to protect citizens not only from a tyrannical king, but also from other citizens.[22] They had no illusions that all people are virtuous. The framers understood the nature of the social contract, the basis for a civilized society, in which individuals give up a little bit of their freedom for the good of the whole, the community. The framers were influenced by the famed philosopher John Locke and other social-contract theorists, who asserted that freedom is not the freedom for each individual to do as they want; it is instead the freedom to live in peace governed by laws for the good of all. In light of this research, asserting that there is an individual right to possess guns is a terribly tragic misreading of the Constitution and its guarantees of liberties.

Parenthetically, a case very similar to *Heller, McDonald v. City of Chicago*, was decided in 2010, with the same outcome: the Court maintained the right of individuals to keep firearms for private purposes, while stating that some regulation was possible and constitutional.

United States v. Masciandaro (2011) is another of the cases that followed in the wake of *Heller*. Sean Masciandaro was found with a semiautomatic pistol in his car while he was parked in a lot in a national park. The National Park Service prohibits loaded weapons in the parks, so Masciandaro was arrested. He appealed on the grounds of his Second Amendment rights. The Court ruled that the Park Service regulations were legitimate and did not violate the Second Amendment or the *Heller* decision, because the core of that decision was about the right to self-defense *in the home*. Outside the home, the Court said, rights to firearms are more limited because a concern for public safety can outweigh the individual's right to self-defense.[23] As a person who enjoys spending time in the national parks, I am grateful for the Court's reasoning. And the decision recognized the legitimacy of reasonable gun regulations.

But then in *New York State Rifle and Pistol Association v. Bruen* (2022), the Court struck down a 1911 New York law that required people seeking a license for carrying a concealed handgun in public to demonstrate that they had "proper cause" to carry. The disturbing thing about the *Bruen* case was that the opinion for the majority, written by Justice Clarence Thomas, held that the constitutionality of gun regulations had to be evaluated not for the public good, but rather by historical traditions of firearm ownership, the so-called originalist approach. Shall we travel back to 1790? If so, we will have to recognize all the regulations on firearms at the time. That historical scholarship somehow escaped the attention of the Court.[24]

One juicy detail related to the *Bruen* decision was brought to light by investigative reporters Mike McIntire and Jodi Kantor in 2024.[25] (Kantor is a Pulitzer Prize winner who broke the story about Harvey Weinstein's sexual harassment of women.) As it turns out, in the *Bruen* decision and in other Court decisions, the progun side has cited research by William English, PhD, who is an assistant professor in the business school at Georgetown University. The research, which has not been published or peer reviewed to ensure its quality, is based on a national survey conducted by English. He claims that the results show that gun owners frequently use their weapons for self-defense, which is music to the ears of gun rights activists. People gotta have guns for protection. (See TheReload.com for delighted coverage of the study.) What was covered up in the unpublished paper and its use in court was that the NRA funded the survey and that English served as an expert for progun plaintiffs in multiple cases, charging $250 to $350 per hour. This research, then, which was cited by Justice Alito in his concurring opinion in *Bruen*, has not been published and was paid for by the Gun Lobby. And research from multiple other sources shows that successful defensive use of a gun is extremely rare and having a gun in the home is more likely to result in the death of a member of the household.[26] But this questionable study was influential in a Supreme Court decision that weakened gun restrictions.

In a recognition of reasonable regulations, in 2023 the Court issued a ruling (not a full decision) that upheld a Biden administration regulation on ghost guns, which are kits of parts that can be made into a gun that has no serial number or other identification—thus "ghost"—making it impossible for law enforcement to track them and making it easy for people who cannot buy guns legitimately, such as convicted felons, to buy the makings for a gun.[27]

The Biden administration's regulation did not ban the kits, but did require manufacturers and sellers to obtain licenses like all other manufacturers and sellers, put serial numbers on the product, and conduct background checks. The regulation therefore closed a major loophole.

But then in 2024, in *Garland v. Cargill*, the Court struck down a ban on bump stocks, which are small devices that turn a semiautomatic rifle like an AR-15 into one that fires even more rapidly.[28] The federal ban originated after the 2017 mass shooting at a Las Vegas concert. The decision hinged on technicalities, but in brief, the 6–3 majority said that ATF (the Bureau of Alcohol, Tobacco, Firearms, and Explosives) did not have the authority to ban the devices. The decision left the door open for Congress to pass legislation that would ban them. In the meantime, it's legal to buy a bump stock and install it on an AR-15 so that it can kill even more people in a few minutes.

The good news, also in 2024—and I'm sorry if you're beginning to get whiplash over these decisions—the Court upheld a ban on gun possession by someone with a domestic violence restraining order, in *United States v. Rahimi.* The majority opinion recognized the constitutionality of reasonable regulations on guns, and said the domestic violence situation is one in which guns can be regulated.[29] This one was a huge victory for those wanting commonsense gun laws, and it will truly save lives.

> **GOOD NEWS**
>
> In 2024 SCOTUS upheld a ban on gun possession by someone with a domestic violence restraining order. This decision recognized the constitutionality of reasonable regulations on guns.

And that, my friends, is where we are today in regard to the Second Amendment, individual rights to own guns, and how much those rights can be regulated. Guns for self-protection in the home are considered a protected right, at least in the eyes of the current Court, but guns in the hands of a domestic abuser can be regulated, and it will take one case after another to define which regulations are possible and which are not.

FEDERAL LEGISLATION

As explained earlier in the chapter, major pieces of federal legislation regulating guns were passed in 1934 (the National Firearms Act) and 1968 (the Federal Gun Control Act). What kinds of federal legislation have been passed, or not, since then?

Federal Assault Weapons Ban (1994)

In 1994, during the Clinton administration, Congress passed the Federal Assault Weapons Ban (AWB) as part of the Public Safety and Recreational Firearms Use Protection Act. The legislation was supported by former presidents Gerald Ford (R), Jimmy Carter (D), and Ronald Reagan (R), as well as 77 percent of Americans, according to polls. Responding to three deadly mass shootings between 1989 and 1993, the legislation prohibited the manufacture, transfer, or possession of semiautomatic assault weapons, as well as high-capacity magazines.

The bill was in effect for a period of 10 years. At that point, it had to be renewed, but Congress refused to do so in 2004.

It is important to recognize that the United States did have an assault weapons ban from 1994 to 2004, and it was successful. Some people find current proposals for an assault weapons ban to be frightening. Second Amendment activists use a "slippery slope" argument: first they take away our assault weapons, then they take all of our guns. But the fact is that we had an assault weapons ban for 10 years and the government did not seize everyone's other guns. And the rate of gun deaths was reduced during those 10 years. Figure 8.1 shows the reduction in deaths during the ban, as well as the reduction in deaths following other federal gun safety legislation.

On the theme of smart choices saving lives, researchers have estimated that had the Federal Assault Weapons Ban been extended it would have saved 339 lives by 2020.[30] It's smart legislation.

The Bipartisan Safer Communities Act (2022)

It was a regular Monday morning on October 24, 2022, at a magnet high school in St. Louis. Then a 19-year-old, a graduate of the school, entered with an AR-15 rifle and 600 rounds of ammunition saying "You all are going to die!" In

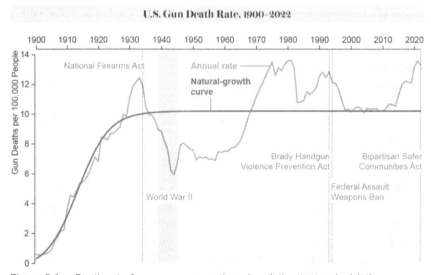

Figure 8.1.   Death rate from guns across time, in relation to gun legislation.

the end, he killed one student and one teacher and injured many others before police arrived and shot him, interrupting yet another school shooting.

The shooter had had serious mental health issues over the years, so serious that his family had him committed on multiple occasions. When he tried to purchase a gun at a licensed dealer 16 days before his killing spree, he was rejected by the federal background check system because of the mental health issues. He turned to Armslist (it's like Craigslist, but for firearms) and easily bought the gun online with no background check, from an unlicensed dealer.

That was the legal situation in the United States in 2022. While licensed dealers—roughly 80,000 of them—were required to conduct a background check before selling a gun, "private" sales had no such requirement. Private sales included gun shows, and the oh-so-convenient online sales on sites such as Armslist, which are quickly eclipsing sales at gun shows.

It was in this legal context that Congress, during the Biden administration, passed the Bipartisan Safer Communities Act (BSCA) in 2022, the first federal gun legislation since 1994. It has many provisions, one of which is to require expanded background checks, including checks of mental health records, for purchasers under 21 years of age (the St. Louis shooter was 19). It also closed the "gun-show loophole" by expanding the definition of gun sellers who must be federally licensed to include anyone who sells multiple times, for example, on Armslist. A federally licensed seller must conduct background checks. This provision closed the gaping loophole that allowed the St. Louis shooter to acquire a gun.

> ## GOOD NEWS
>
> The Bipartisan Safer Communities Act (2022) closed the "gun show loophole" and expanded the definition of gun sellers so that many more of them are required to be federally licensed and conduct criminal background checks.

Criminal background checks are made possible through the NICS (not to be confused with the popular TV show *NCIS*), which stands for National Instant Criminal Background Check System.

The BSCA also closed the so-called boyfriend loophole. Previously, gun purchases were forbidden for those convicted of domestic violence against a spouse, which is definitely important. However, domestic assault against a cohabiting partner was not covered. With the Bipartisan Safer Communities

Act, anyone who has been convicted of domestic assault is prohibited from purchasing a gun for a period of five years.

The act cracks down on trafficking of guns and on "straw purchases," which refers to a situation in which someone buys a gun for another person, usually because the latter is barred from purchasing a gun because of their criminal background or for other reasons.

Readers may notice that the BSCA was signed into law in June 2022, and the St. Louis school shooting occurred in October 2022. Was the BSCA ineffective? The answer is that it takes some time to implement complex new rules such as those that are part of the BSCA. It doesn't happen overnight. Implementation was not far enough along by October to prevent the shooter from acquiring the AR-15. The good news is that by May 2023, a year later, the Department of Justice (DOJ) had denied 160 firearm purchases because of enhanced background checks for those under 21. Any one of those sales, had they not been stopped, could have resulted in a school shooting. The DOJ's prosecutions of unlicensed dealers had increased 52 percent from the previous year. And in May 2024, the DOJ fully implemented the requirement for all sellers—including gun shows and online sellers—to be licensed and conduct full criminal background checks.

STATE LAWS ON GUNS

It would be an impossible task to summarize the current laws of all 50 states on guns. And that, of course, is part of the problem—the inconsistency from state to state. It would be so much simpler and more effective if the basic, essential gun regulations were federal law.

In general, states may or may not have laws that*

- Require background checks on all gun sales, including those at gun shows and online purchases.
- Provide for Extreme Risk Protection Orders (ERPO) that allow law enforcement to temporarily remove guns from individuals who are deemed a risk to themselves or others.
- Require a waiting period for the purchase of a gun.
- Block concealed carry.

---

* Those marked [Weaken] are laws that weaken restrictions on guns and thereby weaken safety requirements. All the others strengthen gun regulations.

- Permit "stand your ground" shooting, also known as "shoot first" laws. [Weaken]
- Prohibit guns in schools and other sensitive areas.
- Protect gun manufacturers and sellers from being sued (held accountable) for irresponsible, negligent sales and manufacturing practices. [Weaken]
- Prohibit assault weapons.
- Prohibit high-capacity magazines.

To learn about your state's laws, go to everytown.org/states/. Everytown for Gun Safety is a nonprofit organization dedicated to promoting gun safety. Everytown's research division ranks states for the strength or weakness of their gun laws.

The Top Eight States with the Strictest Gun Laws

- California
- New York
- Hawaii
- New Jersey
- Connecticut
- Massachusetts
- Illinois
- Maryland

The Ten States with the Weakest Gun Laws

- Alaska
- Arizona
- Oklahoma
- Wyoming
- South Dakota
- Montana
- Georgia

- Idaho
- Arkansas
- Mississippi

Mississippi wins the prize for having the weakest gun laws in the nation.

Are Gun Laws Effective?

It was July 3, 2023, and folks were out in their Philadelphia neighborhood celebrating the Fourth. Suddenly shots rang out, although many thought they were just fireworks. A man in body armor, with an AR-15, fired seemingly at random, resulting in the deaths of five and the wounding of two, one of them a 2-year-old child.[31] A total of 50 shell casings were recovered by the police.

In retrospect, there had been warning signs. One neighbor said that when he had met the man the previous week, the man had introduced himself as the "town watchman." The shooter shared a house with seven others, who noticed that his behavior had become more agitated in the past few days and that he had started wearing a bulletproof vest around the house. The housemates dealt with his erratic behavior by avoiding him. Importantly, the state of Pennsylvania had no Red Flag law.

Imagine how this story might have unfolded differently. Suppose that Pennsylvania had a Red Flag law and it was publicized widely so that most people knew what it was and how they might access it. Imagine that one, just one, of the housemates had said to themselves, "This guy is agitated and is wearing a bulletproof vest around the house. He could be dangerous, and he has guns." The housemate remembered about the Red Flag law and reported the man to the authorities, who took away his gun temporarily and got him into mental health treatment. Five people's lives would have been saved and a neighborhood would not have been traumatized.

What does the scientific evidence say on whether stricter gun laws are effective in reducing gun violence? We have a substantial number of studies on this question. Different researchers have included different kinds of gun laws, making it a bit more difficult to sort through the findings. But the devil is in the details, and we want to know both whether stricter gun laws in general reduce gun homicides, and which specific gun laws are the most effective, so the complexity is important. I rely, in part, on a massive report, *The Science of Gun Policy: A Critical Synthesis of Research Evidence on the Effects of Gun Policies in the United States* from the RAND Corporation, which is a research powerhouse.[32] Here are important takeaways from these studies.

1. *The 13 states with the weakest gun laws have three times the gun death rates of the 8 states with the strongest gun laws.*[33]

   Mississippi has the highest rate of gun deaths and the weakest gun laws in the country. The two states with the lowest rates of gun violence—Massachusetts and Hawaii—are in the top four for strength of gun laws. Another study found that the rate of school shootings is higher in states with weak gun laws.[34] And the rate of handgun carrying by youth is lower in states with stricter gun laws, carrying being a major precursor to shooting.[35] The scientific evidence clearly indicates that strong gun laws reduce gun deaths.

2. *Universal background check laws are one of the most effective policies for reducing gun deaths.*[36]

   The evidence indicates that when a state passes such a law the rate of gun homicides declines substantially.[37] The key is to require background checks not only by licensed dealers, but also by private sellers. And the background checks must be paired with laws requiring the licensing of handgun purchasers.[38] The evidence also indicates that universal background checks lower the child mortality rate.[39] "Universal background checks" usually apply to gun purchases, but laws can also require background checks for ammunition purchases. According to a 2022 Gallup poll, 92 percent of all Americans favor a requirement of background checks on all gun sales. There's broad consensus on this one. Can we get Congress to act?

3. *Child-access protection (CAP) laws reduce firearm deaths.*[40]

   CAP laws focus on requirements for safe storage of firearms, and their main effect is to reduce the rate of youth deaths by suicide. They also reduce homicides and unintentional firearm injuries and deaths among youth.

4. *Laws prohibiting firearm ownership for individuals with domestic violence restraining orders decrease intimate-partner homicides.*[41]

   Domestic violence and firearms are a lethal combination.[42] Firearms can also be used as a powerful tool of coercive control of a domestic partner; approximately 4.5 million women in the United States have had an intimate partner threaten them with a gun.[43] Approximately 50 percent of intimate partner homicides are committed with firearms. State laws that prohibit those with a domestic violence restraining order from possessing a gun reduce intimate-partner homicide by 16 percent.[44]

5. *Stand-your-ground laws (SYG) increase firearm homicides.*

The purported purpose of SYG laws ("shoot first" laws) is to authorize people to shoot in self-defense when they feel "threatened." There are many problems with these laws. What if someone feels threatened but the situation, objectively, is not threatening? Is the shooter's subjective fear a legitimate reason for murdering someone? Moreover, the US Constitution guarantees each of us due process in criminal cases, including trial by jury. With SYG laws, one person acts as judge, jury, and executioner. And the scientific evidence indicates that these laws increase homicides. States would be best advised to get rid of them.

THE RIGHTS OF THE GUNSENSE MAJORITY

On July 4, 2022, the joy of an Independence Day parade in Highland Park, Illinois, was shattered when a gunman began firing. In all, seven people were killed and 48 others were injured by bullets or shrapnel. The shooter used a Smith & Wesson M&P15 semiautomatic rifle, firing a total of 83 times in rapid succession. It took a while for police to capture him, and in that time he drove to Madison, Wisconsin, where I live, so he was within just a couple of miles of me—a sobering thought.

In some ways, this is another tale of a mass shooting, but the point is different in this case. Those folks in Highland Park had a right to be out celebrating Independence Day, and doing so without being shot or the fear of being shot. According to a survey commissioned by the American Psychological Association, 33 percent of adult Americans say that fear of mass shootings prevents them from going to certain places or events.[45] That's not right.

Earlier in this book, I presented the example of the successful reduction in smoking and smoking deaths as a model for how we can reduce firearm deaths. One force that contributed to the success with smoking was a movement that emerged in the 1970s, advocating for the Rights of Nonsmokers.[46] America is a rights-based nation, so this approach was appealing to many. Is there a parallel argument for the rights of the GunSense Majority?

The GunSense Majority are people who are just that—sensible and smart about guns. They choose not to own any, or if they do, they keep them very securely locked up. GunSense folks would like some relief from those who are reckless with guns. The GunSense Majority would like to be able to go to an outdoor concert in Las Vegas, or a Fourth of July parade in Highland Park, without being shot and without fear of being shot. GunSense folks should have those freedoms. Moreover, polls show they are in the majority. A majority of

Americans do not own firearms, and a majority of Americans, including many who are gun owners, favor commonsense gun regulations. That's why we could call them the *GunSense Majority*.

In the 1960s, when smoking was still allowed on airplanes, a smoker wrote a letter to advice columnist Ann Landers. On a recent flight, he had asked the woman next to him if she minded if he smoked. Yes, she minded. The smoker said that her answer irritated him—he actually suggested she move to a different seat and she did—since he was a heavy smoker and he felt that she was interfering with his rights. Ann Landers's firm response: "Your right to smoke ends where the other fellow's nose begins." This is a difficult concept for many Americans to understand—that my individual rights may have to be curtailed if they impinge on someone else's rights. The real question is: how can we balance the rights of different groups of people?

In 1971, a grassroots activist movement called Group Against Smoking Pollution (GASP) was started by Clara Gouin in her living room in College Park, Maryland.[47] She produced buttons saying "GASP—Nonsmokers Have Rights Too." Chapters quickly sprang up across the country. These activists, together with those pursuing legal protections for nonsmokers, created an identity for nonsmokers.

Over a period of several years, the group gradually achieved some legislative successes with clean indoor air bills. The Tobacco Institute fought back. Over time, though, the nonsmokers' movement succeeded in promoting the idea that smoking was a public problem because it infringed on nonsmokers' rights.

Applied to gun violence, the GunSense Majority could assert their rights to be in public spaces without the threat of an assault weapon being used against them. They could assert the right of children in schools not to have to experience active shooter drills that frighten them and the right of children to be protected from school shootings. To be clear, that protection does not involve arming teachers, which only succeeds in placing guns in schools, where they can do so much damage.

Psychologically, a movement to recognize the rights of the GunSense Majority could accomplish two important goals. It would create an identity for those who choose not to possess firearms or are extremely careful if they do have them. It would also contribute to a sense of group cohesion among GunSense citizens, empowering them to collective political action on behalf of themselves.

One particularly stark example concerns laws that permit open carry of firearms. Research shows that most Americans would feel unsafe if they were in the presence of an unknown person who was openly carrying a firearm.[48] Imagine a case in which a group wants to hold a peaceful protest outside the state capitol. Their right to do so is guaranteed by the First Amendment, with stated rights to freedom of assembly and freedom of speech. Now suppose that 10 men who are opposed to the view of the protesters show up, all openly carrying AR-15s. What a chilling effect on the protesters! In this case, guns are not used in self-defense but rather as instruments of intimidation. The protesters might choose to flee the scene, fearing for their own safety. In this case, the Second Amendment rights of the second group are trampling the First Amendment rights of the first group. Is the Second Amendment so powerful that it cancels other rights guaranteed by the Constitution? Legal scholars are beginning to address this issue.[49]

A closely related concept is the right to *freedom from gun violence*. It was on full display on the fourth and final night of the 2024 Democratic National Convention in Chicago. A whole segment of the evening was devoted to freedom from gun violence, with those words on a large screen. Testimonials came from folks like a teacher who had survived a shooting in her school and a survivor of domestic violence involving a gun. Presidential candidate Kamala Harris spoke about it. The idea is to think of freedom from gun violence as one of our basic rights.

Solutions

Recently, some legal solutions have emerged that don't involve anything like overturning the Second Amendment. These include suing gun manufacturers and sellers, and holding adults responsible when they could have prevented their child from committing a murder by gun.

Suing Manufacturers and Sellers

If a car manufacturer produces a car with a major defect that kills your spouse in a crash, you have a right to sue the manufacturer for damages. If a car company produced numerous cars with these fatal defects, they would be the object of many costly lawsuits and they would eventually go out of business. Shouldn't gun manufacturers and sellers be held accountable in this same way?

The Gun Lobby has manipulated Congress into passing various pieces of legislation protecting gun manufacturers from lawsuits in a way no other manufacturers of consumer products are protected. The most impactful one is the Protection of Lawful Commerce in Arms Act (PLCAA, 2005), which generally gives immunity from lawsuits to gun manufacturers and sellers, for products including firearms, ammunition, and component parts. Those laws need to change and you can help by working to change them. In case this seems like an awfully heavy lift, I have an inspiring story about a very feasible strategy that seems to have succeeded despite the PLCAA—suing gun sellers.[50]

In July 2023, an Indiana gun store, Westforth Sports, announced that it would close and liquidate its inventory.[51] That's one less major, high-volume, unethical seller. The plot line leading up to the closure is fascinating and provides a model that can be used in other cases.

The State of Illinois and the City of Chicago have strict gun laws, yet gun homicide rates in Chicago remain high. Why? The answer is Indiana. That state has weak gun laws, which allowed Westforth Sports of Indiana—just 10 miles from the Illinois border—to conduct a thriving business, including straw purchases, gun trafficking, and sales of assault weapons to people from Chicago, despite Chicago's ban on assault weapons. Westforth Sports was the largest out-of-state supplier of guns recovered by Chicago police from crime scenes.

The City of Chicago partnered with Everytown Law to seek a remedy. They sued Westforth and contacted ATF (the Bureau of Alcohol, Tobacco, Firearms, and Explosives, the federal agency responsible for enforcing firearm laws), sharing the evidence of Westforth's illegal activities. For example, from 2014 to 2021, more than 300 guns had been straw purchased from Westforth, including 19 guns sold to a single person. No one buys 19 guns except to sell them to others, usually to people who cannot legally purchase firearms, such as convicted felons. The usual wrangling between sides occurred over time and more evidence of misconduct emerged. With the case still in process, Westforth decided to cease operations. Chicago will be safer as a result.

Following on this success, in 2024 the City of Chicago again partnered with Everytown Law to sue Glock! Glock produces semiautomatic pistols that can easily be converted into machine guns (which are illegal) in a few minutes with a cheap device the size of a quarter. The pistol then can fire as fast as US military fully automatic firearms. Moreover, police data from Chicago indicate that 1,100 of these modified Glock pistols were recovered from crime scenes in Chicago in just the two years before the lawsuit. Glock must be held accountable.

In 2024, the families of the schoolchildren killed in Uvalde filed a lawsuit against Daniel Defense, the manufacturer of the assault rifle used in the murders there.[52] They also sued the publisher of the *Call of Duty* video game, which the shooter had played incessantly.

Lawsuits such as these will test the limits of the PLCAA. It's also worth noting that the PLCAA lists six exceptions, that is, situations in which manufacturers or sellers can be sued. I won't drag you into the details, but the point is that even the PLCAA allows some lawsuits against the gun industry.

THE PSYCHOLOGY OF GUN VIOLENCE

The overall moral to this story is that, even with the Second Amendment and *Heller*, there are ways to stop bad actors, such as lodging a complaint with ATF or suing a gun seller or manufacturer. If your city is in a situation like Chicago's, consider one of these strategies. Or if a loved one was killed by a gun, think about suing the manufacturer or seller of the gun. Too often after gun homicides or mass shootings, anguished survivors go after the obvious, low-hanging fruit, like school security guards who failed at their jobs. They should be held accountable, but if that shooter hadn't had a gun and ammo in the first place because a seller was all too happy to let them purchase it, often illegally, the tragedy wouldn't have occurred.

Holding Adults Accountable

In a follow-up to the 2022 Highland Park Fourth of July shooting—in 2023, the shooter's father was prosecuted and pled guilty to multiple crimes in connection with the shooting.[53] In 2019, the father had sponsored his son's application for a state gun ownership permit, the sponsorship being required because the son was only 19 at the time. The father also knew that his son had threatened to commit violence against his family and others, but did nothing—except authorize the gun permit.

In 2024 the parents of the Oxford High School shooter in Michigan were both convicted and sentenced to at least 10 years in prison.[54] They had failed in their responsibility as parents in so many ways. In school on the morning of the shooting, their son drew a violent picture and his parents were summoned to the school to take him home, but they refused to do so. Before that, there were many signs that the shooter's mental health was failing, but the parents ignored the signs. The mother even took him to a gun range just days before the shooting. This conviction received widespread publicity and it may have been a tipping point because it was the first time that parents had been convicted of manslaughter in conjunction with their child committing a shooting (in other cases, parents had been charged with things like neglect or reckless conduct). In addition to holding the parents responsible, the conviction sent a clear message to parents around the nation. Don't give your 15-year-old a gun for Christmas. Don't ignore warning signs that your child is seriously considering violence. The outcome in this highly publicized case is probably saving lives at this very moment, as parents nationwide think more carefully about their responsibilities in relation to guns.

We need to hold the gun industry accountable, but we also need to hold parents accountable when they engage in reckless behavior and fail in their obligations as parents.

CHAPTER NINE

Smart Choices Save Lives

IN JUST THE FIRST THREE MONTHS OF 2024, THE TSA INTERCEPTED 1,503 firearms at airport security checkpoints around the United States.[1] That's about 17 every day! And this even though firearms are forbidden at checkpoints and in the cabin of a plane. You can't check in for a flight without seeing that warning. To make matters worse, 93 percent of those guns were loaded. We don't know what psychological processes lead passengers to make this serious error—some may want to see if they can get away with it, and others may just be so used to having a gun with them at all times they forget they have it. The Gun Lobby has promoted the myth of the "good guy with a gun," but these episodes explode that myth, demonstrating how many individuals with guns break federal regulations by having a gun with them in an airport, and how frequent the violations of secure storage are, with almost all of the guns loaded. If TSA didn't catch them, those guns would be a danger to everyone on the aircraft.

In the 1500s and 1600s, in both Britain and America, many people held a fearsome belief in witches and witchcraft.[2] King James VI of Scotland personally supervised a trial in which three witches were accused of attempting to kill him. One of them, under torture, confessed to hurling a cat and limbs from a dead man's body into the sea to produce a wild storm that would wreck the king's ship. James recalled the storm as particularly fierce and here was an explanation. A belief in witchcraft gave people such as King James a belief that they understood why bad things happened, and they could control those bad things by executing a witch. Today we live in a culture enriched by science and we know there is no scientific evidence of witchcraft and, in fact, convincing evidence against it.

Some Americans' beliefs in the "good guy with a gun" who protects his family from home invasion, children from school shootings, and everyone else from random acts of gun violence is not so different from earlier views about witchcraft. It helps folks make sense of a tumultuous world and gives believers faith that they can control bad things that might happen. But science informs us those beliefs are simply false. Most often, shooters are stopped by police, by someone tackling them, or when they shoot themselves. And those protection guns in the home are unlikely to kill an intruder and are much more likely to kill a member of the household.

> ## GOOD NEWS
>
> We can make smart choices, based on the best available science, to reduce deaths from guns.

An essential theme running through this book is that we—as individuals, as a society—can take action to reduce deaths from gun violence, not relying on the mythical good guy with a gun but on the best available science. We can make smart choices.

Some people believe that solving our gun problem is impossible. To bolster the case that change is possible, let's return to the story of the reduction in smoking deaths in America, which resulted from a powerful combination of psychological and public health approaches.

A SUCCESS STORY: REDUCING DEATHS FROM SMOKING

In the twentieth century, cigarette smoking rates rose dramatically up to about 1964.[3] Smoking was pervasive in the mid-twentieth century. Smoking causes cancer, which causes fatalities. Prevent smoking and you save lives. It's just that simple.

By 1953, 47 percent of American adults smoked cigarettes and there was no sign the practice would decline.[4] But a watershed moment occurred in 1964, when the US Surgeon General issued a major report on the dangers of smoking. Public attitudes began to shift, as did patterns of smoking. Beginning in 1966, regulations required manufacturers to put a label on cigarette packs stating that cigarette smoking "may be hazardous to your health." Cigarette ads were banned from TV beginning in 1971. By 2011, less than 20 percent of Americans smoked. What an inspiring public health victory!

A nonsmokers' rights movement also emerged, demanding smokefree environments in public places like restaurants, and the movement gained traction first at the local and state levels and later at the national level.[5] Today, smoking is not permitted in most public places, so nonsmokers are not forced to inhale secondhand smoke. Nonsmokers have some rights.

This story of the reduction in smoking and smoking deaths provides concrete evidence that it is possible to change a deeply entrenched, unhealthy culture into a more sensible, healthy one. It can take decades, though, of scientific research and persistent activism to accomplish the goal.

RECAP: SOLUTIONS FROM PREVIOUS CHAPTERS

To highlight some solutions from previous chapters, I will recap them here. But first, a reminder—it is crucial that we follow evidence-based policies as we work to address America's gun problem. Folks have plenty of guesses or intuitions about what might help, such as arming teachers in the schools, but research shows that many of these intuitive ideas are not effective and often make us less safe, not more. The emphasis here, therefore, is on solutions that are backed by scientific evidence, that is, evidence-based solutions. Solutions from previous chapters include

1. *Promote social norms that encourage gun safety*—Most gun owners favor universal criminal background checks for gun purchases, but they believe that members of their group (gun owners) are opposed to them, so they say nothing. Widespread advertising on the real statistics about approval for gun regulations will increase public support. The same can be done with norms for secure storage of firearms. (Chapter 3, "A Gun Will Make You a Real Man")

2. *Implement and fund community violence interventions in cities around the country*—Research shows they are effective in reducing gun homicides. (Chapter 4, "The Volatile Mix of Race, Racism, and Guns")

3. *If you have friends or family who are Christian Evangelicals or hold other progun attitudes, try having some deep conversations with them, using deep canvassing techniques*—In a low-key, nonthreatening way, share your personal story and beliefs about gun violence. Don't try to persuade, try only to tell your own story, and listen carefully to theirs. You may be surprised by what happens, and we must start talking across the gun divide. (Chapter 5, "The Tortured Relationship Between Religion and Guns")

4. *Learn to recognize the signs of suicide, and if there is even a hint of it from someone in your household, be super conscientious about secure storage of any firearms*—The safest approach is to have no guns in the home. If you have a gun, store it elsewhere. If you keep it in the house, be sure that it is locked and unloaded

and that ammunition is stored separately. Guns are a uniquely lethal method for suicide. (Chapter 6, "A Highly Effective Method of Suicide")

5. *Promote a GunSense citizen identity for those who want to end the insanity*— The NRA has successfully promoted a gun-owner identity and uses it to drive everything from gun sales to voting for certain politicians. We need to promote a group identity for those who want to prevent gun deaths and everything that goes into prevention, including secure storage. (Chapter 7, "How the Gun Lobby Uses Psychology for Profit and Power")

6. *Recognize and promote the right to freedom from gun violence*—In the United States we have a right to peaceful protests, freedom of speech, and, importantly, a right to public safety. Children have a right to go to school without lockdown drills, much less an active shooter. When armed gunmen appear at a rally or parade, they are taking away the rights of the peaceful GunSense Majority. We should recognize that we have a right to freedom from gun violence. (Chapter 8, "The Second Amendment Does Not Doom Us")

In the sections that follow, I elaborate on ways in which we can take action as individuals, as parents, in schools, in the workplace, in our communities, and with policies at the state and federal levels.

SMART CHOICES FOR INDIVIDUALS
Certainly there are dozens of actions that individuals can take to reduce gun violence in America. Here, let me highlight three: be safe around guns, vote in a gun-safety-informed way, and join a grassroots activist organization.

Be Safe Around Guns
You and those around you are safest if you have no guns in your home or vehicle. If you feel you must have a gun, be sure to store it securely locked up and unloaded, with ammunition stored separately. Also, consider the possibility of trading in your old firearm for one of the new biometric guns that can be set so that only you can fire it.

Vote in a Gun-Safety-Informed Way
We know which laws save lives from gun violence, but the US Congress and many state legislatures have failed to pass those laws. Use your power as a voter to elect politicians who are committed to passing lifesaving gun laws. GunSenseVoter.org

lists all candidates for elected office who pledge to pass these desperately needed laws. This project is run by Everytown for Gun Safety and is nonpartisan. All candidates for a particular office receive a questionnaire on which they can declare their views on gun legislation. If they indicate a commitment to voting for commonsense gun laws, they gain the distinction of being a Gun Sense Candidate and appear on the website. The website allows you to easily find out whether particular candidates are committed to gun safety legislation, so you can make smart choices when you vote. And tell your friends about it.

Join a Grassroots Activist Organization

When important legislation in your state or in Congress is up for a vote—and it might be a law that strengthens gun regulations, or a law that weakens them—you want your voice to be heard. By affiliating with an organization such as Moms Demand Action, you will receive notifications at critical junctures as legislation moves forward, with an easy way to convey your views to your elected representatives. You can also do more with these organizations, such as attending meetings and participating in rallies. The amount of effort you put in is up to you. There is strength in numbers, and your commitment to a group like Moms boosts the strength of the gun safety movement.

SMART CHOICES FOR PARENTS

You see them in the headlines—parents whose teenager has gone on a rampage, shooting multiple people at a school or a shopping mall. What can you do so that your child or grandchild or niece or nephew does not become involved with guns and shoot someone?

How to Stop the Cycle: Recognize and Address Antisocial Behavior

Antisocial behavior can emerge in childhood or adolescence and includes rule-breaking and aggressiveness.[6] These kids are poor at controlling their behavior, even though it hurts others. They are often bullies who intimidate other kids and pick fights, and they can be cruel to people or animals. It might not disturb them to shoot another person.

Kids who exhibit antisocial behavior are not a homogeneous group. One important distinction is between early-onset antisocial behavior and adolescent onset.[7] Antisocial behavior that appears in the preschool years (early childhood) is the early-onset variety; it is more serious and more likely to persist into late adolescence and adulthood.

The *coercive cycle* is a pattern in which the child's misbehavior evokes harsh and inconsistent parenting, which only fuels more misbehavior.[8] Harsh parenting includes physical punishment like hitting, or yelling at and demeaning the child. As we've seen elsewhere in this book, punishment is drearily ineffective at shaping behavior in a positive direction. Inconsistent parenting involves just that—inconsistency, such as harsh punishment for a behavior one day, ignoring the same behavior the next day, and being hypernurturing the next. All of this leaves the child confused, and the antisocial behavior escalates, triggering more harsh parenting. In school, the aggressiveness leads to academic failures, again escalating the nasty behaviors. And the other kids don't like a bully, so he is rejected by his peers and associates with the few rule-breakers who are like him. The antisocial behavior escalates even more. This is the cycle that must be stopped.

The message here is not parent blaming. When a child displays behavior problems, it's not necessarily the parent's fault. Some children are difficult to raise from the get-go and they can test a parent's patience. And many other factors are in play, including neighborhood violence and poverty.

Research indicates that family poverty is an environmental factor that contributes to antisocial behavior.[9] Poverty and financial instability are severe stressors on parents, leaving them short of emotional resources to put into parenting. It's tough to be warm and supportive when you're wondering where the rent money is coming from and whether you might be evicted. In that context, too, it's difficult for parents to support wholesome organized activities for their child (see below).

Neighborhood disadvantage is another factor that has been linked to antisocial behavior. Kids growing up in a neighborhood with widespread poverty and frequent violence are more likely to develop antisocial behavior for multiple reasons, including the exposure to traumatizing neighborhood violence, schools that don't function well, and exposure to lead and other toxic environmental substances that affect the brain.

Psychological testing reveals that kids with antisocial behavior, on average, have less inhibitory control than other kids their age. That is, they have difficulty inhibiting behavior when that's what they need to do, such as sitting quietly at their desk in school instead of running around the room. They also tend to have trouble keeping their attention focused and regulating emotions such as anger. These patterns have led researchers to ask whether the brain regions responsible for these functions might show deficits in these youth and, indeed, some regions of the prefrontal cortex and the amygdala differ, on average, between antisocial kids and others.[10] The prefrontal cortex is crucial for inhibiting behavior and the amygdala is integral to emotion processing.

Again, the message is not about parent blaming. But we do know that kids who have a warm relationship with at least one parent have better outcomes. That doesn't mean a parent who is a pushover and sets no rules. It means a parent who expresses their love and caring for their child and does so consistently, while also remaining firm about rules.

Parenting skills are not something we're born with, they are learned, and therefore they can be trained. Psychologists have devised training programs for parents whose children are more challenging or who have fallen into these coercive cycles, or even just for parents who are stressed and want additional ideas about parenting.[11] The programs can be carried out with parents even when the child is just a toddler, the idea being to prevent early conduct problems before they occur. Overall, the goal is to reduce negative parenting behaviors such as criticizing, threatening, using sarcasm, and yelling, and replace those with positive, proactive parenting such as suggesting constructive activities to the child, rewarding good behavior, resolving issues playfully, and using these strategies proactively, before problem behaviors occur. Evaluations show that parent training interventions like these are effective at reducing child behavior problems. We need to make these training programs widely available, and Head Start centers and WIC (Women, Infants, and Children) centers often offer these resources.

What if you're a parent who suspects that your child is developing behavior problems? The trick here is not to be too sensitive and not to be insensitive. You don't want to overreact to small problems, but neither do you want to ignore big problems. You can talk to your child's pediatrician, or search online for a child psychologist in your area who has experience with "parent management training" or some other type of parent training. Branded packages include The Incredible Years and Triple P (Positive Parenting Program). Tell your pediatrician or child psychologist your concerns and ask for an opportunity to learn more about parent training.

"Bibliotherapy" is actually a thing, too. It refers to reading a self-help book by a qualified psychologist and following the recommendations. DIY. One example is *Everyday Parenting* by Thomas Dishion, a noted researcher.

The bottom line: children's antisocial behavior can be overcome if it is addressed early, using evidence-based positive parenting techniques.

Reduce Exposure to Firearm Violence in Media

Media researchers Dan Romer, Brad Bushman, and Michael Rich have put together the scientific evidence on firearm violence in the media and its harmful effects on children.[12] Here are some of the key takeaways.

- The scientific evidence linking media consumption to firearm violence is strong.

- The industry rating systems allow children 13 and older to watch media with firearms.

- The portrayal of guns in PG-13 movies has tripled over the last 30 years. This is combined with sanitizing so that no blood or other serious harm from a gunshot wound are shown. A reasonable kid might infer that gunshot wounds don't really hurt people.

- The link between playing violent video games and later aggression peaks at 13 to 15 years of age. That's an especially sensitive period for kids, one that parents should pay attention to.

- In the movies, firearm violence is often portrayed as virtuous. Overall, the media normalizes the use of guns.

- Research shows that the increase in gun violence in popular TV shows from 2000 to 2018 was paralleled by an increase in gun homicides among 15- to 24-year-olds over that same period.

In short, the portrayal of guns on TV, in movies, and in active shooter games is a real problem. Parents need to place firm limits on screen time and monitor the content of what their kids are watching, perhaps implementing parental controls. And the media could help by reducing the representation of guns in movies and television.

Promote Participation in Organized Activities

Multiple studies have shown that exposure to violence—such as media violence, neighborhood violence, or knowing someone who has been shot—increases the risk that a teen will engage in firearm aggression themselves.[13] The good news is that participating in positive organized activities can protect youth from the damaging effects of exposure to violence.[14] Dozens of organized activities are possible, such as playing on a basketball team, going to a church or temple youth group, or regular volunteering at a local food pantry. This doesn't have to mean an overscheduled kid, it just means a major, regular commitment to some reasonably healthy, structured activity.

Organized activities have protective effects for multiple reasons.[15] The activities provide an opportunity to be mentored by responsible adults in the community, who themselves model positive, responsible behavior. Kids are likely to observe peaceful methods for resolving conflicts, and they gain a network of social support. Even for youth whose parents condone retaliatory attitudes (conveying the message that revenge is a good thing), therefore increasing the risk the youth will use violence, participation in an organized activity such as a religious youth group exposes them to a network of adults and peers who don't advocate violence or retaliation.

These findings offer hope even for parents who are raising kids in neighborhoods afflicted with high levels of violence. Commitment to even one regular organized activity could provide a lifeline.

Think Carefully About Male Socialization

In the chapter on masculinity and guns, we saw the evidence of how socializing boys for qualities like aggressiveness and toughness leads to gun violence and the preponderance of boys and men among mass shooters. Experts are calling for a new approach to socialization, termed *progressive masculinities*.[16] Much of it is aimed at reducing men's sexual violence, but it applies to gun violence as well, and to boys' and men's mental health more broadly.

Challenging the belief that boys and men must be emotionally invincible, star athletes such as Alex Rodriguez and Michael Phelps have openly discussed their mental health struggles. See the website headsupguys.org, which provides a wealth of resources. Everyone, and especially parents, need to think more progressively about socializing boys.

Smart Choices for Schools

I was talking with a 40-something friend who, as a teenager, experienced a shooting at her high school. She was not in the room where it occurred, so she was physically distanced from it. But she says that it forever shattered her belief that her school was a safe place to be. What an enormous change in worldview, in just a matter of minutes. We simply must stop school shootings, not only to save lives, but also to halt all the collateral damage to those who survive.

While rampage shootings attract the most attention, they account for only about 19 percent of the gun deaths in schools.[17] The remainder occur in a multitude of situations such as parking lot altercations and robberies that happen to occur on school grounds. There are patterns to gunfire on school grounds, though. The shooter usually has a connection to the school, either as a current or former student. The guns that are used typically come from home, family, or friends; that means the shooter did not purchase the gun directly. There are nearly always warning signs in advance of the shooting. And gun violence in schools disproportionately impacts students of color.

The prestigious Everytown for Gun Safety's Research and Policy unit issued a report, "How to Stop Shootings and Gun Violence in Schools: A Plan to Keep Students Safe," which presents evidence-based solutions.[18] Many of their key recommendations pertain to state and national policies such as enacting Extreme Risk Protection Order (Red Flag) laws and secure storage laws. Those are covered elsewhere in this chapter. Here I will summarize their recommendations for schools specifically: foster a safe and trusting school climate; create evidence-based crisis assessment/prevention programs; implement specific school security upgrades; and engage in trauma-informed emergency planning. In addition, based on media effects research, I explain media and information literacy training, which must become part of the curriculum.

> **GOOD NEWS**
>
> We have evidence-based solutions to prevent gun violence in schools: foster a trusting school climate; implement specific school security upgrades; and create crisis assessment/prevention teams.

You can take action by making sure that the decision-makers in your school district have access to the Everytown report and its list of evidence-based solutions. Too often, school officials adopt strategies that have an intuitive appeal or that are demanded by parents, but unfortunately, those strategies are not backed by the scientific evidence. To address shootings at schools, we need policies that work, and research shows what works.

Foster a Safe and Trusting School Climate

At the top of the list for preventing gun violence in schools is school climate.[19] It is impossible to overstate its importance. A positive, warm, supportive school climate is essential in preventing violence, and the goal should be prevention, not addressing the aftermath of a shooting that already occurred. What follows are the recommendations from the Division for Emotional and Behavioral Health of the Council for Children with Behavioral Disorders.[20]

A central component is to promote the success of all learners through schoolwide positive behavior interventions.[21] Expectations for students' behavior are clearly defined, taught, and reinforced. We know from learning theory and decades of research in psychology that punishment is not effective at shaping behavior whereas positive reinforcement works amazingly well. It is also much better at creating a positive school climate. Positive reinforcement is at the heart of these schoolwide positive behavior interventions. That doesn't mean popping some M&Ms in a kid's mouth every time they do something good. Positive reinforcement can be as simple and low calorie as praise. Screening for mental health issues and providing mental health services should also be part of the plan. Intervening with mental health problems works so much better if it is done early, rather than later, when a student is far into a downward spiral.

Create Evidence-Based Crisis Assessment and Prevention Programs

Even with all that positive energy, schools should still have a threat assessment protocol in place. The National Threat Assessment Center (NTAC), which is part of the US Secret Service, has issued a report on protecting America's schools.[22] The report reveals there is no single profile of a student attacker, so there is no profile based on gender, race, or similar characteristics. Instead, threat can be assessed using multiple behavior, social, and psychological indicators. No one single indicator is sufficient. The strategy is to identify a kid who has multiple converging risk factors. According to the NTAC study, most attackers had psychological symptoms such as depression, suicidal ideation, or defiant behavior. Half were interested in violent topics. All had experienced stressors in their relationships with peers, half of them within two days of the attack; many of them had been bullied, and many of them were in crisis. Nearly every attacker had negative factors in their home life such as domestic abuse or criminal charges among family members. Most attackers had a history of disciplinary actions at school, and all exhibited concerning behaviors, such as communicating their intent to engage in violence.

Each school should have a team that is charged with spotting a constellation of problems like this in a student. The Secret Service website has a guide for schools on how to put together a threat assessment team, when law enforcement should be involved, and so on. The National Threat Assessment Center provides trainings for school personnel. All of this must run in the background, though, or it risks sapping away positive school climate.

Perhaps you find it disturbing to think about the Secret Service in relation to schools. I have a twinge of that myself. But the Secret Service has amassed decades of experience in threat assessment, with the goal of protecting people like the president. That knowledge of how to assess threats can be applied to keeping schools safe.

At the risk of sounding like a broken record, this report also concluded that most attackers used firearms and most firearms were obtained from the home.

In his book *Trigger Points: Inside the Mission to Stop Mass Shootings in America*, journalist Mark Follman provides a fascinating, inside look at behavioral threat assessment and how it is used to prevent mass shootings.[23] We rarely hear about the shootings that are foiled, much less how they were foiled. This book shines a light on that behind-the-scenes work. Later in this chapter, I describe how this approach is being applied to preventing workplace shootings.

Implement Specific School Security Upgrades

In terms of physical security practices, at the top of the list are so-called access control measures that keep a possible shooter out of the school.[24] Depending on the situation, this may include a single entrance to the school with all other doors locked. It may include a metal-detecting scanner that students walk through as they enter, similar to those used at airports.

The other essential physical security measure is locks on the inside of classroom doors so that if a shooter should gain access to the school, teachers can secure their own classrooms and the children in them. I watched locks like that being installed in my own building at the University of Wisconsin a few years ago. I am grateful I never had to use them.

By way of giving a balanced view, I should note there are two issues with these security upgrades. First, they cost money, and it is money that comes out of the school's budget, which might otherwise go to purchase new curriculum materials or increase teachers' salaries. Ideally, states should provide the funding. Second, if a school goes too far with these security upgrades, the school could seem like a maximum-security prison, which works against the strategy of creating a safe and trusting school climate. The two security measures described here—access control and locks inside classroom doors—are probably enough, and more could be overkill that unintentionally harms school climate.

Engage in Trauma-Informed Emergency Planning

Threat assessment aims at prevention by identifying a potentially high-risk individual before an incident occurs. Emergency planning, in contrast, has to do with the protocol to be followed if gun violence actually occurs at the school. Both the American Federation of Teachers (AFT) and the National Education Association (NEA) recommend that school personnel plan for a gun violence emergency by practicing regularly and collaborating with law enforcement.[25] The collaboration might mean, for example, that local law enforcement has the floor plan for each school so that they can quickly locate classrooms at points of danger.

The "trauma-informed" part of the approach involves a recognition that childhood trauma is common and its effects can be long-lasting.[26] School personnel should be educated about how common it is and how to recognize the signs of trauma exposure in a student. A cornerstone of trauma-informed approaches is to make sure that a child is not retraumatized. For that reason, active shooter drills should not be used because they might retraumatize some children.

Another practice to be avoided is arming teachers, an approach that is fraught at best.[27] Can you imagine what it would be like for a child who saw their brother killed with a gun, to now see their trusted teacher with a gun?

One approach that has been intuitively appealing in many school districts is to hire police as guards or School Resource Officers (SROs), a term apparently designed to soften the image of armed police in the school. The evidence actually indicates that SROs do not improve school safety.[28] And they may work against creating a positive and trusting school climate.[29] That said, it depends on the SRO. If the officer is approachable and builds trusting relationships with students, those students may be more likely to report a threat of violence, and that could prevent a shooting.[30]

Media and Information Literacy

Many school systems, at the level of middle school and high school, provide students with training in media and information literacy (MIL).[31] That's a good thing! And research gives us reason to believe that if students receive MIL training, it will help them recognize misinformation on specific issues such as guns. They learn to spot things like fearmongering and conspiracy theories, often from businesses that sell guns by frightening you. Here are some things you can do to further the cause.

- Check to see if your local schools incorporate media literacy training in the curriculum. If they don't, advocate for it with principals and the superintendent of schools.

- Provide resources that teachers can use, such as the *Bad News* game (www.getbadnews.com), which teaches media literacy. In comments on the game, one teacher said they had used it with their fifth and sixth graders and it was very successful. There are similar comments from many other teachers.

SMART CHOICES FOR THE WORKPLACE

Although school shootings receive the most publicity, workplace shootings are actually more common. Following the 2019 mass shooting by an employee at the Virginia Beach Municipal Center in which 17 individuals were shot, 12 of whom died, psychologists analyzed whether the threat could have been anticipated.[32] To do this, they used the *Workplace Assessment of Violence Risk* or WAVR. With the WAVR, the threat assessment team considers the following 21 items in relation to the individual who is exhibiting concerning behavior.

1. Motives for Violence

2. Homicidal Ideas, Violent Preoccupations or Identifications

3. Threatening Communications or Expressed Intent

4. Weapons Skill and/or Access

5. Pre-attack Planning and Preparation

6. Stalking or Menacing Behavior

7. Current Job or Academic Problems

8. Extreme Job or Academic Attachment

9. Loss, Personal Stressors and Negative Coping

10. Entitlement and Other Negative Traits

11. Lack of Conscience and Irresponsibility

12. Anger Problems

13. Suicidality and/or Depressive Mood

14. Irrationally Suspicious or Bizarre Beliefs

15. Substance Abuse and/or Dependence

16. Increasing Isolation

17. History of Violence, Criminality, and/or Conflict

18. Domestic/Intimate Partner Violence

19. Situational and Organizational Contributors to Violence

20. Stabilizers and Buffers Against Violence

21. Organizational Impact of Real or Perceived Threats[33]

The team scores each item as absent, present, or prominent (more than just present). Each of these items is a risk factor for workplace violence and if enough of them are present, the supervisor or the team should address the situation with the individual. This same method can be used in schools.

In the Virginia Beach case, the shooter was killed on the scene by Special Weapons and Tactics officers, ending the killing but also making it impossible for researchers to interview him and find out his thinking directly. Therefore, for the analysis, the researchers accessed numerous documents such as the perpetrator's work emails, photos of his office, his internet search history, and a transcript of a police interview with his ex-wife. The shooter was 40 years old with a degree in engineering and worked in an engineering capacity for the city—not what you might expect for a mass shooter, but we have to dig deeper.

Based on the information the researchers collected, the warning signs were there. For example, for item 1, Motives for Violence, the gunman, beginning five years earlier, had expressed workplace grievances repeatedly, to such an extent that the experts termed him a "grievance collector."[34] A person like that begins to think they are being victimized, even if the slights are, objectively, minor or nonexistent. The shooter believed that he was given more than his fair share of work and less than his fair share of compensation and recognition, over and over again.

For item 2, Homicidal Ideas, Violent Preoccupations or Identifications, the perpetrator identified strongly with violent characters such as those in the Detective Comics Universe and Marvel Comics. Identifications like these are a red flag.

For item 4, Weapons Skill and/or Access, the shooter had been in the Virginia Army National Guard and received weapons training there. After his home was burglarized, he purchased his first firearm in 2005, and in the three years before the attack, he purchased at least six additional weapons.

He engaged in Pre-attack Planning (item 5), although he kept it secret, searching on websites for other mass shootings. A few months before the attack, he purchased body armor, another red flag. He also made several financial errors at work and was reported for them (item 7), and he resigned on the morning of the shooting, apparently thinking he would be fired.

I could go on with more details, but you get the picture—this individual displayed numerous risk factors for workplace violence.

Could this mass shooting have been anticipated and prevented, given what we know about the psychology of workplace violence? The answer is complicated.[35] Some of the indicators, such as the internet searches, couldn't have been known to supervisors or coworkers. And information can be siloed within the organization, so that a few people knew about all the emails with grievances, whereas others knew about identification with violent characters as demonstrated by the Funko Mopeez Deadshot figure displayed on his desk. Perhaps no one individual knew about the multiple warning signs.

That said, any one of these indicators is so concerning that a well-informed supervisor or coworker should talk to others in the workplace and collect more information. If a colleague has a long string of unresolved, perhaps paranoid grievances over time, report it to a supervisor and collect more information on other possible risk factors. You have the list of them above. If a colleague has a Funko Mopeez Deadshot figure on their desk, do the same. You might prevent a mass shooting and, in the process, get help for someone who desperately needs it.

We must also have some cooperation from credit card companies. If an individual purchases six firearms plus body armor, it should be flagged for law enforcement. Some will say that every American has the right to make those purchases. I would say those rights must be balanced against the death of 12 human beings, and the flag could just be for law enforcement to seek more information, not necessarily make an immediate arrest.

More broadly, we must boost capacity for *leakage-based prevention of mass shootings*. Researchers examined mass shootings that occurred between 2000 and 2019, 92 of them completed and 142 of them foiled.[36] It's good to know that so many were foiled! The purpose of threat assessment is to identify and assess potential offenders with the goal of preventing a violent act. In threat assessment, "leakage" refers to the potential offender communicating to someone else their intent to commit a violent act. The leakage may occur through any number of channels including face-to-face interaction, emails, or online posts. The two most common kinds of leakage are in-person and online. Among the *foiled* mass shooters who leaked online, the greatest number were identified by law enforcement and the shooting was prevented. That kind of monitoring of potential threats is a good use of taxpayer money. With *completed* mass shootings, leak-

> ## GOOD NEWS
>
> The majority of mass shooting plans are foiled through leakage-based prevention efforts, most often by law enforcement.

age to family and wife or girlfriend was common but went unreported. Overall, workplace shootings were more likely to be completed and school shootings were more likely to be foiled, and the school shootings were most often foiled because the suspicious behavior was reported by classmates. Employee training programs could aim to bring the level of reporting by adults up to the level of schoolchildren.

SMART CHOICES FOR COMMUNITIES AND CULTURES

Here I explore ways to make communities and cultures safer, using trusted messengers, and the power of humans to change their culture.

Trusted Messengers

In both psychology and public health, we learned a lot from the Covid-19 pandemic. One key takeaway was the crucial role of trusted messengers in persuading people to engage in health behaviors. Although a large percentage of the population was persuaded to get vaccinated by scientific evidence and leading scientists like Dr. Anthony Fauci, another chunk of the population refused vaccination or experienced vaccine hesitancy. It became apparent that a way to reach this last group was through *trusted messengers*: individuals or organizations they know and trust. Influential messengers include doctors, nurses, and religious leaders such as ministers, priests, and rabbis.[37] We must mobilize these trusted leaders to persuade people about the importance of gun safety. And, in fact, many pediatricians across the nation are taking this action with their patients. Because physicians are held in high regard, they can also play an influential role in advocating for gun safety legislation.[38]

Actions for Cultures

Humans shape culture and culture shapes humans. It's a two-way street. The question is, can American humans change some aspects of our culture so that we don't have 43,000 people dying by guns every year? We could be talking about a broad culture, such as American Gun Culture, or a narrower, more specific one, such as police training or police culture in a Texas city.

Culture has been defined as a socially meaningful system of shared ideas, histories, policies, norms, and products that structure the behavior of individuals.[39] Cultures tell us what is good and valuable, and they organize people's interactions, whether with other people or with institutions (e.g., government, religion).

Social psychologists have put a good deal of thought into *intentional culture change*, that is, when some members of a culture decide it should change and they work toward that goal.[40] Here are some of the key points.

- *Humans shape culture, so they can change a culture.* To do so, they must change both people and their social environment.

- *Culture exists at multiple levels* (see figure 9.1): ideas (cultural assumptions about what is good or dangerous, who is powerful, etc.); institutions (governments, schools, media); interactions with other people (e.g., family, the police), groups (e.g., teams, gun clubs), and products (e.g., violent video games); and individuals (e.g., a person's behavior, thoughts, feelings, and identities). Analyzing these multiple levels helps us know where to target change and how to change multiple levels.

- *Culture change can be stimulated from the top down or the bottom up.* An example of top-down change would be the US president declaring gun safety policies. Grassroots activists working for gun safety would be a bottom-up change initiative. Effective change is most likely if the top and bottom levels agree on the needed change.

- *Culture change is easier if it leverages existing core values.* For example, freedom is a deeply held value in America. The Gun Lobby emphasizes the freedom to keep and bear arms. To foster culture change, the GunSense Majority must emphasize freedom from gun violence.

To apply these ideas to changing Gun Culture, let's suppose that your goal is to change one aspect of the culture of your small town, Shootsville, where the custom is to fire guns in the air in celebration on the evening of the Fourth of July. The gunfire wakes your baby and frightens your dog. You also wonder what happens to those bullets discharged into the sky. After consulting with the emergency department at your local hospital, you learn that the practice is called "celebratory gunfire" and serious injuries and even deaths from it have been reported nationwide.[41] Bullets fired vertically arc up and then return to earth some distance away at a velocity that can penetrate skin and bone. This has got to stop! But it's the

> **GOOD NEWS**
>
> Humans can change culture, so we can change Gun Culture. Think about how quickly we adopted laptop computers. Cultures can change quickly.

custom, the culture in your small town. What can you do? Oh, and you'd like to remain friends with your neighbors.

In terms of the model shown in figure 9.1, the celebratory gunfire involves several levels of local culture. At the level of Ideas, many of your neighbors believe that firing guns is a great way to celebrate Independence Day. Their parents did it before them, and their grandparents before them. It's part of what it means to be a Shootsan. At the level of Institutions, the police do nothing about the celebratory firing because it's one of the cherished traditions of Shootsville. The mayor and members of the city council are among those who participate.

How can you intervene to stop this annoying and perhaps even deadly practice? You'll need to start months in advance of Independence Day to have any chance of making a change in the celebratory gunfire culture. The box in figure

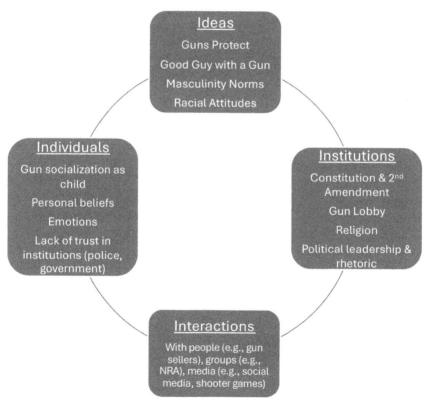

Figure 9.1   The multiple levels of culture applied to Gun Culture.

9.1 labeled Interactions shows some promise. As you talk face-to-face with your neighbors, you could mention in a low-key way how awful it is in the middle of the night when gunfire wakes the baby and scares the dog—and you. See how they react. If they are part of the celebratory gunfire crowd, they may never have thought of the unintended consequences of their actions. They're only thinking of the fun of firing guns on the Fourth. You are helping them see another perspective and think through the consequences of their actions.

In addition, you could sound out some other parents with small children like yourself. You are probably not the only one who is disturbed by the gunfire and would like to change the custom. You could enlist 10 or 20 other like-minded parents across the town to have in-person conversations with their celebratory neighbors to explain their point of view about the mode of celebration. If the group of parents seems to be getting some positive responses in their conversations, you could move on to the next step.

You prepare a statement in which residents voluntarily pledge not to fire guns in celebration this Fourth of July, with a background statement about how the custom is disruptive to families and tears at the community-mindedness of Shootsville. The idea is to leverage core values. You and the other parents go door to door and ask neighbors to take the voluntary pledge. Once you have a few signatures, you're creating a new social norm. It just might work!

Notice that everything about this approach is very low key. Social psychologists have documented a phenomenon known as *reactance*. If you press a person too hard to change their mind about a particular topic, they are likely to react against your persuasion attempt and become even more rigidly convinced of their original opinion.[42] You get exactly the opposite result from the one you hoped for. The approaches outlined here are therefore designed to be nonthreatening so as not to touch off reactance.

Reactance can be stimulated if the persuasive message seems to threaten the person's sense of freedom, and freedom is a core American value. That's why it's important that signing the pledge be completely voluntary. There's no threat to anyone's freedom.

To extend the analysis to leverage existing core values, what are some core values of Shootsville? Perhaps the cultural belief is that it's a great place to raise kids. But isn't that incompatible with shooting off guns in the middle of the night?

These ideas are a beginning at thinking about how we could bring about some of the culture change that is necessary to reduce dependence on guns and reduce gun deaths in America, beginning at the local level.

Even more basic than that, we can all work on changing culture through everyday conversations with folks who are progun activists, as shown in table 9.1.

Table 9.1 Arguments from Progun Activists and How You Can Respond

Progun Activist Says	You Could Respond
No one is taking away my Second Amendment rights.	Let's take out our phones and google "Second Amendment" to see what it actually says. Ah, it says "well-regulated militia." We've had regulations on guns since colonial times.
You're trying to take away my guns.	No, I'm just trying to save lives.
Did you know that "assault weapon" is not even in the dictionary?	Dictionary.com defines "assault weapon" as "any of various automatic and semiautomatic military firearms utilizing an intermediate-power cartridge, designed for individual use."
I have a right to own a gun.	With rights come responsibilities, including safe storage. Do you store your gun locked up, with ammunition removed?
First you ban assault weapons, then you take away all our guns.	That's a slippery slope argument. The fact is that we had an assault weapons ban from 1994 to 2004 and the government did not take away all the other guns. During that time, homicide rates went down. Don't you agree that we want to reduce the number of homicides?
The only thing that stops a bad guy with a gun is a good guy with a gun.	The evidence indicates that's not true. It's very rare for an active shooter to be stopped by a bystander with a gun. More often, the police stop the shooter, or a bystander tackles the shooter.
I can't lock up my gun because I need quick access to it.	Biometric locks are available that require only your fingerprint to open them.

Source: Janet Hyde.

SMART POLICIES: STATE AND FEDERAL GOVERNMENT

Researchers have put a great deal of effort into determining which laws are effective in reducing gun deaths, often by studying what happens in states that pass various gun regulations compared with states that do not. We don't have to guess which regulations are effective, and I have explained the rationale for each of these in previous chapters. Here is a list of the top 10.[43]

1. Mandate background checks on all gun sales and a waiting period between purchase and actually taking possession of the gun.

2. Pass Red Flag or ERPO (Extreme Risk Protection Order) laws to temporarily remove firearms from a person who is a danger to themselves or others.

3. Repeal Shoot First (stand your ground) laws.

4. Require a permit to carry a concealed gun in public.

5. Stop arming teachers.

6. Require secure gun storage.

7. Prohibit downloadable guns.

8. Prohibit assault weapons and high-capacity magazines for civilians.

9. Prohibit bump stocks and other devices that create rapid-fire guns.

10. Repeal gun industry immunity from prosecution.

Let's move forward with each of these laws!

THE BOTTOM LINE

I have a dream, of an America free from gun violence.

You want to end gun violence in America. I want to end gun violence in America. We're in this together and we want to save lives. Let's get to work! I have offered dozens of strategies for solutions—smart choices. The problem will not be solved by a single initiative. Because the problem is very complex, it will take a multipronged approach. Which solution will you work on?

Notes

Chapter One: Introduction

1. National Center for Health Statistics. 2023. *CDC Annual Mortality Data Files for WISQARS Fatal Data*. National Center for Health Statistics. https://wisqars.cdc.gov/reports/.

2. Kegler, Scott R. et al. 2022. "Vital Signs: Changes in Firearm Homicide and Suicide Rates—United States, 2019–2020." *MMWR, 71(19)*.

3. Goldstick, Jason E. et al. 2022. "Current Causes of Death in Children and Adolescents in the United States." *New England Journal of Medicine, 386*, 1955–56.

4. Everytown for Gun Safety. 2023. *Gun Violence in the United States*. EveryStat.org.

5. Kegler, "Vital Signs: Changes in Firearm Homicide and Suicide Rates."

6. Miller, Ted R., and Bruce Lawrence. 2019. "Analysis of CDC Fatal Injury: 2019 and HCUP Nonfatal Injury." Everystat.org.

7. Zeineddin, Suhail et al. 2023. "Disfiguring Firearm Injuries in Children in the United States." *The American Surgeon, 89*, 2070–72.

8. Chapman, S. et al. 2006. "Australia's 1996 Gun Law Reforms: Faster Falls in Firearm Deaths, Firearms Suicides, and a Decade Without Mass Shootings." *Injury Prevention, 12*, 365–72.

9. Stroebe, Wolfgang et al. 2022. "When Mass Shootings Fail to Change Minds About the Causes of Violence: How Gun Beliefs Shape Causal Attributions." *Psychology of Violence, 12*, 305–13.

10. Everytown for Gun Safety. 2023. "Gun Violence in the United States." EveryStat.org; Meghan Phadke et al. 2024. "Arming Teachers: Who Will Bear the Burden?" *Educational Studies*, https://doi.org/10.1080/00131946.2024.2308696; Paul Reeping et al. 2022. "State Firearm Laws, Gun Ownership, and K–12 School Shootings: Implications for School Safety." *Journal of School Violence, 21*, 132–46.

11. McGinty, Emma E., and Daniel W. Webster. 2016. "Gun Violence and Serious Mental Illness." In *Gun Violence and Mental Illness*, edited by Liza H. Gold and Robert I. Simon. American Psychiatric Association.

12. McGinty and Webster, "Gun Violence and Serious Mental Illness."

13. Brucato, Gary et al. 2022. "Psychotic Symptoms in Mass Shootings v. Mass Murders Not Involving Firearms: Findings from the Columbia Mass Murder Database." *Psychological Medicine, 52*, 3422–30.

14. Charlson, Fiona J. et al. 2018. "Global Epidemiology and Burden of Schizophrenia: Findings from the Global Burden of Disease Study 2016." *Schizophrenia Bulletin, 44,* 1195–203.

15. Small Arms Survey. 2020. "Global Firearms Holdings." Smallarmssurvey.org.

16. Boglioli, Marc. 2009. *A Matter of Life and Death: Hunting in Contemporary Vermont.* Amherst: University of Massachusetts Press.

17. US Surgeon General. 2024. *Firearm Violence: A Public Health Crisis in America.* https://www.hhs.gov/surgeongeneral/priorities/firearm-violence/index.html.

18. Hemenway, David, and Lois K. Lee. 2022. "Lessons from the Continuing 21st Century Motor Vehicle Success." *Injury Prevention, 28,* 480–82.

19. Hemenway and Lee, "Lessons from the Continuing 21st Century Motor Vehicle Success."

CHAPTER TWO: EMOTIONS MAKE US BUY THEM

1. Boine, Claire et al. 2022. "Who Are Gun Owners in the United States? A Latent Class Analysis of the 2019 National Lawful Use of Guns Survey." *Sociological Perspectives, 65,* 35–57.

2. Boglioli, Marc. 2009. *A Matter of Life and Death: Hunting in Contemporary Vermont.* Amherst: University of Massachusetts Press.

3. Heberlein, Tom. 2016. "Sweden May Have the Answer to America's Gun Problem." *Vox.* https://www.vox.com/2016/8/8/12351824/gun-control-sweden-solution.

4. Miller, Matthew et al. 2021. "Firearm Purchasing during the COVID-19 Pandemic: Results from the 2021 National Firearms Survey." *Annals of Internal Medicine, 175,* 219–25.

5. Buttrick, Nicholas. 2020. "Protective Gun Ownership as a Coping Mechanism." *Perspectives on Psychological Science, 15,* 835–55.

6. Buttrick, "Protective Gun Ownership as a Coping Mechanism."

7. Homsher, Deborah. 2001. *Women and Guns: Politics and the Culture of Firearms in America.* M. E. Sharpe, 8.

8. Mencken, F. Carson, and Paul Froese. 2019. "Gun Culture in Action." *Social Problems, 66,* 3–27.

9. Hogg, Michael A. 2023. "Walls Between Groups: Self-uncertainty, Social Identity, and Intergroup Leadership." *Journal of Social Issues, 79,* 825–40; Simon Ozer et al. 2020. "Group Membership and Radicalization: A Cross-National Investigation of Collective Self-Esteem Underlying Extremism." *Group Processes & Intergroup Relations, 23,* 1230–48.

10. Hemenway, David, and Sara J. Solnick. 2015. "The Epidemiology of Self-Defense Gun Use: Evidence from the National Crime Victimization Surveys 2007–2011." *Preventive Medicine, 79,* 22–27.

11. Anglemyer, Andrew et al. 2014. "The Accessibility of Firearms and Risk for Suicide and Homicide Victimization Among Household Members." *Annals of Internal Medicine, 160,* 101–10; L. L. Dahlberg et al. 2004. "Guns in the Home and Risk of a Violent Death in the Home: Findings from a National Study." *American Journal of Epidemiology, 160,*

929–36; David M. Studdert et al. 2022. "Homicide Deaths Among Adult Cohabitants of Handgun Owners in California, 2004 to 2016." *Annals of Internal Medicine, 175*, 804–11.

12. Anglemyer, "The Accessibility of Firearms and Risk for Suicide and Homicide Victimization."

13. Shapira, Harel, and Samantha J. Simon. 2018. "Learning to Need a Gun." *Qualitative Sociology, 41*, 1–20.

14. Tversky, Amos, and Daniel Kahneman. 1974. "Judgment Under Uncertainty: Heuristics and Biases." *Science, 185*, 1124–31.

15. Festinger, Leon. 1957. *A Theory of Cognitive Dissonance*. Redwood City: Stanford University Press.

16. Naughton, Felix et al. 2013. Dissonance and Disengagement in Pregnant Smokers. *Journal of Smoking Cessation, 8*, 24–32.

17. Pierre, Joseph M. 2019. "The Psychology of Guns: Risk, Fear, and Motivated Reasoning." *Palgrave Communications, 5*, 159. https://doi.org/10.1057/s41599-019-0373-z.

18. Pew Research Center. 2023. *For Most U.S. Gun Owners, Protection Is the Main Reason They Own a Gun*. August 16. https://www.pewresearch.org/politics/2023/08/16/for-most-u-s-gun-owners-protection-is-the-main-reason-they-own-a-gun/.

19. Schutten, Nathaniel et al. 2023. "Understanding Gun Ownership in the Twenty-First Century: Why Some Americans Own Guns, But Most Do Not." *Justice Quarterly, 40*, 27–250.

20. Schutten et al. 2023.

21. Peterson, Jillian K. et al. 2022. "Psychosis and Mass Shootings: A Systematic Examination Using Publicly Available Data." *Psychology, Public Policy, and Law, 28*, 280–91.

22. Peterson et al. 2022.

23. Langman, Peter. 2009. "Rampage School Shooters: A Typology." *Aggression and Violent Behavior, 14*, 79–86.

24. Silver, James et al. 2018. *A Study of the Pre-Attack Behaviors of Active Shooters in the United States Between 2000–2013*. Federal Bureau of Investigation, US Department of Justice.

25. Slemaker, Alexandra. 2023. "Studying Mass Shooters' Words: Warning Behavior Prior to Attacks." *Journal of Threat Assessment and Management, 10*, 1–17.

26. Cox, John Woodrow. 2021. *Children Under Fire*. New York: HarperCollins.

27. Rossin-Slater, Maya et al. 2020. "Local Exposure to School Shootings and Youth Antidepressant Use." *PNAS, 117*, 23484–89.

28. Sharkey, Patrick. 2010. "The Acute Effect of Local Homicides on Children's Cognitive Performance." *PNAS, 107*, 11733–38.

29. Cabral, Marika et al. 2022. "Trauma at School: The Impacts of Shootings on Students' Human Capital and Economic Outcomes." NBER Working Paper Series, Working Paper 28311.

30. Jaffee, Sara R. et al. 2023. "Differential Exposure to Gun or Knife Violence over Two Decades Is Associated with Sibling Differences in Depression." *Development and Psychopathology, 35*, 2096–102.

31. Lowe, Sarah R., and Sandro Galea. 2017. "The Mental Health Consequences of Mass Shootings." *Trauma, Violence, and Abuse, 18,* 62–82.

32. Song, Zirui et al. 2023. "The Clinical and Economic Impact of Child and Adolescent Firearm Injuries on Survivors and Family Members." *Journal of General Internal Medicine, 38(Suppl2),* S97–S98.

33. El Sherief, Mai et al. 2021. "Impacts of School Shooter Drills on the Psychological Well-Being of American K–12 School Communities: A Social Media Study." *Humanities and Social Sciences Communications, 8,* 315.

34. Schildkraut, Jaclyn et al. 2023. "Can School Lockdowns Save Lives? An Assessment of Drills and Use in Real-World Events." *Journal of School Violence, 22,* 167–83.

35. Schildkraut, Jaclyn et al. 2020. "Locks, Lights, Out of Sight: Assessing Students' Perceptions of Emergency Preparedness across Multiple Lockdown Drills." *Journal of School Violence, 19,* 93–106.

36. Schonfeld, David J. et al. 2020. "Participation of Children and Adolescents in Live Crisis Drills and Exercises." *Pediatrics, 146,* e2020015503.

37. Aftab, Awais, and Benjamin G. Druss. 2023. "Addressing the Mental Health Crisis in Youth: Sick Individuals or Sick Societies?" *JAMA Psychiatry, 80,* 863–64.

38. Bancalari, Pilar et al. 2022. "Youth Exposure to Endemic Community Gun Violence: A Systematic Review." *Adolescent Research Review, 7,* 383–417.

39. Bancalari et al. 2022.

40. Liebbrand, Christine et al. 2020. "Invisible Wounds: Community Exposure to Gun Homicides and Adolescents' Mental Health and Behavioral Outcomes." *SSM—Population Health, 12,* 100689.

41. Cowan, Rebecca G. et al. 2024. "'It Will Stay with Me Forever': The Experiences of Physicians Treating Victims of Public Mass Shootings." *Traumatology, 30(3),* 432–38.

42. Bandura, Albert et al. 1986. *Social Foundations of Thought and Action: A Social Cognitive Theory.* Prentice Hall.

43. Bandura, Albert et al. 1963. "Imitation of Film-Mediated Aggressive Models." *Journal of Abnormal and Social Psychology, 66,* 3–11.

44. Huesmann, L. Rowell et al. 2021. "Longitudinal Predictions of Young Adults' Weapons Use and Criminal Behavior from Their Childhood Exposure to Violence." *Aggressive Behavior, 47,* 621–34.

45. Tulchinsky, Theodore, and Elena Varavikova. 2014. "A History of Public Health." *The New Public Health,* 1–42. DOI: https://doi.org/10.1016%2FB978-0-12-415766-8.00001-X.

46. Brownson, Ross C. et al. 2018. *Evidence-Based Public Health.* New York: Oxford University Press.

47. Schneider, Mary-Jane. 2021. *Introduction to Public Health,* 6th ed. Burlington, MA: Jones & Bartlett.

48. Cummings, K. Michael, and Robert N. Proctor. 2014. "The Changing Public Image of Smoking in the United States: 1964–2014." *Cancer Epidemiology, Biomarkers and Prevention, 23,* 32–36.

49. Brandt, Allan M. 2007. *The Cigarette Century: The Rise, Fall, and Deadly Persistence of the Product That Defined America.* New York: Basic Books.

50. Cummings and Proctor, "The Changing Public Image of Smoking in the United States."

51. Brandt 2007.

52. Brandt 2007.

53. Cummings and Proctor, "The Changing Public Image of Smoking in the United States."

54. Milov, Sarah. 2019. *The Cigarette: A Political History.* Cambridge: Harvard University Press.

55. Brandt 2007.

56. Gurrey, Sixtine, et al. 2021. "Firearm-Related Research Articles in Health Sciences by Funding Status and Type: A Scoping Review." *Preventive Medicine Reports, 24,* 101604.

CHAPTER THREE: A GUN WILL MAKE YOU A REAL MAN

1. Violence Prevention Project. 2021. "Gender of Perpetrator from 1966 to 2021." Hamline University, https://www.theviolenceproject.org/data-on-social-media/gender-of-perpetrator-from-1966-2021/.

2. Pleck, Joseph R. 1981. *The Myth of Masculinity.* Cambridge, MA: MIT Press.

3. Rosenberg, Rosalind. 1983. *Beyond Separate Spheres: Intellectual Roots of Modern Feminism.* New Haven: Yale University Press.

4. Pleck, Joseph R. 1995. "The Gender Role Strain Paradigm: An Update." In *A New Psychology of Men,* edited by R. F. Levant and W. S. Pollack, 11–32. New York: Basic Books.

5. Levant, Ronald F. 2022. "Examining the Gender Role Strain Paradigm to Account for U.S. Males' Gun Violence." *Psychology of Men & Masculinities, 23,* 151–59.

6. Stroud, Angela. 2015. *Good Guys with Guns: The Appeal and Consequences of Concealed Carry.* Chapel Hill: University of North Carolina Press.

7. Ingram, Katherine M. et al. 2019. "Longitudinal Associations Between Features of Toxic Masculinity and Bystander Willingness to Intervene in Bullying Among Middle School Boys." *Journal of School Psychology, 77,* 139–51.

8. Parent, Mike C. et al. 2019. "Social Media Behavior, Toxic Masculinity, and Depression." *Psychology of Men & Masculinity, 20,* 277–87.

9. Bridges, Tristan, and Tara L. Tober. 2022. *Mass Shootings and Masculinity.* Report for the Mass Casualty Commission.

10. Willer, Robb et al. 2013. "Overdoing Gender: A Test of the Masculine Overcompensation Thesis." *American Journal of Sociology, 118,* 980–1022.

11. DiMuccio, Sarah H., and Eric D. Knowles. 2023. "Something to Prove? Manhood Threats Increase Political Aggression Among Liberal Men." *Sex Roles, 88,* 240–67.

12. Borgogna, Nicholas C. et al. 2022. "The Precarious Masculinity of Firearm Ownership." *Psychology of Men & Masculinities, 23,* 173–82.

13. Vescio, Theresa K. et al. 2025. "Masculinity Threats Sequentially Arouse Public Discomfort, Anger, and Positive Attitudes Toward Sexual Violence." *Personality and Social Psychology Bulletin, 51(1),* 96–109.

14. DiMuccio and Knowles, "Something to Prove?"

15. Brooks, Robert C. 2022. "Incel Activity on Social Media Linked to Local Mating Ecology." *Psychological Science, 33,* 249–58.

16. Follman, Mark. 2022. *Trigger Points.* New York: Dey Street Books.

17. Levant 2022.

18. Greenberger, Marcia D., and Deborah L. Blake. 1996. "The VMI Decision: Shattering Sexual Stereotypes." *Chronicle of Higher Education,* July 5, A52.

19. Plant, E. Ashby, and Janet S. Hyde et al. 2000. "The Gender Stereotyping of Emotions." *Psychology of Women Quarterly, 24,* 81–92.

20. Feder, June et al. 2007. "Boys and Violence: A Gender-Informed Analysis." *Professional Psychology: Research and Practice, 38,* 385–91; Ruth Whippman. 2024. *BoyMom: Reimagining Boyhood in an Age of Impossible Masculinity.* New York: Harmony.

21. Levant, Ronald F., and Shana Pryor. 2024. *Assessing and Treating Emotionally Inexpressive Men.* New York: Routledge.

22. Ghavami, Negin, and Anne L. Peplau. 2013. "An Intersectional Analysis of Gender and Ethnic Stereotypes: Testing Three Hypotheses." *Psychology of Women Quarterly, 37,* 113–27.

23. Blakemore, Judith et al. 2009. *Gender Development.* New York: Psychology Press.

24. American Academy of Pediatrics. 2015. "Tackling in Youth Football." *Pediatrics, 136(5),* e1419–30.

25. Mascaro, Jennifer S. et al. 2017. "Child Gender Influences Paternal Behavior, Language, and Brain Function." *Behavioral Neuroscience, 131,* 262–73.

26. Littlefield, Jon, and Julie L. Ozanne. 2011. "Socialization into Consumer Culture: Hunters Learning to Be Men." *Consumption Markets & Culture, 14,* 333–60.

27. Witkowski, Terrence H. 2020. "Guns for Christmas: Advertising in *Boys' Life* Magazine, 1911–2012." *Journal of Macromarketing, 40,* 396–414.

28. Stroud 2015.

29. Oliphant, Stephen N. 2023. "Bullying Victimization and Weapon Carrying: A Partial Test of General Strain Theory." *Youth & Society, 55,* 122–42.

30. Bushman, Brad J., and L. R. Huesmann. 2006. "Short-Term and Long-Term Effects of Violent Media on Aggression in Children and Adults." *Archives of Pediatrics & Adolescent Medicine, 160,* 358–52.

31. Paik, H., and G. Comstock. 1994. "The Effects of Television Violence on Antisocial Behavior: A Meta-Analysis." *Communication Research, 21,* 516–46; Joanne Savage and Christina Yancey. 2008. "The Effects of Media Violence Exposure on Criminal Aggression: A Meta-Analysis." *Criminal Justice and Behavior, 35,* 772–91.

32. Calvert, Sandra L. et al. 2017. "The American Psychological Association Task Force Assessment of Violent Video Games." *American Psychologist, 72,* 126–43.

33. Bushman and Huesmann, "Short-Term and Long-Term Effects of Violent Media."

34. Fikkers, Karin M. et al. 2017. "A Matter of Style? Exploring the Effects of Parental Mediation Styles on Early Adolescents' Media Violence Exposure and Aggression." *Computers in Human Behavior, 70,* 407–15.

35. Bushman, Brad J. et al. 2016. "Youth Violence: What We Know and What We Need to Know." *American Psychologist, 71,* 17–39.

36. Buchanan, Larry, and Lauren Leatherby. 2022. "Who Stops a "Bad Guy with a Gun?" *New York Times,* June 22.

37. Carlson, Jennifer. 2015. "Mourning Mayberry: Guns, Masculinity, and Socioeconomic Decline." *Gender & Society, 29,* 386–409.

38. Carlson 2020.

39. Leverso, John, and Chris Hess. 2021. "From the Hood to the Home: Masculinity Maturation of Chicago Street Gang Members." *Sociological Perspectives, 64,* 1206–23; Paul B. Stretesky and Mark R. Pogrebin. 2007. "Gang-Related Gun Violence: Socialization, Identity, and Self." *Journal of Contemporary Ethnography, 36,* 85–115.

40. Goldman, Liran et al. 2014. "Going to Extremes: Social Identity and Communication Processes Associated with Gang Membership." *Group Processes and Intergroup Relations, 17,* 813–32.

41. Goldman et al. 2014.

42. Stretesky and Pogrebin 2007.

43. Stretesky and Pogrebin 2007.

44. Patton, Desmond U. et al. 2019. "Guns on Social Media: Complex Interpretations of Gun Images Posted by Chicago Youth." *Palgrave Communications 5:119.*

45. Liverso and Hess 2021.

46. Gul, Pelin et al. 2021. "Implications of Culture of Honor Theory and Research for Practitioners and Prevention Researchers." *American Psychologist, 76,* 502–15; Richard E. Nisbett. 1993. "Violence and U.S. Regional Culture." *American Psychologist, 48,* 441–49.

47. Gul, "Implications of Culture of Honor Theory."

48. McCartin, Hadley R. et al. 2023. "Boys Round Here: The Relationship Between Masculine Honor Ideology, Aggressive Behavior, Race, and Regional Affiliation." *Journal of Interpersonal Violence, 38,* 5305–28.

49. McMartin et al. 2023.

50. Anderson, Elijah. 1999. *Code of the Street: Decency, Violence, and the Moral Life of the Inner City.* New York: W.W. Norton.

51. Whaley, Arthur L. 2022. "The Cultural Ecology of Gun Violence: Culture of Honor and Code of the Street." *Du Bois Review, 19,* 193–203.

52. Leemis, Ruth W. et al. 2022. *The National Intimate Partner and Sexual Violence Survey: 2016/2017 Report on Intimate Partner Violence.* National Center for Injury Prevention and Control, Centers for Disease Control and Prevention.

53. Leemis et al. 2022.

54. Leemis et al. 2022.

55. Leemis et al. 2022.

56. Wallace, Maeve E. et al. 2021. "Firearm Relinquishment Laws Associated with Substantial Reduction in Homicide of Pregnant and Postpartum Women." *Health Affairs, 40,* 1654–62.

57. Leemis et al. 2022

58. Johnson, Lisette. 2023. "Shameless Survivors." https://momentsthatsurvive.org/tribute/lisette-johnson/.

59. Leemis, *The National Intimate Partner and Sexual Violence Survey: 2016/2017.*

60. Clare, Camille A. et al. 2021. "Risk Factors for Male Perpetration of Intimate Partner Violence: A Review." *Aggression and Violent Behavior, 56,* 101532.

61. Clare et al. 2021.

62. Wallin, Mikaela A. et al. 2022. "The Association of Federal and State-level Firearm Restriction Policies with Intimate Partner Homicide: A Re-Analysis by Race of the Victim." *Journal of Interpersonal Violence, 27(17–18)*.

63. Spencer, Chelsea M., and Sandra M. Stith. 2020. "Risk Factors for Male Perpetration and Female Victimization of Intimate Partner Homicide: A Meta-Analysis." *Trauma, Violence, and Abuse, 21,* 527–40.

64. Geller, Lisa B. et al. 2021. "The Role of Domestic Violence in Fatal Mass Shootings in the United States, 2014–2019." *Injury Epidemiology, 8(1),* 38.

65. Sivaraman, Josie J. et al. 2019. "Association of State Firearm Legislation with Female Intimate Partner Homicide." *American Journal of Preventive Medicine, 56,* 125–33; April M. Zeoli et al. 2018. "Analysis of the Strength of Legal Firearms Restrictions for Perpetrators of Domestic Violence and Their Associations with Intimate Partner Homicide." *American Journal of Epidemiology, 187,* 2365–71.

66. Sivaraman et al. 2029.

67. Campbell, Jacquelyn C. et al. 2003. "Risk Factors for Femicide in Abusive Relationships: Results from a Multisite Case Control Study." *American Journal of Public Health, 93,* 1089–97.

68. Zeoli, April M. et al. 2022. "Effectiveness of Firearm Restriction, Background Checks, and Licensing Laws in Reducing Gun Violence." *Annals of the American Academy of Political and Social Science, 704,* 118–36.

69. Lynch, Kellie R. et al. 2022. "Firearm-Related Abuse and Protective Order Requests Among Intimate Partner Violence Victims." *Journal of Interpersonal Violence, 37(15–16)*.

70. Koppa, Vijetha, and Jill T. Messing. 2021. "Can Justice System Interventions Prevent Intimate Partner Homicides? An Analysis of Rates of Help Seeking Prior to Fatality." *Journal of Interpersonal Violence, 36,* 8792–816.

71. Liptak, Adam. 2023. "Supreme Court's Devotion to Gun Rights Faces a Challenging Test." *New York Times,* November 6.

72. Zeoli et al. 2022. "Firearm-Related Abuse and Protective Order Requests."

73. Aronson, Elliot et al. 2019. *Social Psychology,* 10th ed. New York: Pearson.

74. Pascoe, C. J. 2007. *Dude, You're a Fag: Masculinity and Sexuality in High School.* Oakland: University of California Press.

75. Dixon, Graham et al. 2020. "Public Opinion Perceptions, Private Support, and Public Actions of US Adults Regarding Gun Safety Policy." *JAMA Network Open, 3(12),* e2029571; Mark W. Susmann et al. 2022. "Correcting Misperceptions of Gun Policy Support Can Foster Intergroup Cooperation Between Gun Owners and Non-Gun Owners." *PLOS ONE, 17(6),* e0268601.

76. Aitken, Mary E. et al. 2020. "Parents' Perspectives on Safe Storage of Firearms." *Journal of Community Health, 45,* 469–77.

77. Miller, Matthew, and Deborah Azrael. 2022. "Firearm Storage in US Households with Children: Findings from the 2021 National Firearm Survey." *JAMA Network Open, 5(2),* e2148823.

78. Pew Research Center. 2023. *For Most U.S. Gun Owners, Protection Is the Main Reason They Own a Gun.* https://www.pewresearch.org/politics/2023/08/16/for-most-u -s-gun-owners-protection-is-the-main-reason-they-own-a-gun/.

CHAPTER FOUR: THE VOLATILE MIX OF RACE, RACISM, AND GUNS

1. Martin, Rachel et al. 2022. "Racial Disparities in Child Exposure to Firearm Violence Before and During COVID-19." *American Journal of Preventive Medicine, 63,* 204–12.

2. Allport, Gordon. 1954. *The Nature of Prejudice.* Boston: Addison-Wesley.

3. Anderson, Carol. 2021. *The Second: Race and Guns in a Fatally Unequal America.* New York: Bloomsbury Publishing.

4. Gillman, Howard et al. 2021. *American Constitutionalism. Volume II: Rights and Liberties,* 3rd ed. New York: Oxford University Press.

5. Buttrick, Nicholas, and Jessica Mazen. 2022. "Historical Prevalence of Slavery Predicts Contemporary American Gun Ownership." *PNAS Nexus, 1,* 1–10.

6. Buttrick and Mazen, "Historical Prevalence of Slavery Predicts Contemporary Gun Ownership."

7. Buttrick and Mazen, "Historical Prevalence of Slavery Predicts Contemporary Gun Ownership."

8. Blackhawk, Ned. 2023. *The Rediscovery of America: Native Peoples and the Unmaking of U.S. History.* New Haven: Yale University Press.

9. Blackhawk, *The Rediscovery of America.*

10. Pope Alexander VI. 1493. *Inter Caetera.* www.nim.nih.gov/nativevoices/time line/171.html.

11. Blackhawk 2023.

12. Blackhawk 2023.

13. Blackhawk, *The Rediscovery of America.*

14. Blackhawk 2023.

15. Slotkin, Richard. 1973. *Regeneration Through Violence: The Mythology of the American Frontier, 1600-1860.* Norman: University of Oklahoma Press.

16. Slotkin, Richard. 1992. *Gunfighter Nation: The Myth of the Frontier in Twentieth-Century America.* Harper Perennial.

17. Jones, Robert P. 2023. *The Hidden Roots of White Supremacy and the Path to a Shared American Future.* New York: Simon & Schuster.

18. Everytown Research and Policy. 2022. *Misogyny, Extremism, and Gun Violence.* https://everytownresearch.org/report/misogyny-extremism-and-gun-violence/.

19. Reyna, Christine et al. 2022. "The Psychology of White Nationalism: Ambivalence Toward a Changing America." *Social Issues and Policy Review, 16,* 79–124.

20. Reyna et al. 2022.

21. Brewer, Marilynn. 2007. "The Importance of Being 'We': Human Nature and Intergroup Relations." *American Psychologist, 62,* 728–38.

22. Miller, C. B. 2009. "Yes, We Did! Basking in Reflected Glory and Cutting Off Reflected Failure in the 2008 Presidential Election." *Analyses of Social Issues and Public Policy, 9,* 283–96.

23. Boatwright, Brandon et al. 2019. "The 2016 U.S. Presidential Election and Transition Events: A Social Media Volume and Sentiment Analysis." *Southern Communication Journal, 84,* 196–209; Eliana DuBosar et al. 2023. "Celebrating Wins, Lamenting Losses in the Aftermath of Presidential Elections." *Journal of Media Psychology.* https://doi .org/10.1027/1864-1105/a000394.

24. Reyna et al. 2022.

25. Reyna et al. 2022.

26. Reyna et al. 2022.

27. Miller-Idriss 2020.

28. Darby, Seyward. 2020. *Sisters in Hate: American Women on the Front Lines of White Nationalism.* New York: Little, Brown.

29. Roberts, Steven O., and M. T. Rizzo. 2021. "The Psychology of American Racism." *American Psychologist, 76,* 475–87.

30. Bigler, Rebecca, and Lynn Liben. 2007. "Developmental Intergroup Theory: Explaining and Reducing Children's Social Stereotyping and Prejudice." *Current Directions in Psychological Science, 16,* 162–66.

31. Paolini, Stefania et al. 2021. "Intergroup Contact Research in the 21st Century: Lessons Learned and Forward Progress If We Remain Open." *Journal of Social Issues, 77,* 11–37.

32. Roberts and Rizzo 2021.

33. Davis-Delano, Laurel R. et al. 2021. "Representations of Native Americans in U.S. Culture? A Case of Omissions and Commissions." *The Social Science Journal.* https://doi .org/10.1080/03623319.2021.1975086.

34. Swim, Janet K. et al. 1995. "Sexism and Racism: Old-Fashioned and Modern Prejudices." *Journal of Personality and Social Psychology, 68,* 199–214.

35. Charlesworth, Tessa, and Mahzarin Banaji. 2022. "Patterns of Implicit and Explicit Attitudes: IV. Change and Stability from 2007 to 2020." *Psychological Science, 33,* 1347–71.

36. Johnson, David J., and William J. Chopik. 2019. "Geographic Variation in the Black-Violence Stereotype." *Social Psychological and Personality Science, 10,* 287–94; Brian A. Nosek et al. 2007. "Pervasiveness and Correlates of Implicit Attitudes and Stereotypes." *European Review of Social Psychology, 18,* 36–88.

37. Ellyson, Alice M. et al. 2023. "Implicit Racial and Gender Bias about Handguns: A New Implicit Association Test." *Journal of Interpersonal Violence, 38,* 5190–210.

38. Hollingsworth, Heath. 2023. "White Man Will Stand Trial for Shooting Black Teen Ralph Yarl, Who Went to Wrong House, Judge Rules." Associated Press. August 31.

39. Correll, Joshua et al. 2007. "Across the Thin Blue Line: Officers and Racial Bias in the Decision to Shoot." *Journal of Personality and Social Psychology, 92,* 1006–23; Jessica J. Sim et al. 2013. "Understanding Police and Expert Performance: When Training Attenuates (vs. Exacerbates) Stereotypic Bias in the Decision to Shoot." *Personality and Social Psychology Bulletin, 39,* 291–304.

40. Correll, "Across the Thin Blue Line"; Sim, "Understanding Police and Expert Performance."

41. Correll et al. 2007.

42. Sim et al. 2013.

43. Sadler, Melody, and Thierry Devos. 2020. "Ethnic Diversity Matters: Putting Implicit Associations Between Weapons and Ethnicity in Context." *Group Processes and Intergroup Relations, 23,* 285–300.

44. Clark, Dartunorro. 2021. "GOP Sen. Ron Johnson Says He Never Felt Threatened During Jan. 6 Capitol Attack." NBC News. https://www.nbcnews.com/politics/congress/ gop-sen-ron-johnson-says-he-never-felt-threatened-during-n1261024.

45. Devine, Patricia G. et al. 2012. "Long-Term Reduction in Implicit Race Bias: A Prejudice Habit-Breaking Intervention." *Journal of Experimental Social Psychology, 48,* 1267–78. (For a review of numerous interventions to reduce race bias, see Calvin K. Lai et al. 2014. "Reducing Implicit Racial Preferences: I. A Comparative Investigation of 17 Interventions." *Journal of Experimental Psychology: General, 143,* 1765–85.

46. Forscher, Patrick S. et al. 2017. "Breaking the Prejudice Habit: Mechanisms, Timecourse, and Longevity." *Journal of Experimental Social Psychology, 72,* 133–46.

47. Forscher et al. 2017.

48. Guo, Kayla, and Nicholas Bogel-Burroughs. 2023. "A Baltimore Party, a Hail of Gunfire and a Neighborhood Shattered." *New York Times,* July 3.

49. Guo and Bogel-Burroughs 2023.

50. Robertson, Campbell et al. 2023. "In Philadelphia, a Mass Shooting Leaves Five Dead." *New York Times,* July 4.

51. Jewett, Patricia I. et al. 2022. "US Mass Public Shootings Since Columbine: Victims per Incident by Race and Ethnicity of the Perpetrator." *Preventive Medicine, 162,* 107176.

52. Bottiani, Jessika H. et al. 2021. "Youth Firearm Violence Disparities in the United States and Implications for Prevention." *Journal of Child Psychology and Psychiatry, 62,* 563–79.

53. Bottiani et al. 2021.

54. Martin et al. 2022.

55. Ranney, Megan et al. 2019. "What Are the Long-Term Consequences of Youth Exposure to Firearm Injury, and How Do We Prevent Them? A Scoping Review." *Journal of Behavioral Medicine, 42,* 724–40.

56. Webster, Daniel W. et al. 2023. *Estimating the Effects of Safe Streets Baltimore on Gun Violence.* Center for Gun Violence Solutions, Johns Hopkins University, Bloomberg School of Public Health. https://publichealth.jhu.edu/sites/default/files/2023–03/estimating-the-effects-of-safe-streets-baltimore-on-gun-violence-march-2023.pdf.

57. O'Toole, Megan, and Mackey O'Keefe. 2023. *The Changing Demographics of Gun Homicide Victims and How Community Violence Intervention Programs Can Help.* Everytownresearch.org.

58. Everytown Research and Policy. 2024. *Hospital-Based Violence Intervention Programs: A Guide to Implementation and Costing.* https://everytownresearch.org/report/hospital-based-violence-intervention-programs-a-guide-to-implementation-and-costing/?source=emfe_20240501-newsletter&refcode.

Chapter Five: The Tortured Relationship Between Religion and Guns

1. Pew Research Center. 2014. *Religious Landscape Study.* https://www.pewresearch.org/religion/religious-landscape-study/.

2. Merino, Stephen M. 2018. "God and Guns: Examining Religious Influences on Gun Control Attitudes in the United States." *Religions, 9,* 189.

3. Merino 2018.

4. Moore, Russell. 2023. *Losing Our Religion: An Altar Call for Evangelical America.* New York: Sentinel.

5. Alberta, Tim. 2023. *The Kingdom, the Power, and the Glory: American Evangelicals in an Age of Extremism.* New York: HarperCollins.

6. Alberta 2023.

7. Schwadel, Philip. 2014. "Are White Evangelical Protestants Lower Class? A Partial Test of Church-Sect Theory." *Social Science Research, 46,* 100–116.

8. Reese, Thomas. 2022. "The Catholic Bishops Support Gun Control. Why Don't We Hear More About It?" *National Catholic Reporter.* June 14, 2022. https://www .ncronline.org/news/opinion/catholic-bishops-support-gun-control-why-dont-we-hear -more-about-it.

9. Reese 2022.

10. Religious Action Center of Reform Judaism. 2023. *Gun Violence Prevention.* https://rac.org/issues/gun-violence-prevention?_gl=1*e2n7ma*_ga*OTU3Mzk2NjcxL jE2OTkxNDIwOTY.*_ga_6WX143SJW5*MTY5OTE0MjA5NS4xLjEuMTY5O TE0MjEzMi4yMy4wLjA.

11. Rabbinical Assembly. 2016. *Resolution on American Gun Violence.* https://www .rabbinicalassembly.org/story/resolution-american-gun-violence.

12. Hennessy-Fiske, Molly. 2023. "House Speaker Mike Johnson's Louisiana Hometown Guided by Faith and Family." *The Washington Post,* October 29.

13. Petri, Alexandra. 2023. "The Problem Is the Human Heart. It's Not Guns." *Washington Post*, October 27.

14. Seto, Christopher H., and Laura Openieks. 2023. "Under God and Under Threat: Christian Nationalism and Conspiratorial Thinking as Links Between Political Orientation and Gun Ownership." *Justice Quarterly, 41,* 291–316.

15. Seto and Openieks 2023.

16. Graham, David A. 2018. "Wayne LaPierre's Cynical Exploitation of Outrage." *The Atlantic*, February 22.

17. Dawson, Jessica. 2019. "Shall Not Be Infringed: How the NRA Used Religious Language to Transform the Meaning of the Second Amendment." *Palgrave Communications, 5,* 58.

18. Whitehead, Andrew L. et al. 2018. "Gun Control in the Crosshairs: Christian Nationalism and Opposition to Stricter Gun Laws." *Socius, 4,* 1–13.

19. Davis, Joshua T. et al. 2024. "Liberty for Us, Limits for Them: Christian Nationalism and Americans' View on Citizens' Rights." *Sociology of Religion, 85,* 60–82.

20. Brewer, Marilynn, and R. J. Brown. 1998. *Intergroup Relations.* New York: McGraw-Hill; Henri Tajfel and J. C. Turner. 1986. "The Social Identity Theory of Intergroup Behavior." In *Psychology of Intergroup Relations*, edited by S. Worchel and W. G. Austin. Newton: Nelson-Hall.

21. Vegter, Abigail, and Kevin R. den Dulk. 2021. "Clinging to Guns and Religion? A Research Note Testing the Role of Protestantism in Shaping Gun Identity in the United States." *Politics and Religion, 14,* 809–824.

22. Jung, Jong Hyun. 2020. "Belief in Supernatural Evil and Mental Health: Do Secure Attachment to God and Gender Matter?" *Journal for the Scientific Study of Religion, 59,* 141–60.

23. Pike, Sarah M. 2009. "Dark Teens and Born-Again Martyrs: Captivity Narratives After Columbine." *Journal of the American Academy of Religion, 77,* 647–79.

24 Pike 2009.

25. Dawson 2019.

26. Ellison, Christopher G. et al. 2021. "Peace Through Superior Firepower: Belief in Supernatural Evil and Attitudes Toward Gun Policy in the United States." *Social Science Research, 99,* 102595.

27. Ausubel, Jacob. 2021. *Christians, Religiously Unaffiliated Differ on Whether Most Things in Society Can Be Divided into Good, Evil.* Pew Research Center.

28. Austin, Michael W. 2020. *God and Guns in America.* Grand Rapids, MI: Wm. B. Eerdmans Publishing Co.

29. Hays, Christopher B. 2021. "'Do Not Be Afraid': The Walls of Jerusalem and the Guns of America. In *God and Guns*," edited by C. Hays and C. Crouch, 57–75. Louisville, KY: Westminster John Knox Press.

30. Austin, *God and Guns in America.*

31. Pratt, Erich. 2022. "The Bible, Guns, and the Second Amendment." Gunowners .org.

32. Austin 2020.

33. Jones, Serene. 2023. "The 'God-Given Right' to Guns Is a Cash-Fueled Sham." *Salon.* https://utsnyc.edu/the-god-given-right-to-guns-is-a-cash-fueled-sham/.

34. Schenck, Robert. 2020. Foreword to *God and Guns in America*, by Michael W. Austin. Grand Rapids, MI: Wm. B. Eerdmans Publishing Co.

35. Austin, *God and Guns in America*, 108.

36. Oppenheimer, Mark. 2021. *Squirrel Hill: The Tree of Life Synagogue Shooting and the Soul of a Neighborhood.* New York: Knopf.

37. Hannebrink, Paul. 2018. *A Specter Haunting Europe: The Myth of Judeo-Bolshevism.* Cambridge, MA: Harvard University Press; Francesca Trivellato. 2019. *The Promise and Peril of Credit: What a Forgotten Legend about Jews and Finance Tells Us About the Making of European Commercial Society.* Princeton: Princeton University Press.

38. Wolfe, Elizabeth, and Artemie Moshtaghian. 2023. "Authorities Investigating Online Threats of Violence Against Jewish Students at Cornell University, School's President Says." CNN. October 30. https://www.cnn.com/2023/10/29/us/cornell-uni versity-antisemitic-threats-online-investigation/index.html.

39. Chicago Project on Security & Threat. 2023. *Antisemitism and Support for Political Violence.* Chicago: University of Chicago.

40. Broockman, David, and Joshua Kalla. 2016. "Durably Reducing Transphobia: A Field Experiment on Door-to-Door Canvassing." *Science, 352,* 220–24; David McRaney. 2022. *How Minds Change: The Surprising Science of Belief, Opinion, and Persuasion.* New York: Penguin.

41. Kalla, Joshua L., and David E. Broockman. 2020. "Reducing Exclusionary Attitudes Through Interpersonal Conversation: Evidence from Three Field Experiments." *American Political Science Review, 114,* 410–25.

42. Broockman and Kalla 2016.

43. Kalla, Joshua L., and David E. Broockman. 2023. "Which Narrative Strategies Durably Reduce Prejudice? Evidence from Field and Survey Experiments Supporting the Efficacy of Perspective-Getting." *American Journal of Political Science, 67,* 185–204.

44. Kalla, Joshua L. et al. 2022. "Personalizing Moral Reframing in Interpersonal Conversation: A Field Experiment." *The Journal of Politics, 84,* 1239–43.

45. Kubin, Emily et al. 2021. "Personal Experiences Bridge Moral and Political Divides Better Than Facts. *Proceedings of the National Academy of Sciences (PNAS), 118,* no. 6.

46. Kosek, Joseph Kip. 2009. *Acts of Conscience: Christian Nonviolence and Modern American Democracy.* Columbia University Press; Keith L. Neigenfind. 2020. "Is Nonviolence and Pacifism in Christian and Buddhist Ethics Obligatory or Supererogatory?" *Buddhist-Christian Studies, 40,* 387–401; Angie O'Gorman, ed. 1990. *The Universe Bends Toward Justice: A Reader on Christian Nonviolence in the U.S.* Gabriola Island, BC: New Society Publishers; Murray Polner and Naomi Goodman, eds. 1994. *The Challenge of Shalom: The Jewish Tradition of Peace and Justice.* Gabriola Island, BC: New Society Publishers.

47. Babyak, Joyce K. 2021. "Christian Commitments to Political Nonviolence: When Jewish and Muslim Perspectives Make a Difference." *Journal of Religious Ethics, 49,* 519–45; Neigenfind, "Is Nonviolence and Pacifism in Christian and Buddhist Ethics Obligatory or Supererogatory?"

48. Chernus, Ira. 2004. *American Nonviolence: The History of an Idea.* Ossining, NY: Orbis Books.

49. Chernus 2004.

50. Crozier, Karen D. 2021. *Fannie Lou Hamer's Revolutionary Practical Theology.* Leiden: Brill; Chana Kai Lee. 1999. *For Freedom's Sake: The Life of Fannie Lou Hamer.* Champaign: University of Illinois Press.

51. Sprinkle, Preston. 2021. *Nonviolence: The Revolutionary Way of Jesus.* Colorado Springs: David C Cook.

CHAPTER SIX: A HIGHLY EFFECTIVE METHOD FOR SUICIDE

1. Moments That Survive. 2024. *Luc-John.* https://momentsthatsurvive.org/tribute/luc-john/.

2. Case, Anne, and Angus Deaton. 2020. *Deaths of Despair and the Future of Capitalism.* Princeton University Press.

3. Everytown Research & Policy. 2023. *Firearm Suicide in the United States.* https://everytownresearch.org/report/firearm-suicide-in-the-united-states/.

4. Conner, Andrew et al. 2019. "Suicide Case-Fatality Rates in the United States, 2007 to 2014." *Annals of Internal Medicine, 171,* 885–95.

5. Conner et al. 2019.

6. Demesmaeker, Alice et al. 2022. "Suicide Mortality After a Nonfatal Suicide Attempt: A Systematic Review and Meta-Analysis." *Australian & New Zealand Journal of Psychiatry, 56,* 603–16.

7. Akbar, Rahat et al. 2023. "Posttraumatic Stress Disorder and Risk of Suicidal Behavior: A Systematic Review and Meta-Analysis." *Suicide and Life-Threatening Behavior, 53,* 163–84; Christoph U. Correll et al. 2022. "Mortality in People with Schizophrenia: A Systematic Review and Meta-Analysis of Relative Risk and Aggravating or Attenuating Factors." *World Psychiatry, 21,* 248–71; Richard T. Liu et al. 2017. "A Behav-

ioral and Cognitive Neuroscience Perspective on Impulsivity, Suicide, and Non-Suicidal Self-Injury: Meta-Analysis and Recommendations for Future Research." *Neuroscience and Biobehavioral Reviews, 83*, 440–50; Mathilde Septier et al. 2019. "Association Between Suicidal Spectrum Behaviors and Attention-Deficit/Hyperactivity Disorder: A Systematic Review and Meta-Analysis." *Neuroscience and Biobehavioral Reviews, 103*, 109–18; Giulia Serra et al. 2022. "Suicidal Behavior in Juvenile Bipolar Disorder and Major Depressive Disorder Patients: Systematic Review and Meta-Analysis." *Journal of Affective Disorders, 311*, 572–81.

8. Klonsky, E. David, and Alexis M. May. 2015. "The Three-Step Theory (3ST): A New Theory of Suicide Rooted in the 'Ideation-to-Action' Framework." *International Journal of Cognitive Therapy, 8*, 114–29.

9. Ribeiro, Jessica D. et al. 2018. "Depression and Hopelessness as Risk Factors for Suicide Ideation, Attempts and Death: Meta-Analysis of Longitudinal Studies." *British Journal of Psychiatry, 212*, 279–86.

10. Xiao, Yunyu et al. 2024. "Decoding Suicide Decedent Profiles and Signs of Suicidal Intent Using Latent Class Analysis." *JAMA Psychiatry, 81*, 595–605.

11. Chu, Carol et al. 2017. "The Interpersonal Theory of Suicide: A Systematic Review and Meta-Analysis of a Decade of Cross-National Research." *Psychological Bulletin, 143*, 1313–45.

12. McKinnon, Britt et al. 2016. "Adolescent Suicidal Behaviours in 32 Low- and Middle-Income Countries." *Bulletin of the World Health Organization, 94*, 340–50.

13. Calati, Raffaella et al. 2019. "Suicidal Thoughts and Behaviors and Social Isolation: A Narrative Review of the Literature." *Journal of Affective Disorders, 245*, 653–67; Heather McClelland et al. 2020. "Loneliness as a Predictor of Suicidal Ideation and Behaviour: A Systematic Review and Meta-Analysis of Prospective Studies." *Journal of Affective Disorders, 274*, 880–96.

14. Whitlock, Janis et al. 2014. "Connectedness and Suicide Prevention in Adolescents: Pathways and Implications." *Suicide and Life–Threatening Behavior, 44*, 246–72.

15. Hou, Xiaofei et al. 2022. "Methods and Efficacy of Social Support Interventions in Preventing Suicide: A Systematic Review and Meta-Analysis." *Evidence-Based Mental Health, 25*, 29–35.

16. Mueller, Anna S. 2017. "Does the Media Matter to Suicide? Examining the Social Dynamics Surrounding Media Reporting on Suicide in a Suicide-Prone Community." *Social Science & Medicine, 180*, 152–59.

17. Mueller 2017.

18. Division of Adolescent and School Health, Centers for Disease Control. 2023. *Youth Risk Behavior Survey: Data Summary & Trends Report, 2011–2021.* https://www.cdc.gov/healthyyouth/data/yrbs/pdf/YRBS_Data-Summary-Trends_Report2023_508.pdf

19. Centers for Disease Control. 2024. *Youth Risk Behavior Survey: Data Summary & Trends Report.* US Department of Health and Human Services.

20. Division of Adolescent and School Health 2023.

21. Reinbergs, Erik J. et al. 2024. "Firearm Carrying and Adolescent Suicide Risk Outcomes Between 2015 and 2021 Across Nationally Representative Samples." *Suicide and Life-Threatening Behavior, 54*, 302–9.

22. Bennett, Susanna et al. 2023. "Male Suicide Risk and Recovery Factors: A Systematic Review and Qualitative Metasynthesis of Two Decades of Research." *Psychological Bulletin, 149,* 371–417.

23. Centers for Disease Control. 2023. *Suicide Data and Statistics.* https://www.cdc.gov/suicide/suicide-data-statistics.html#print.

24. Bennett et al. 2023.

25. Cleary, A. 2012. "Suicidal Action, Emotional Expression, and the Performance of Masculinities." *Social Science & Medicine, 74,* 498–505.

26. Bennett et al. 2023.

27. Bennett et al. 2023.

28. Bennett et al. 2023.

29. Seidler, Zac E. et al. 2024. "A Randomized Wait-List Controlled Trial of Men in Mind: Enhancing Mental Health Practitioners' Self-Rated Clinical Competencies to Work with Men." *American Psychologist, 79,* 423–36.

30. Case and Deaton, *Deaths of Despair and the Future of Capitalism.*

31. Case and Deaton, *Deaths of Despair and the Future of Capitalism.*

32. Case and Deaton 2020.

33. Friedman, Joseph, and Helena Hansen. 2024. "Trends in Deaths of Despair by Race and Ethnicity from 1999 to 2022." *JAMA Psychiatry, 81,* 731–32.

34. Everytown Research & Policy. 2024. *Those Who Serve: Addressing Firearm Suicide Among Military Veterans.* https://everytownresearch.org/report/those-who-serve/.

35. Everytown Policy and Research 2024.

36. Everytown Policy and Research 2024.

37. Kang, Han K. et al. 2015. "Suicide Risk Among 1.3 Million Veterans Who Were on Active Duty During the Iraq and Afghanistan Wars." *Annals of Epidemiology, 25,* 96–100.

38. White House. 2021. *Reducing Military and Veteran Suicide: Advancing a Comprehensive, Cross-Sector, Evidence-Informed Public Health Strategy.* https://www.whitehouse.gov/wp-content/uploads/2021/11/Military-and-Veteran-Suicide-Prevention-Strategy.pdf.

39. Cuijpers, Kim. 2024. "How to Improve Outcomes of Psychological Treatment of Depression." *American Psychologist, 79,* 1407–17.

40. Iyengar, Udita et al. 2018. "A Further Look at Therapeutic Interventions for Suicide Attempts and Self-Harm in Adolescents: An Updated Systematic Review of Randomized Controlled Trials." *Frontiers in Psychiatry, 9 (583)*; Dennis Ougrin et al. 2015. "Therapeutic Interventions for Suicide Attempts and Self-Harm in Adolescents: Systematic Review and Meta-Analysis." *Journal of the American Academy of Child and Adolescent Psychiatry, 54,* 97–107.

41. Bryan, Craig J. et al. 2018. "Mechanisms of Action Contributing to Reductions in Suicide Attempts Following Brief Cognitive Behavioral Therapy for Military Personnel: A Test of the Interpersonal-Psychological Theory of Suicide." *Archives of Suicide Research, 22,* 241–53; Gregory E. Simon. 2024. "Management of Depression in Adults: A Review." *JAMA, 332,* 141–52.

42. Jobes, David A. 2012. "The Collaborative Assessment and Management of Suicidality (CAMS): An Evolving Evidence-Based Clinical Approach to Suicidal Risk." *Suicide*

and Life-Threatening Behavior, 42, 640–53; Joshua K. Swift. 2021. "The Effectiveness of the Collaborative Assessment and Management of Suicidality (CAMS) Compared to Alternative Treatment Conditions: A Meta-Analysis." *Suicide and Life-Threatening Behavior, 51,* 882–96.

43. Franklin, Joseph C. et al. 2017. "Risk Factors for Suicidal Thoughts and Behaviors: A Meta-Analysis of 50 Years of Research." *Psychological Bulletin, 143,* 187–232; Joel Paris. 2021. "Can We Predict or Prevent Suicide? An Update." *Preventive Medicine, 152,* 106353.

44. Meza, Jocelyn I. et al. 2023. "Practitioner Review: Common Elements in Treatments for Youth Suicide Attempts and Self-Harm—a Practitioner Review Based on Review of Treatment Elements Associated with Intervention Benefits." *Journal of Child Psychology and Psychiatry, 64,* 1409–21.

45. Frey, Laura M. et al. 2022. "Review of Family-Based Treatments from 2010 to 2019 for Suicidal Ideation and Behavior." *Journal of Marital and Family Therapy, 48,* 154–77.

46. Zalewski, Maureen et al. 2023. "Integrating Dialectical Behavior Therapy with Child and Parent Training Interventions: A Narrative and Theoretical Review." *Clinical Psychology: Science and Practice, 30,* 365–76.

47. Rudd, M. David et al. 2015. "Brief Cognitive-Behavioral Therapy Effects on Post-Treatment Suicide Attempts in a Military Sample: Results of a Randomized Clinical Trial with 2-Year Follow-Up." *American Journal of Psychiatry, 172,* 441–49.

48. Linehan, Marsha M., and Chelsey R. Wilks. 2015. "The Course and Evolution of Dialectical Behavior Therapy." *American Journal of Psychotherapy, 69,* 97–110.

49. Frey et al. 2022; Zalewski et al. 2023.

50. Jobes 2012.

51. Mann, J. John et al. 2021. "Improving Suicide Prevention Through Evidence-Based Strategies: A Systematic Review." *American Journal of Psychiatry, 178,* 611–24.

52. Dutton, Megan et al. 2023. "Oral Ketamine May Offer a Solution to the Ketamine Conundrum." *Psychopharmacology, 240,* 2483–97.

53. Nierenberg, Andrew A. et al. 2023. "Diagnosis and Treatment of Bipolar Disorder: A Review." *JAMA, 330,* 1370–80.

54. Gartlehner, Gerald et al. 2021. "Pharmacological Treatment for Borderline Personality Disorder: A Systematic Review and Meta-Analysis." *CNS Drugs, 35,* 1053–67.

55. Zainal, Nur Hani. 2024. "Is Combined Antidepressant Medication (ADM) and Psychotherapy Better Than Either Monotherapy at Preventing Suicide Attempts and Other Psychiatric Serious Adverse Events for Depressed Patients? A Rare Events Meta-Analysis." *Psychological Medicine, 54,* 457–72.

56. Hong, Barry et al. 2024. "The Saint Louis Bridges Program: A Mental Health Network of More Than One Hundred Churches and the Mental Health Community." *Journal of the National Medical Association, 116,* 16–23.

57. Molock, Sherry D. et al. 2008. "Developing Suicide Prevention Programs for African American Youth in African American Churches." *Suicide and Life-Threatening Behavior, 38,* 323–33.

58. Hong et al. 2024.

59. Molock et al. 2008.

60. Hong et al. 2024.

61. Mann et al. 2021.

62. Anestis, Michael D. 2024. "Firearm Access and Suicide Rates: An Unambiguously Robust Association." *Archives of Suicide Research, 28,* 701–5; Tyler J. Lane. 2023. "Associations Between Firearm and Suicide Rates: A Replication of Kleck (2021)." *Archives of Suicide Research, 27,* 880–95; Colin Pritchard et al. 2023. "USA Suicides Compared to Other Western Countries in the 21st Century: Is There a Relationship with Gun Ownership?" *Archives of Suicide Research, 27,* 135–47.

63. Lane 2023.

64. Pritchard et al. 2023.

65. McGough, Matt et al. 2023. *Child and Teen Firearm Mortality in the US and Peer Countries.* KFF. https://www.kff.org/mental-health/issue-brief/child-and-teen-firearm-mortality-in-the-u-s-and-peer-countries/# .

66. Lane 2023.

67. Barber, Catherine et al. 2022. "Who Owned the Gun in Firearm Suicides of Men, Women, and Youth in Five US States?" *Preventive Medicine, 164,* 107066.

68. Liu et al. 2017.

69. Simon, Thomas R. et al. 2001. "Characteristics of Impulsive Suicide Attempts and Attempters." *Suicide and Life-Threatening Behavior, 32(supp),* 49–59.

70. Morris-Perez, Pamela et al. 2023. "Preventing Adolescent Suicide: Recommendations for Policymakers, Practitioners, Program Developers, and Researchers." *SRCD Social Policy Report, 36,* 2–32.

71. Mann et al. 2021.

72. Morris-Perez et al. 2023.

73. Gallup Poll. 2023. "Guns." https://news.gallup.com/poll/1645/guns.aspx.

74. Aubel, Amanda J. et al. 2022. "A Comparative Content Analysis of Newspaper Coverage About Extreme Risk Protection Order Policies in Passing and Non-Passing US States." *BMC Public Health, 22,* 981.

75. Lemle, Russell B. 2024. "Bridging the Sociopolitical Divide: Transforming Efforts to Prevent Firearm Suicide." *American Psychologist,* 79, 1361–65.

CHAPTER SEVEN: HOW THE GUN LOBBY USES PSYCHOLOGY FOR PROFIT AND POWER

1. Lacombe, Matthew J. 2021. *Firepower: How the NRA Turned Gun Owners into a Political Force.* Princeton: Princeton University Press.

2. Lacombe 2021.

3. Lacombe, *Firepower.*

4. Lacombe 2021.

5. Lacombe, *Firepower,* 53.

6. Dawson, Jessica, and Dana B. Weinberg. 2022. "These Honored Dead: Sacrifice Narratives in the NRA's *American Rifleman* Magazine." *American Journal of Cultural Sociology, 10,* 110–35.

7. Lacombe 2021.

8. Horwitz, Joshua, and Casey Anderson. 2009. *Guns, Democracy, and the Insurrectionist Idea.* Ann Arbor: University of Michigan Press.

9. Stroud, Angela. 2012. "Good Guys with Guns: Hegemonic Masculinity and Concealed Handguns." *Gender & Society, 26,* 216–38.

10. Hakim, Danny. 2024. "LaPierre, Longtime N.R.A. Leader, Faces Trial That Could End His Reign." *New York Times,* January 2.

11. McKinley, Jesse et al. 2024. "N.R.A. Stung by Corruption Verdict Tied to Millions of Misspent Dollars." *New York Times,* February 23.

12. Carlson, Jennifer. 2023. *Merchants of the Right: Gun Sellers and the Crisis of American Democracy.* Princeton: Princeton University Press.

13. Everytown Research. 2023. *Inside the Gun Shop: Firearms Dealers and Their Impact.* https://everytownresearch.org/report/firearms-dealers-and-their-impact/.

14. Carlson, *Merchants of the Right.*

15. Carlson, *Merchants of the Right,* 119.

16. Carlson, *Merchants of the Right,* 54.

17. McIntire, Mike et al. 2022. "How Gun Makers Harness Fear to Supercharge Sales." *New York Times,* June 19.

18. McWhirter, Cameron, and Zusha Elinson. 2023. *American Gun: The True Story of the AR-15.* New York: Farrar, Straus and Giroux.

19. McWhirter and Elinson, *American Gun.*

20. McWhirter and Elinson 2023.

21. McWhirter and Elinson 2023.

22. McWhirter and Elinson 2023.

23. McIntire et al. 2022; McWhirter and Elinson 2023.

24. McWhirter and Elinson 2023.

25. McWhirter and Elinson, *American Gun,* 247.

26. FBI. 2021. *Investigative Report on the August 4, 2019, Attack in Dayton, Ohio.* https://www.fbi.gov/contact-us/field-offices/cincinnati/news/press-releases/investigative-report-on-the-august-4-2019-attack-in-dayton-ohio.

27. Hussain, Zain et al. 2023. "A Qualitative Framing Analysis of How Firearm Manufacturers and Related Bodies Communicate to the Public on Gun-Related Harms and Solutions." *Preventive Medicine, 166,* 107346.

28. Stroud 2015.

29. Stroud 2015.

30. Light, Caroline E. 2021. "'What Real Empowerment Looks Like': White Rage and the Necropolitics of Armed Womanhood." *Signs: Journal of Women in Culture and Society, 46(4),* 911–37.

31. Light 2021.

32. Carlson, Jennifer. 2015. *Citizen-Protectors: The Everyday Politics of Guns in an Age of Decline.* New York: Oxford University Press.

33. Carlson 2015.

34. Carlson 2015.

35. Carlson, *Citizen-Protectors,* 74.

36. Carlson, *Citizen-Protectors,* 78.

37. Öhman, A., and Susan Mineka. 2001. "Fears, Phobias, and Preparedness: Towards an Evolved Module of Fear and Fear Learning." *Psychological Review, 108,* 483–522.

38. LoBue, Vanessa. 2010. "What's So Scary About Needles and Knives? Examining the Role of Experience in Threat Detection." *Cognition and Emotion, 24,* 180–87.

39. LoBue 2010.

40. Van Damme, Stefaan et al. 2008. "Attentional Bias to Threat: A Perceptual Accuracy Approach." *Emotion, 8,* 820–27.

41. Carlson 2015.

42. Carlson. *Citizen-Protectors.*

43. Simon, Samantha J. 2024. *Before the Badge: How Academy Training Shapes Police Violence.* New York University Press.

44. Hemenway, David et al. 2019. "Variation in Rates of Fatal Police Shootings Across US States: The Role of Firearm Availability." *Journal of Urban Health, 96,* 63–73.

45. Martaindale, M. Hunter. 2021. "Improving the Accuracy of Firearm Identification in a Dynamic Use of Force Scenario." *Police Quarterly, 24,* 104–30.

46. Giaccardi, Soraya et al. 2022. *Shooting Straight: What TV Stories Tell Us About Gun Safety, How These Depictions Affect Audiences, and How We Can Do Better.* Everytown for Gun Safety. https://everytownsupportfund.org/report/gun-safety-depictions-on-tv/?_gl=1*kfkqj*_ga*ODA2NjM5NTgyLjE2OTc5MTY3MDU.*_ga_LT0FWV3EK3*MTY5OTM5NzA4Ni4zLjEuMTY5OTM5Nzc5MS4wLjAuMA.

47. Giaccardi et al. 2022.

48. World Economic Forum. 2024. *The Global Risks Report 2024,* 19th ed. www3.weforum.org.

49. Roozenbeek, Jon, and Sander van der Linden. 2024. *The Psychology of Misinformation.* New York: Cambridge University Press.

50. Compton, Josh et al. 2021. "Inoculation Theory in the Post-Truth Era: Extant Findings and New Frontiers for Contested Science, Misinformation, and Conspiracy Theories." *Social and Personality Psychology Compass, 15(6),* article e12602; Alice H. Eagly and Shelly Chaiken. 1993. *The Psychology of Attitudes.* Harcourt Brace Jovanovich; William J. McGuire and Demetrios Papageorgis. 1961. "The Relative Efficacy of Various Types of Prior Belief Defense in Producing Immunity Against Persuasion." *Journal of Abnormal and Social Psychology, 62,* 327–37.

51. Maertens, Rakoen et al. 2021. "Long-Term Effectiveness of Inoculation Against Misinformation: Three Longitudinal Experiments." *Journal of Experimental Psychology: Applied, 27,* 1–16; Jon Roozenbeek et al. 2022. "Psychological Inoculation Improves Resilience Against Misinformation on Social Media." *Science Advances, 8,* eabo6254.

52. Mason, Alicia M. et al. 2024. "Analyzing the Prophylactic and Therapeutic Role of Inoculation to Facilitate Resistance to Conspiracy Theory Beliefs." *Communication Reports, 37,* 13–27.

53. Mason et al. 2024.

54. Mason, "Analyzing the Prophylactic and Therapeutic Role of Inoculation."

55. Boyd, Michelle J., and Julie Dobrow. 2011. "Media Literacy and Positive Youth Development." In *Advances in Child Development and Behavior,* edited by R. Lerner et al., 251–71. London: Elsevier.

56. Maertens, "Long-Term Effectiveness of Inoculation Against Misinformation"; Roozenbeek and Van der Linden, *The Psychology of Misinformation.*

CHAPTER EIGHT: THE SECOND AMENDMENT DOES NOT DOOM US

1. Anderson, Carol. 2021. *The Second: Race and Guns in a Fatally Unequal America.* New York: Bloomsbury Publishing.

2. Anderson 2021.

3. Anderson 2021.

4. Anderson 2021.

5. Anderson 2021.

6. Erdozain, Dominic. 2024. *One Nation Under Guns: How Gun Culture Distorts Our History and Threatens Our Democracy.* New York: Crown.

7. Ingraham, Christopher. 2018. "One in Five Americans Wants the Second Amendment to Be Repealed, National Survey Finds." *Washington Post,* March 27.

8. Blocher, Joseph, and Darrell Miller. 2018. *The Positive Second Amendment: Rights, Regulation, and the Future of Heller.* New York: Cambridge University Press.

9. Erdozain 2024.

10. Blocher and Miller 2018.

11. Blocher and Miller 2018.

12. Blocher and Miller 2018.

13. Blocher and Miller 2018.

14. Blocher and Miller 2018.

15. Erdozain 2024.

16. Blocher and Miller 2018.

17. Blocher and Miller 2018.

18. Blocher and Miller 2018.

19. Everytown for Gun Safety. 2023. *Gun Violence in the United States.* EveryStat.org.

20. Blocher and Miller 2018.

21. Blocher and Miller 2018.

22. Erdozain "One Nation Under Guns."

23. Blocher and Miller 2018.

24. Erdozain 2024.

25. McIntire, Mike, and Jodi Kantor. 2024. "The Gun Lobby's Hidden Hand in the 2nd Amendment Battle." *New York Times,* June 18.

26. Anglemyer, Andrew et al. 2014. "The Accessibility of Firearms and Risk for Suicide and Homicide Victimization Among Household Members." *Annals of Internal Medicine, 160,* 101–10; David Hemenway and Sara J. Solnick. 2015. "The Epidemiology of Self-Defense Gun Use: Evidence from the National Crime Victimization Surveys 2007–2011." *Preventive Medicine, 79,* 22–27.

27. Liptak, Adam. 2023. "By 5–4 Vote, Supreme Court Revives Biden's Regulation of 'Ghost Guns.'" *New York Times,* August 8.

28. VanSickle, Abbie. 2024. "Supreme Court Rejects Trump-Era Ban on Gun Bump Stocks." *New York Times,* June 14.

29. Howe, Amy. 2024. "United States v. Rahimi." SCOTUSblog. June 21. https://www.scotusblog.com/case-files/cases/united-states-v-rahimi/.

30. Post, Lori et al. 2021. Impact of Firearm Surveillance on Gun Control Policy: Regression Discontinuity Analysis. *JMIR Public Health and Surveillance 7,* e26042, https://doi.org/10.2196/26042.

31. Wolfram, Joel, and Campbell Robertson. 2023. "Suspect Showed Troubling Signs Before Philadelphia Rampage, D.A. Says." *New York Times*, July 5.

32. Smart, Rosanna et al. 2023. *The Science of Gun Policy: A Critical Synthesis of Research Evidence on the Effects of Gun Policies in the United States*, 3rd ed. RAND Corporation. https://www.rand.org/pubs/research_reports/RRA243-4.html.

33. Everytown for Gun Safety. 2022. "Everytown Launches New Nationwide Interactive Gun Law Platform Analyzing 50 Policies in All 50 States." https://everytownsupportfund.org/press/everytown-launches-new-nationwide-interactive-gun-law-platform-analyzing-50-policies-in-all-50-states/?_gl=1*1krbz1g*_ga*MTgxNDYwNDIwMy4xNjg3MjczODg4*_ga_LT0FWV3EK3*MTY4ODY5MTczNS4zLjEuMTY4ODY5MjkzOS4wLjAuMA.

34. Reeping, Paul M. et al. 2022. "State Firearm Laws, Gun Ownership, and K-12 School Shootings: Implications for School Safety." *Journal of School Violence, 21*, 132–46.

35. Dong, Beidi, and David B. Wilson. 2022. "State Firearm Legislation and Youth/Young Adult Handgun Carrying in the United States." *Journal of Adolescent Health, 71*, 751–56.

36. Gobaud, Ariana N. et al. 2022. "Gun Shows and Universal Background Check Laws Across State Lines." *Preventive Medicine, 165*, 107094; Lois K. Lee et al. 2017. "Firearm Laws and Firearm Homicides: A Systematic Review." *JAMA Internal Medicine, 177*, 106–19.

37. Kaufman, E. J. et al. 2020. "Universal Background Checks for Handgun Purchases Can Reduce Homicide Rates of African Americans." *Journal of Trauma and Acute Care Surgery, 88*, 825–31.

38. McCourt, Alexander D. et al. 2020. "Purchaser Licensing, Point-of-Sale Background Check Laws, and Firearm Homicide and Suicide in 4 US States, 1985–2017." *American Journal of Public Health, 110*, no. 10.

39. Goyal, Monika K. et al. 2019. "State Gun Laws and Pediatric Firearm-Related Mortality." *Pediatrics, 144*, no. 2.

40. Schell, Terry L. et al. 2020. "Changes in Firearm Mortality Following the Implementation of State Laws Regulating Firearm Access and Use." *PNAS, 117*, 14906–10.

41. Wallin, Mikaela A. et al. 2022. "The Association of Federal and State-Level Firearm Restriction Policies with Intimate Partner Homicide: A Re-Analysis by Race of Victim." *Journal of Interpersonal Violence, 27*, issue 17–18; April M. Zeoli et al. 2016. "Risks and Targeted Interventions: Firearms in Intimate Partner Violence." *Epidemiologic Review, 38*, 125–39.

42. Sorenson, Susan B., and Rebecca A. Schut. 2018. "Nonfatal Gun Use in Intimate Partner Violence: A Systematic Review of the Literature." *Trauma, Violence, & Abuse, 19*, 431–42.

43. Valente, Rob, and Rachel Graber. 2022. "Firearms, Domestic Violence, and Dating Violence: Abusers' Use of Firearms Violence to Exert Coercive Control and Commit Intimate Partner Homicides. In *Handbook of Interpersonal Violence and Abuse Across the Lifespan*, edited by R. Geffner et al., 2815–37. Springer.

44. Wallin et al. 2022.

45. American Psychological Association. 2019. *One-Third of US Adults Say Fear of Mass Shootings Prevents Them from Going to Certain Places or Events*. August 15. https://www.apa.org/news/press/releases/2019/08/fear-mass-shooting.

46. Milov, Sarah. 2019. *The Cigarette: A Political History*. Cambridge: Harvard University Press.

47. Milov 2019.

48. Wallace, Lacey N. 2019. "Implied Threat or Part of the Scenery: Americans' Perceptions of Open Carry." *Journal of Risk Research, 22,* 817–32.

49. Blocher, Joseph, and Darrell Miller. 2018. *The Positive Second Amendment: Rights, Regulation, and the Future of Heller.* New York: Cambridge University Press; Gregory P. Magarian. 2012. "Speaking Truth to Firepower: How the First Amendment Destabilizes the Second." *Texas Law Review, 91,* 49–99; Timothy Zick. 2018. "Arming Public Protests." *Iowa Law Review, 104,* 223–85.

50. Gabbatt, Adam. 2023. "Wave of Lawsuits Against US Gun Makers Raises Hope of End to Mass Shootings." May 27. www.theguardian.com.

51. Everytown Law. 2023. "Westforth Sports, Long-Time Dealer of Crime Guns, to Close After Lawsuit Exposed Persistent Violations of Federal and State Gun Laws." https://everytownlaw.org/press/westforth-sports-long-time-dealer-of-crime-guns-to -close-after-lawsuit-exposed-persistent-violations-of-federal-and-state-gun-laws/ #:~:text=Over%20300%20guns%20have%20been,%2Dfatal%20shootings%2C%20 and%20assaults.

52. Goodman, J. David. 2024. "Uvalde Families Accuse Instagram, 'Call of Duty' and Rifle Maker of 'Grooming' Gunman." *New York Times,* May 24.

53. Bosman, Julie. 2023. "Man Whose Son Is Accused of Parade Shooting Pleads Guilty to Misdemeanors." *New York Times,* November 6.

54. Fortin, Jacey, and Anna Betts. 2024. "Parents of Michigan School Shooter Sentenced to 10 to 15 Years in Prison." *New York Times,* April 9.

CHAPTER NINE: SMART CHOICES SAVE LIVES

1. TSA. 2024. "TSA Intercepted More Than 1,500 Firearms at Airport Checkpoints Nationwide During the First Quarter of 2024." Press release. April 11. https:// www.tsa.gov/news/press/releases/2024/04/11/tsa-intercepted-more-1500-firearms-air port-checkpoints-nationwide.

2. Gaskill, Malcolm. 2022. *The Ruin of All Witches: Life and Death in the New World.* New York: Knopf; Ramie Targoff. 2024. *Shakespeare's Sisters: How Women Wrote the Renaissance.* New York: Knopf.

3. Cummings, K. Michael, and Robert N. Proctor. 2014. "The Changing Public Image of Smoking in the United States: 1964–2014." *Cancer Epidemiology, Biomarkers and Prevention, 23,* 32–36.

4. Cummings and Proctor 2014.

5. Milov, Sarah. 2019. *The Cigarette: A Political History.* Cambridge, MA: Harvard University Press.

6. American Psychiatric Association. 2022. *DSM-5-TR.* American Psychiatric Association Publishing.

7. Hyde, Luke W. et al. 2025. "An Ecological Neurodevelopmental Model of the Development of Youth Antisocial Behavior and Callous-Unemotional Traits." *Annual Review of Developmental Psychology* (in press).

8. Patterson, G. R. et al. 1989. "A Developmental Perspective on Antisocial Behavior." *American Psychologist, 44,* 329–35.

9. Hyde et al. 2025.

10. Hyde et al. 2025.

11. Shaw, D. S., and E. C. Shelleby. 2014. "Early-Onset Conduct Problems: Intersection of Conduct Problems and Poverty." *Annual Review of Clinical Psychology, 10,* 503–28; Frances Gardner et al. 2007. "Randomized Prevention Trial for Early Conduct Problems: Effects on Proactive Parenting and Link to Toddler Disruptive Behavior." *Journal of Family Psychology, 21,* 398–406.

12. Romer, Dan et al. 2023. "Media Influences on Children and Advice for Parents to Reduce Harmful Exposure to Firearm Violence in Media." *Pediatric Clinics of North America, 70,* 1217–24.

13. Lee, Daniel B. et al. 2022. "Retaliatory Attitudes as Mediator of Exposure to Violence and Firearm Aggression Among Youth: The Protective Role of Organized Activity Involvement." *Developmental Psychology, 58,* 990–1002.

14. Lee et al. 2022.

15. Lee et al. 2022.

16. Levant, Ronald F., and Shana Pryor. 2020. *The Tough Standard: The Hard Truths About Masculinity and Violence.* New York: Oxford University Press.

17. Everytown Research and Policy. 2022. *How to Stop Shootings and Gun Violence in Schools.* https://everytownresearch.org/report/how-to-stop-shootings-and-gun-violence-in-schools/.

18. Everytown Research and Policy. *How to Stop Shootings and Gun Violence in Schools.*

19. Flannery, Daniel J. et al. 2021. "Guns, School Shooters, and School Safety: What We Know and Directions for Change." *School Psychology Review, 50,* 237–53.

20. Division for Emotional and Behavioral Health, Council for Children with Behavioral Disorders. 2024. "School Shootings: Current Status and Recommendations for Research and Practice." *Behavioral Disorders, 49,* 116–27.

21. McIntosh, K. et al. 2010. "Principles of Sustainable Prevention: Designing the Scale-up of School-wide Positive Behavior Support to Promote Durable Systems." *Psychology in the Schools, 47,* 5–21.

22. Alathari, Lina et al. 2019. *Protecting America's Schools: A U.S. Secret Service Analysis of Targeted School Violence.* https://www.secretservice.gov/sites/default/files/2020-04/Protecting_Americas_Schools.pdf.

23. Follman, Mark. 2022. *Trigger Points: Inside the Mission to Stop Mass Shootings in America.* New York: Dey Street Books.

24. Everytown Research and Policy 2022.

25. Everytown Research and Policy 2022.

26. Davis, Whitney et al. 2022. "Centering Trauma-Informed Approaches in Schools Within a Social Justice Framework." *Psychology in the Schools, 59,* 2453–70.

27. Everytown Research and Policy 2022.

28. Flannery et al. 2021.

29. Tocci, Charles et al. 2023. "Statement on the Effects of Law Enforcement in School Settings." *American Journal of Community Psychology,* 1–18.

30. Crichlow-Ball, Caroline et al. 2022. "Student Perceptions of School Resource Officers and Threat Reporting." *Journal of School Violence, 21,* 222–36.

31. Roozenbeek, Jon et al. 2022. "Psychological Inoculation Improves Resilience Against Misinformation on Social Media." *Science Advances, 8,* eabo6254.

32. Cowan, Rebecca G., and Adam Lankford. 2024. "The Virginia Beach Municipal Center Mass Shooting: A Retrospective Threat Assessment Using the WAVR-21." *Journal of Threat Assessment and Management, 11(2),* 83–105.

33. Stephen G. White and J. Reid Meloy. 2016. WAVR-21™, 3rd ed. https://www.wavr21.com.

34. Cowan and Lankford 2022.

35. Cowan and Lankford 2022.

36. Silva, Jason R., and Emily A. Greene-Colozzi. 2024. "Assessing Leakage-Based Mass Shooting Prevention: A Comparison of Foiled and Completed Attacks." *Journal of Threat Assessment and Management, 11(4),* 203–17.

37. Klein, Lauren M. et al. 2024. "Parents' Trust in COVID-19 Messengers and Implications for Vaccination." *American Journal of Health Promotion, 38,* 364–74; Lois Privor-Dumm and Terris King. 2020. "Community-Based Strategies to Engage Pastors Can Help Address Vaccine Hesitancy and Health Disparities in Black Communities." *Journal of Health Communication, 25,* 827–30; Rachel S. Purvis et al. 2023. "Key Conversations and Trusted Information Among Hesitant Adopters of the COVID-19 Vaccine." *Journal of Health Communication, 28,* 595–604.

38. Behrens, Deanna et al. 2023. "Firearm Injury Prevention Advocacy: Lessons Learned and Future Directions." *Pediatric Clinics of North America, 70,* 67–82.

39. Hamedani, MarYam G. et al. 2024. "We Built This Culture (So We Can Change It): Seven Principles for Intentional Culture Change." *American Psychologist, 79,* 384–402.

40. Hamedani, "We Built This Culture."

41. Lacy, Aaron J. et al. 2022. "A Celebration with Unforeseen Consequences: Celebratory Gunfire Causing Injury." *American Journal of Emergency Medicine, 58,* 350. e1–350.e3; Grace S. Liu et al. 2023. Surveillance for Violent Deaths—National Violent Death Reporting System, 48 States, the District of Columbia, and Puerto Rico, 2020." *MMWR, 72(5).*

42. Brehm, Sharon S., and Jack W. Brehm. 1981. *Psychological Reactance: A Theory of Freedom and Control.* New York: Academic Press; Adam S. Richards et al. 2021. "Freedom-Prompting Reactance Mitigation Strategies Function Differently Across Levels of Trait Reactance." *Communication Quarterly, 69,* 238–58.

43. US Surgeon General. 2024. *Firearm Violence: A Public Health Crisis in America.* https://www.hhs.gov/surgeongeneral/priorities/firearm-violence/index.html.

BIBLIOGRAPHY

Aftab, Awais, and Benjamin G. Druss. 2023. "Addressing the Mental Health Crisis in Youth: Sick Individuals or Sick Societies?" *JAMA Psychiatry, 80,* 863–64.

Aitken, Mary E. et al. 2020. "Parents' Perspectives on Safe Storage of Firearms." *Journal of Community Health, 45,* 469–77.

Akbar, Rahat et al. 2023. "Posttraumatic Stress Disorder and Risk of Suicidal Behavior: A Systematic Review and Meta-Analysis." *Suicide and Life-Threatening Behavior, 53,* 163–84.

Alathari, Lina et al. 2019. *Protecting America's Schools: A U.S. Secret Service Analysis of Targeted School Violence.* https://www.secretservice.gov/sites/default/files/2020–04/Protecting_Americas_Schools.pdf.

Alberta, Tim. 2023. *The Kingdom, the Power, and the Glory: American Evangelicals in an Age of Extremism.* New York: HarperCollins.

Allport, Gordon. 1954. *The Nature of Prejudice.* Boston: Addison-Wesley.

American Academy of Pediatrics. 2015. "Tackling in Youth Football." *Pediatrics, 136(5),* e1419–30.

American Psychiatric Association. 2022. *DSM-5-TR.* American Psychiatric Association Publishing.

American Psychological Association. 2019. *One-Third of US Adults Say Fear of Mass Shootings Prevents Them from Going to Certain Places or Events.* August 15. https://www.apa.org/news/press/releases/2019/08/fear-mass-shooting.

Anderson, Carol. 2021. *The Second: Race and Guns in a Fatally Unequal America.* New York: Bloomsbury Publishing.

Anderson, Elijah. 1999. *Code of the Street: Decency, Violence, and the Moral Life of the Inner City.* New York: W.W. Norton.

Anestis, Michael D. 2024. "Firearm Access and Suicide Rates: An Unambiguously Robust Association." *Archives of Suicide Research, 28,* 701–5.

Anglemyer, Andrew et al. 2014. "The Accessibility of Firearms and Risk for Suicide and Homicide Victimization Among Household Members." *Annals of Internal Medicine, 160,* 101–10.

Aronson, Elliot et al. 2019. *Social Psychology,* 10th ed. New York: Pearson.

Aubel, Amanda J. et al. 2022. "A Comparative Content Analysis of Newspaper Coverage About Extreme Risk Protection Order Policies in Passing and Non-Passing US States." *BMC Public Health, 22,* 981.

Austin, Michael W. 2020. *God and Guns in America.* Grand Rapids, MI: Wm. B. Eerdmans Publishing Co.

Ausubel, Jacob. 2021. *Christians, Religiously Unaffiliated Differ on Whether Most Things in Society Can Be Divided into Good, Evil.* Pew Research Center.

Babyak, Joyce K. 2021. "Christian Commitments to Political Nonviolence: When Jewish and Muslim Perspectives Make a Difference." *Journal of Religious Ethics, 49,* 519–45.

Bancalari, Pilar et al. 2022. "Youth Exposure to Endemic Community Gun Violence: A Systematic Review." *Adolescent Research Review, 7,* 383–417.

Bandura, Albert. 1986. *Social Foundations of Thought and Action: A Social Cognitive Theory.* Prentice Hall.

Bandura, Albert et al. 1963. "Imitation of Film-Mediated Aggressive Models." *Journal of Abnormal and Social Psychology, 66,* 3–11.

Barber, Catherine et al. 2022. "Who Owned the Gun in Firearm Suicides of Men, Women, and Youth in Five US States?" *Preventive Medicine, 164,* 107066.

Behrens, Deanna et al. 2023. "Firearm Injury Prevention Advocacy: Lessons Learned and Future Directions." *Pediatric Clinics of North America, 70,* 67–82.

Bennett, Susanna et al. 2023. "Male Suicide Risk and Recovery Factors: A Systematic Review and Qualitative Metasynthesis of Two Decades of Research." *Psychological Bulletin, 149,* 371–417.

Bigler, Rebecca, and Lynn Liben. 2007. "Developmental Intergroup Theory: Explaining and Reducing Children's Social Stereotyping and Prejudice." *Current Directions in Psychological Science, 16,* 162–66.

Blackhawk, Ned. 2023. *The Rediscovery of America: Native Peoples and the Unmaking of U.S. History.* New Haven: Yale University Press.

Blakemore, Judith et al. 2009. *Gender Development.* New York: Psychology Press.

Blocher, Joseph, and Darrell Miller. 2018. *The Positive Second Amendment: Rights, Regulation, and the Future of Heller.* New York: Cambridge University Press.

Boatwright, Brandon et al. 2019. "The 2016 U.S. Presidential Election and Transition Events: A Social Media Volume and Sentiment Analysis." *Southern Communication Journal, 84,* 196–209.

Boglioli, Marc. 2009. *A Matter of Life and Death: Hunting in Contemporary Vermont.* Amherst: University of Massachusetts Press.

Boine, Claire et al. 2022. "Who Are Gun Owners in the United States? A Latent Class Analysis of the 2019 National Lawful Use of Guns Survey." *Sociological Perspectives, 65,* 35–57.

Borgogna, Nicholas C. et al. 2022. "The Precarious Masculinity of Firearm Ownership." *Psychology of Men & Masculinities, 23,* 173–82.

Bosman, Julie. 2023. "Man Whose Son Is Accused of Parade Shooting Pleads Guilty to Misdemeanors." *New York Times,* November 6.

Bottiani, Jessika H. et al. 2021. "Youth Firearm Violence Disparities in the United States and Implications for Prevention." *Journal of Child Psychology and Psychiatry, 62,* 563–79.

Boyd, Michelle J., and Julie Dobrow. 2011. "Media Literacy and Positive Youth Development." In *Advances in Child Development and Behavior*, edited by R. Lerner et al., 251–71. London: Elsevier.

Brandt, Allan M. 2007. *The Cigarette Century: The Rise, Fall, and Deadly Persistence of the Product That Defined America*. New York: Basic Books.

Brehm, Sharon S., and Jack W. Brehm. 1981. *Psychological Reactance: A Theory of Freedom and Control*. New York: Academic Press.

Brewer, Marilynn. 2007. "The Importance of Being 'We': Human Nature and Intergroup Relations." *American Psychologist, 62*, 728–38.

Brewer, Marilynn, and R. J. Brown. 1998. *Intergroup Relations*. New York: McGraw-Hill.

Bridges, Tristan, and Tara L. Tober. 2022. *Mass Shootings and Masculinity*. Report for the Mass Casualty Commission.

Broockman, David, and Joshua Kalla. 2016. "Durably Reducing Transphobia: A Field Experiment on Door-to-Door Canvassing." *Science, 352*, 220–24.

Brooks, Robert C. 2022. "Incel Activity on Social Media Linked to Local Mating Ecology." *Psychological Science, 33*, 249–58.

Brownson, Ross C. et al. 2018. *Evidence-Based Public Health*. New York: Oxford University Press.

Brucato, Gary et al. 2022. "Psychotic Symptoms in Mass Shootings v. Mass Murders Not Involving Firearms: Findings from the Columbia Mass Murder Database." *Psychological Medicine, 52*, 3422–30.

Bryan, Craig J. et al. 2018. "Mechanisms of Action Contributing to Reductions in Suicide Attempts Following Brief Cognitive Behavioral Therapy for Military Personnel: A Test of the Interpersonal-Psychological Theory of Suicide." *Archives of Suicide Research, 22*, 241–53.

Buchanan, Larry, and Lauren Leatherby. 2022. "Who Stops a "Bad Guy with a Gun?" *New York Times*, June 22.

Bushman, Brad J., and L. R. Huesmann. 2006. "Short-Term and Long-Term Effects of Violent Media on Aggression in Children and Adults." *Archives of Pediatrics & Adolescent Medicine, 160*, 358–52.

Bushman, Brad J. et al. 2016. "Youth Violence: What We Know and What We Need to Know." *American Psychologist, 71*, 17–39.

Buttrick, Nicholas. 2020. "Protective Gun Ownership as a Coping Mechanism." *Perspectives on Psychological Science, 15*, 835–55.

Buttrick, Nicholas, and Jessica Mazen. 2022. "Historical Prevalence of Slavery Predicts Contemporary American Gun Ownership." *PNAS Nexus, 1*, 1–10.

Cabral, Marika et al. 2022. "Trauma at School: The Impacts of Shootings on Students' Human Capital and Economic Outcomes." NBER Working Paper Series, Working Paper 28311.

Calati, Raffaella et al. 2019. "Suicidal Thoughts and Behaviors and Social Isolation: A Narrative Review of the Literature." *Journal of Affective Disorders, 245*, 653–67.

Calvert, Sandra L. et al. 2017. "The American Psychological Association Task Force Assessment of Violent Video Games." *American Psychologist, 72*, 126–43.

Campbell, Jacquelyn C. et al. 2003. "Risk Factors for Femicide in Abusive Relationships: Results from a Multisite Case Control Study." *American Journal of Public Health, 93,* 1089–97.

Carlson, Jennifer. 2015. *Citizen-Protectors: The Everyday Politics of Guns in an Age of Decline.* New York: Oxford University Press.

———. 2015. "Mourning Mayberry: Guns, Masculinity, and Socioeconomic Decline." *Gender & Society, 29,* 386–409.

———. 2023. *Merchants of the Right: Gun Sellers and the Crisis of American Democracy.* Princeton: Princeton University Press.

Case, Anne, and Angus Deaton. 2020. *Deaths of Despair and the Future of Capitalism.* Princeton University Press.

Centers for Disease Control. 2023. *Suicide Data and Statistics.* https://www.cdc.gov/suicide/suicide-data-statistics.html#print.

———. 2024. *Youth Risk Behavior Survey: Data Summary & Trends Report.* US Department of Health and Human Services.

Chapman, S. et al. 2006. "Australia's 1996 Gun Law Reforms: Faster Falls in Firearm Deaths, Firearms Suicides, and a Decade Without Mass Shootings." *Injury Prevention, 12,* 365–72.

Charlesworth, Tessa, and Mahzarin Banaji. 2022. "Patterns of Implicit and Explicit Attitudes: IV. Change and Stability from 2007 to 2020." *Psychological Science, 33,* 1347–71.

Charlson, Fiona J. et al. 2018. "Global Epidemiology and Burden of Schizophrenia: Findings from the Global Burden of Disease Study 2016." *Schizophrenia Bulletin, 44,* 1195–203.

Chernus, Ira. 2004. *American Nonviolence: The History of an Idea.* Ossining, NY: Orbis Books.

Chicago Project on Security & Threat. 2023. *Antisemitism and Support for Political Violence.* Chicago: University of Chicago.

Chu, Carol et al. 2017. "The Interpersonal Theory of Suicide: A Systematic Review and Meta-Analysis of a Decade of Cross-National Research." *Psychological Bulletin, 143,* 1313–45.

Clare, Camille A. et al. 2021. "Risk Factors for Male Perpetration of Intimate Partner Violence: A Review." *Aggression and Violent Behavior, 56,* 101532.

Clark, Dartunorro. 2021. "GOP Sen. Ron Johnson Says He Never Felt Threatened During Jan. 6 Capitol Attack." NBC News. https://www.nbcnews.com/politics/congress/gop-sen-ron-johnson-says-he-never-felt-threatened-during-n1261024.

Cleary, A. 2012. "Suicidal Action, Emotional Expression, and the Performance of Masculinities." *Social Science & Medicine, 74,* 498–505.

Compton, Josh et al. 2021. "Inoculation Theory in the Post-Truth Era: Extant Findings and New Frontiers for Contested Science, Misinformation, and Conspiracy Theories." *Social and Personality Psychology Compass, 15 (6),* article e12602.

Conner, Andrew et al. 2019. "Suicide Case-Fatality Rates in the United States, 2007 to 2014." *Annals of Internal Medicine, 171,* 885–95.

Correll, Christoph U. et al. 2022. "Mortality in People with Schizophrenia: A Systematic Review and Meta-Analysis of Relative Risk and Aggravating or Attenuating Factors." *World Psychiatry, 21,* 248–71.

Correll, Joshua et al. 2007. "Across the Thin Blue Line: Officers and Racial Bias in the Decision to Shoot." *Journal of Personality and Social Psychology, 92,* 1006–23.

Cowan, Rebecca G. et al. 2024. "'It Will Stay with Me Forever': The Experiences of Physicians Treating Victims of Public Mass Shootings." *Traumatology, 30(3),* 432–38.

Cowan, Rebecca G., and Adam Lankford. 2024. "The Virginia Beach Municipal Center Mass Shooting: A Retrospective Threat Assessment Using the WAVR-21." *Journal of Threat Assessment and Management, 11(2),* 83–105.

Cox, John Woodrow. 2021. *Children Under Fire.* New York: HarperCollins.

Crichlow-Ball, Caroline et al. 2022. "Student Perceptions of School Resource Officers and Threat Reporting." *Journal of School Violence, 21,* 222–36.

Crozier, Karen D. 2021. *Fannie Lou Hamer's Revolutionary Practical Theology.* Leiden: Brill.

Cuijpers, Kim. 2024. "How to Improve Outcomes of Psychological Treatment of Depression." *American Psychologist, 79,* 1407–17.

Cummings, K. Michael, and Robert N. Proctor. 2014. "The Changing Public Image of Smoking in the United States: 1964–2014." *Cancer Epidemiology, Biomarkers and Prevention, 23,* 32–36.

Dahlberg, L. L. et al. 2004. "Guns in the Home and Risk of a Violent Death in the Home: Findings from a National Study." *American Journal of Epidemiology, 160,* 929–36.

Darby, Seyward. 2020. *Sisters in Hate: American Women on the Front Lines of White Nationalism.* New York: Little, Brown.

Davis, Joshua T. et al. 2024. "Liberty for Us, Limits for Them: Christian Nationalism and Americans' View on Citizens' Rights." *Sociology of Religion, 85,* 60–82.

Davis, Whitney et al. 2022. "Centering Trauma-Informed Approaches in Schools Within a Social Justice Framework." *Psychology in the Schools, 59,* 2453–70.

Davis-Delano, Laurel R. et al. 2021. "Representations of Native Americans in U.S. Culture? A Case of Omissions and Commissions." *The Social Science Journal.* https://doi.org/10.1080/03623319.2021.1975086.

Dawson, Jessica. 2019. "Shall Not Be Infringed: How the NRA Used Religious Language to Transform the Meaning of the Second Amendment." *Palgrave Communications, 5,* 58.

Dawson, Jessica, and Dana B. Weinberg. 2022. "These Honored Dead: Sacrifice Narratives in the NRA's *American Rifleman* magazine." *American Journal of Cultural Sociology, 10,* 110–35.

Demesmaeker, Alice et al. 2022. "Suicide Mortality After a Nonfatal Suicide Attempt: A Systematic Review and Meta-Analysis." *Australian & New Zealand Journal of Psychiatry, 56,* 603–16.

Devine, Patricia G. et al. 2012. "Long-Term Reduction in Implicit Race Bias: A Prejudice Habit-Breaking Intervention." *Journal of Experimental Social Psychology, 48,* 1267–78.

DiMuccio, Sarah H., and Eric D. Knowles. 2023. "Something to Prove? Manhood Threats Increase Political Aggression Among Liberal Men." *Sex Roles, 88,* 240–67.

Division for Emotional and Behavioral Health, Council for Children with Behavioral Disorders. 2024. "School Shootings: Current Status and Recommendations for Research and Practice." *Behavioral Disorders, 49,* 116–27.

Division of Adolescent and School Health, Centers for Disease Control. 2023. *Youth Risk Behavior Survey: Data Summary & Trends Report, 2011–2021.* https://www.cdc.gov/healthyyouth/data/yrbs/pdf/YRBS_Data-Summary-Trends_Report2023_508.pdf.

Dixon, Graham et al. 2020. "Public Opinion Perceptions, Private Support, and Public Actions of US Adults Regarding Gun Safety Policy." *JAMA Network Open, 3(12),* e2029571.

Dong, Beidi, and David B. Wilson. 2022. "State Firearm Legislation and Youth/Young Adult Handgun Carrying in the United States." *Journal of Adolescent Health, 71,* 751–56.

DuBosar, Eliana et al. 2023. "Celebrating Wins, Lamenting Losses in the Aftermath of Presidential Elections." *Journal of Media Psychology, 36(3).* https://doi.org/10.1027/1864-1105/a000394.

Dutton, Megan et al. 2023. "Oral Ketamine May Offer a Solution to the Ketamine Conundrum." *Psychopharmacology, 240,* 2483–97.

Eagly, Alice H., and Shelly Chaiken. 1993. *The Psychology of Attitudes.* Harcourt Brace Jovanovich.

El Sherief, Mai et al. 2021. "Impacts of School Shooter Drills on the Psychological Well-Being of American K–12 School Communities: A Social Media Study." *Humanities and Social Sciences Communications, 8,* 315.

Ellison, Christopher G. et al. 2021. "Peace Through Superior Firepower: Belief in Supernatural Evil and Attitudes Toward Gun Policy in the United States." *Social Science Research, 99,* 102595.

Ellyson, Alice M. et al. 2023. "Implicit Racial and Gender Bias about Handguns: A New Implicit Association Test." *Journal of Interpersonal Violence, 38,* 5190–210.

Erdozain, Dominic. 2024. *One Nation Under Guns: How Gun Culture Distorts Our History and Threatens Our Democracy.* New York: Crown.

Everytown for Gun Safety. 2022. "Everytown Launches New Nationwide Interactive Gun Law Platform Analyzing 50 Policies in All 50 States." https://everytownsupportfund.org/press/everytown-launches-new-nationwide-interactive-gun-law-platform-analyzing-50-policies-in-all-50-states/?_gl=1*1krbz1g*_ga*MTgxNDYwNDIwMy4xNjg3MjczODg4*_ga_LT0FWV3EK3*MTY4ODY5MTczNS4zLjEuMTY4ODY5MjkzOS4wLjAuMA.

Everytown for Gun Safety. 2023. *Gun Violence in the United States.* EveryStat.org.

Everytown Law. 2023. "Westforth Sports, Long-time Dealer of Crime Guns, to Close After Lawsuit Exposed Persistent Violations of Federal and State Gun Laws." https://everytownlaw.org/press/westforth-sports-long-time-dealer-of-crime-guns-to-close-after-lawsuit-exposed-persistent-violations-of-federal-and-state-gun-laws/#:~:text=Over%20300%20guns%20have%20been,%2Dfatal%20shootings%2C%20and%20assaults.

Everytown Research and Policy. 2022. *How to Stop Shootings and Gun Violence in Schools.* https://everytownresearch.org/report/how-to-stop-shootings-and-gun-violence-in-schools/.

———. 2023. *Firearm Suicide in the United States.* https://everytownresearch.org/report/firearm-suicide-in-the-united-states/.

———. 2023. *Inside the Gun Shop: Firearms Dealers and Their Impact.* https://everytown research.org/report/firearms-dealers-and-their-impact/.

———. 2024. *Hospital-Based Violence Intervention Programs: A Guide to Implementation and Costing.* https://everytownresearch.org/report/hospital-based-violence-intervention-programs-a-guide-to-implementation-and-costing/?source=emfe_20240501

———. 2024. *Those Who Serve: Addressing Firearm Suicide Among Military Veterans.* https://everytownresearch.org/report/those-who-serve/.

FBI. 2021. *Investigative Report on the August 4, 2019 Attack in Dayton, Ohio.* https://www.fbi.gov/contact-us/field-offices/cincinnati/news/press-releases/investigative-report-on-the-august-4-2019-attack-in-dayton-ohio

Feder, June et al. 2007. "Boys and Violence: A Gender-Informed Analysis." *Professional Psychology: Research and Practice, 38,* 385–91.

Festinger, Leon. 1957. *A Theory of Cognitive Dissonance.* Redwood City: Stanford University Press.

Fikkers, Karin M. et al. 2017. "A Matter of Style? Exploring the Effects of Parental Mediation Styles on Early Adolescents' Media Violence Exposure and Aggression." *Computers in Human Behavior, 70,* 407–15.

Flannery, Daniel J. et al. 2021. "Guns, School Shooters, and School Safety: What We Know and Directions for Change." *School Psychology Review, 50,* 237–53.

Follman, Mark. 2022. *Trigger Points: Inside the Mission to Stop Mass Shootings in America.* New York: Dey Street Books.

Forscher, Patrick S. et al. 2017. "Breaking the Prejudice Habit: Mechanisms, Timecourse, and Longevity." *Journal of Experimental Social Psychology, 72,* 133–46.

Fortin, Jacey, and Anna Betts. 2024. "Parents of Michigan School Shooter Sentenced to 10 to 15 Years in Prison." *New York Times,* April 9.

Franklin, Joseph C. et al. 2017. "Risk Factors for Suicidal Thoughts and Behaviors: A Meta-Analysis of 50 Years of Research." *Psychological Bulletin, 143,* 187–232.

Frey, Laura M. et al. 2022. "Review of Family-Based Treatments from 2010 to 2019 for Suicidal Ideation and Behavior." *Journal of Marital and Family Therapy, 48,* 154–77.

Friedman, Joseph, and Helena Hansen. 2024. "Trends in Deaths of Despair by Race and Ethnicity from 1999 to 2022." *JAMA Psychiatry, 81,* 731–32.

Gabbatt, Adam. 2023. "Wave of Lawsuits Against US Gun Makers Raises Hope of End to Mass Shootings." May 27. www.theguardian.com.

Gallup Poll. 2023. "Guns." https://news.gallup.com/poll/1645/guns.aspx.

Frances Gardner et al. 2007. "Randomized Prevention Trial for Early Conduct Problems: Effects on Proactive Parenting and Link to Toddler Disruptive Behavior." *Journal of Family Psychology, 21,* 398–406.

Gartlehner, Gerald et al. 2021. "Pharmacological Treatment for Borderline Personality Disorder: A Systematic Review and Meta-Analysis." *CNS Drugs, 35,* 1053–67.

Gaskill, Malcolm. 2022. *The Ruin of All Witches: Life and Death in the New World*. New York: Knopf.

Geller, Lisa B. et al. 2021. "The Role of Domestic Violence in Fatal Mass Shootings in the United States, 2014–2019." *Injury Epidemiology, 8(1)*, 38.

Ghavami, Negin, and Anne L. Peplau. 2013. "An Intersectional Analysis of Gender and Ethnic Stereotypes: Testing Three Hypotheses." *Psychology of Women Quarterly, 37*, 113–27.

Giaccardi, Soraya et al. 2022. *Shooting Straight: What TV Stories Tell Us About Gun Safety, How These Depictions Affect Audiences, and How We Can Do Better*. Everytown for Gun Safety. https://everytownsupportfund.org/report/gun-safety-depictions-on-tv/?_gl=1*kfkqj*_ga*ODA2NjM5NTgyLjE2OTc5MTY3MDU.*_ga_LT0F WV3EK3*MTY5OTM5NzA4Ni4zLjEuMTY5OTM5Nzc5MS4wLjAuMA.

Gillman, Howard et al. 2021. *American Constitutionalism. Volume II: Rights and Liberties*, 3rd ed. New York: Oxford University Press.

Gobaud, Ariana N. et al. 2022. "Gun Shows and Universal Background Check Laws Across State Lines." *Preventive Medicine, 165*, 107094.

Goldman, Liran et al. 2014. "Going to Extremes: Social Identity and Communication Processes Associated with Gang Membership." *Group Processes and Intergroup Relations, 17*, 813–32.

Goldstick, Jason E. et al. 2022. "Current Causes of Death in Children and Adolescents in the United States." *New England Journal of Medicine, 386*, 1955–56.

Goodman, J. David. 2024. "Uvalde Families Accuse Instagram, 'Call of Duty' and Rifle Maker of 'Grooming' Gunman." *New York Times*, May 24.

Goyal, Monika K. et al. 2019. "State Gun Laws and Pediatric Firearm-Related Mortality." *Pediatrics, 144*, no. 2.

Graham, David A. 2018. "Wayne LaPierre's Cynical Exploitation of Outrage." *The Atlantic*, February 22.

Greenberger, Marcia D., and Deborah L. Blake. 1996. "The VMI Decision: Shattering Sexual Stereotypes." *Chronicle of Higher Education*, July 5, A52.

Gul, Pelin et al. 2021. "Implications of Culture of Honor Theory and Research for Practitioners and Prevention Researchers." *American Psychologist, 76*, 502–15.

Guo, Kayla, and Nicholas Bogel-Burroughs. 2023. "A Baltimore Party, a Hail of Gunfire and a Neighborhood Shattered." *New York Times*, July 3.

Gurrey, Sixtine et al. 2021. "Firearm-Related Research Articles in Health Sciences by Funding Status and Type: A Scoping Review." *Preventive Medicine Reports, 24*, 101604.

Hakim, Danny. 2024. "LaPierre, Longtime N.R.A. Leader, Faces Trial That Could End His Reign." *New York Times*, January 2.

Hamedani, MarYam G. et al. 2024. "We Built This Culture (So We Can Change It): Seven Principles for Intentional Culture Change." *American Psychologist, 79*, 384–402.

Hannebrink, Paul. 2018. *A Specter Haunting Europe: The Myth of Judeo-Bolshevism*. Cambridge, MA: Harvard University Press.

Hays, Christopher B. 2021. "'Do Not Be Afraid': The Walls of Jerusalem and the Guns of America." In *God and Guns*, edited by C. Hays and C. Crouch, 57–75. Louisville, KY: Westminster John Knox Press.

Heberlein, Tom. 2016. "Sweden May Have the Answer to America's Gun Problem." *Vox*. https://www.vox.com/2016/8/8/12351824/gun-control-sweden-solution.

Hemenway, David, and Lois K. Lee. 2022. "Lessons from the Continuing 21st Century Motor Vehicle Success." *Injury Prevention, 28,* 480–82.

Hemenway, David, and Sara J. Solnick. 2015. "The Epidemiology of Self-Defense Gun Use: Evidence from the National Crime Victimization Surveys 2007–2011." *Preventive Medicine, 79,* 22–27.

Hemenway, David et al. 2019. "Variation in Rates of Fatal Police Shootings Across US States: The Role of Firearm Availability." *Journal of Urban Health, 96,* 63–73.

Hennessy-Fiske, Molly. 2023. "House Speaker Mike Johnson's Louisiana Hometown Guided by Faith and Family." *Washington Post*, October 29.

Hogg, Michael A. 2023. "Walls Between Groups: Self-uncertainty, Social Identity, and Intergroup Leadership." *Journal of Social Issues, 79,* 825–40.

Hollingsworth, Heath. 2023. "White Man Will Stand Trial for Shooting Black Teen Ralph Yarl, Who Went to Wrong House, Judge Rules." Associated Press. August 31.

Homsher, Deborah. 2001. *Women and Guns: Politics and the Culture of Firearms in America.* M. E. Sharpe.

Hong, Barry et al. 2024. "The Saint Louis Bridges Program: A Mental Health Network of More Than One Hundred Churches and the Mental Health Community." *Journal of the National Medical Association, 116,* 16–23.

Horwitz, Joshua, and Casey Anderson. 2009. *Guns, Democracy, and the Insurrectionist Idea.* Ann Arbor: University of Michigan Press.

Hou, Xiaofei et al. 2022. "Methods and Efficacy of Social Support Interventions in Preventing Suicide: A Systematic Review and Meta-Analysis." *Evidence-Based Mental Health, 25,* 29–35.

Howe, Amy. 2024. "United States v. Rahimi." SCOTUSblog. June 21. https://www.scotusblog.com/case-files/cases/united-states-v-rahimi/.

Huesmann, L. Rowell et al. 2021. "Longitudinal Predictions of Young Adults' Weapons Use and Criminal Behavior from Their Childhood Exposure to Violence." *Aggressive Behavior, 47,* 621–34.

Hussain, Zain et al. 2023. "A Qualitative Framing Analysis of How Firearm Manufacturers and Related Bodies Communicate to the Public on Gun-Related Harms and Solutions." *Preventive Medicine, 166,* 107346.

Hyde, Luke W. et al. 2025. "An Ecological Neurodevelopmental Model of the Development of Youth Antisocial Behavior and Callous-Unemotional Traits." *Annual Review of Developmental Psychology* (in press).

Ingraham, Christopher. 2018. "One in Five Americans Wants the Second Amendment to Be Repealed, National Survey Finds." *Washington Post*, March 27.

Ingram, Katherine M. et al. 2019. "Longitudinal Associations Between Features of Toxic Masculinity and Bystander Willingness to Intervene in Bullying Among Middle School Boys." *Journal of School Psychology, 77,* 139–51.

Iyengar, Udita et al. 2018. "A Further Look at Therapeutic Interventions for Suicide Attempts and Self-Harm in Adolescents: An Updated Systematic Review of Randomized Controlled Trials." *Frontiers in Psychiatry, 9 (583)*.

Jaffee, Sara R. et al. 2023. "Differential Exposure to Gun or Knife Violence over Two Decades Is Associated with Sibling Differences in Depression." *Development and Psychopathology, 35*, 2096–102.

Jewett, Patricia I. et al. 2022. "US Mass Public Shootings Since Columbine: Victims per Incident by Race and Ethnicity of the Perpetrator." *Preventive Medicine, 162*, 107176.

Jobes, David A. 2012. "The Collaborative Assessment and Management of Suicidality (CAMS): An Evolving Evidence-Based Clinical Approach to Suicidal Risk." *Suicide and Life-Threatening Behavior, 42*, 640–53.

Johnson, David J., and William J. Chopik. 2019. "Geographic Variation in the Black-Violence Stereotype." *Social Psychological and Personality Science, 10*, 287–94.

Johnson, Lisette. 2023. "Shameless Survivors." https://momentsthatsurvive.org/tribute/lisette-johnson/.

Jones, Robert P. 2023. *The Hidden Roots of White Supremacy and the Path to a Shared American Future.* New York: Simon & Schuster.

Jones, Serene. 2023. "The 'God-Given Right' to Guns Is a Cash-Fueled Sham." *Salon.* https://utsnyc.edu/the-god-given-right-to-guns-is-a-cash-fueled-sham/.

Jung, Jong Hyun. 2020. "Belief in Supernatural Evil and Mental Health: Do Secure Attachment to God and Gender Matter?" *Journal for the Scientific Study of Religion, 59*, 141–60.

Kalla, Joshua L., and David E. Broockman. 2020. "Reducing Exclusionary Attitudes Through Interpersonal Conversation: Evidence from Three Field Experiments." *American Political Science Review, 114*, 410–25.

Kalla, Joshua L., and David E. Broockman. 2023. "Which Narrative Strategies Durably Reduce Prejudice? Evidence from Field and Survey Experiments Supporting the Efficacy of Perspective-Getting." *American Journal of Political Science, 67*, 185–204.

Kalla, Joshua L. et al. 2022. "Personalizing Moral Reframing in Interpersonal Conversation: A Field Experiment." *The Journal of Politics, 84*, 1239–43.

Kang, Han K. et al. 2015. "Suicide Risk Among 1.3 Million Veterans Who Were on Active Duty During the Iraq and Afghanistan Wars." *Annals of Epidemiology, 25*, 96–100.

Kaufman, E. J. et al. 2020. "Universal Background Checks for Handgun Purchases Can Reduce Homicide Rates of African Americans." *Journal of Trauma and Acute Care Surgery, 88*, 825–31.

Kegler, Scott R. et al. 2022. "Vital Signs: Changes in Firearm Homicide and Suicide Rates—United States, 2019–2020." *MMWR, 71(19)*.

Klein, Lauren M. et al. 2024. "Parents' Trust in COVID-19 Messengers and Implications for Vaccination." *American Journal of Health Promotion, 38*, 364–74.

Klonsky, E. David, and Alexis M. May. 2015. "The Three-Step Theory (3ST): A New Theory of Suicide Rooted in the 'Ideation-to-Action' Framework." *International Journal of Cognitive Therapy, 8*, 114–29.

Koppa, Vijetha, and Jill T. Messing. 2021. "Can Justice System Interventions Prevent Intimate Partner Homicides? An Analysis of Rates of Help Seeking Prior to Fatality." *Journal of Interpersonal Violence, 36*, 8792–816.

Kosek, Joseph Kip. 2009. *Acts of Conscience: Christian Nonviolence and Modern American Democracy.* New York: Columbia University Press.

Kubin, Emily et al. 2021. "Personal Experiences Bridge Moral and Political Divides Better than Facts. *Proceedings of the National Academy of Sciences (PNAS), 118(6).*

Lacombe, Matthew J. 2021. *Firepower: How the NRA Turned Gun Owners into a Political Force.* Princeton: Princeton University Press.

Lacy, Aaron J. et al. 2022. "A Celebration with Unforeseen Consequences: Celebratory Gunfire Causing Injury." *American Journal of Emergency Medicine, 58,* 350.e1–350. e3.

Lai, Calvin K. et al. 2014. "Reducing Implicit Racial Preferences: I. A Comparative Investigation of 17 Interventions." *Journal of Experimental Psychology: General, 143,* 1765–85.

Lane, Tyler J. 2023. "Associations Between Firearm and Suicide Rates: A Replication of Kleck (2021)." *Archives of Suicide Research, 27,* 880–95.

Langman, Peter. 2009. "Rampage School Shooters: A Typology." *Aggression and Violent Behavior, 14,* 79–86.

Lee, Chana Kai. 1999. *For Freedom's Sake: The Life of Fannie Lou Hamer.* Champaign: University of Illinois Press.

Lee, Daniel B. et al. 2022. "Retaliatory Attitudes as Mediator of Exposure to Violence and Firearm Aggression Among Youth: The Protective Role of Organized Activity Involvement." *Developmental Psychology, 58,* 990–1002.

Lee, Lois D. et al. 2017. "Firearm Laws and Firearm Homicides: A Systematic Review." *JAMA Internal Medicine, 177,* 106–19.

Leemis, Ruth W. et al. 2022. *The National Intimate Partner and Sexual Violence Survey: 2016/2017 Report on Intimate Partner Violence.* National Center for Injury Prevention and Control, Centers for Disease Control and Prevention.

Lemle, Russell B. 2024. "Bridging the Sociopolitical Divide: Transforming Efforts to Prevent Firearm Suicide." *American Psychologist, 79,* 1361–65.

Levant, Ronald F. 2022. "Examining the Gender Role Strain Paradigm to Account for U.S. Males' Gun Violence." *Psychology of Men & Masculinities, 23,* 151–59.

Levant, Ronald F., and Shana Pryor. 2020. *The Tough Standard: The Hard Truths About Masculinity and Violence.* New York: Oxford University Press.

———. 2024. *Assessing and Treating Emotionally Inexpressive Men.* New York: Routledge.

Leverso, John, and Chris Hess. 2021. "From the Hood to the Home: Masculinity Maturation of Chicago Street Gang Members." *Sociological Perspectives, 64,* 1206–23.

Liebbrand, Christine et al. 2020. "Invisible Wounds: Community Exposure to Gun Homicides and Adolescents' Mental Health and Behavioral Outcomes." *SSM— Population Health, 12,* 100689.

Light, Caroline E. 2021. "'What Real Empowerment Looks Like': White Rage and the Necropolitics of Armed Womanhood." *Signs: Journal of Women in Culture and Society, 46(4),* 911–37.

Linehan, Marsha M., and Chelsey R. Wilks. 2015. "The Course and Evolution of Dialectical Behavior Therapy." *American Journal of Psychotherapy, 69,* 97–110.

Liptak, Adam. 2023. "By 5–4 Vote, Supreme Court Revives Biden's Regulation of 'Ghost Guns.'" *New York Times,* August 8.

———. 2023. "Supreme Court's Devotion to Gun Rights Faces a Challenging Test." *New York Times,* November 6.

Littlefield, Jon, and Julie L. Ozanne. 2011. "Socialization into Consumer Culture: Hunters Learning to Be Men." *Consumption Markets & Culture, 14,* 333–60.

Liu, Grace S. et al. 2023. "Surveillance for Violent Deaths—National Violent Death Reporting System, 48 States, the District of Columbia, and Puerto Rico, 2020." *MMWR, 72(5).*

Liu, Richard T. et al. 2017. "A Behavioral and Cognitive Neuroscience Perspective on Impulsivity, Suicide, and Non-Suicidal Self-Injury: Meta-Analysis and Recommendations for Future Research." *Neuroscience and Biobehavioral Reviews, 83,* 440–50.

LoBue, Vanessa. 2010. "What's So Scary About Needles and Knives? Examining the Role of Experience in Threat Detection." *Cognition and Emotion, 24,* 180–87.

Lowe, Sarah R., and Sandro Galea. 2017. "The Mental Health Consequences of Mass Shootings." *Trauma, Violence, and Abuse, 18,* 62–82.

Lynch, Kellie R. et al. 2022. "Firearm-Related Abuse and Protective Order Requests Among Intimate Partner Violence Victims." *Journal of Interpersonal Violence, 37(15–16).*

Maertens, Rakoen et al. 2021. "Long-Term Effectiveness of Inoculation Against Misinformation: Three Longitudinal Experiments." *Journal of Experimental Psychology: Applied, 27,* 1–16.

Magarian, Gregory P. 2012. "Speaking Truth to Firepower: How the First Amendment Destabilizes the Second." *Texas Law Review, 91,* 49–99.

Mann, J. John et al. 2021. "Improving Suicide Prevention Through Evidence-Based Strategies: A Systematic Review." *American Journal of Psychiatry, 178,* 611–24.

Martaindale, M. Hunter. 2021. "Improving the Accuracy of Firearm Identification in a Dynamic Use of Force Scenario." *Police Quarterly, 24,* 104–30.

Martin, Rachel et al. 2022. "Racial Disparities in Child Exposure to Firearm Violence Before and During COVID-19." *American Journal of Preventive Medicine, 63,* 204–12.

Mascaro, Jennifer S. et al. 2017. "Child Gender Influences Paternal Behavior, Language, and Brain Function." *Behavioral Neuroscience, 131,* 262–73.

Mason, Alicia M. et al. 2024. "Analyzing the Prophylactic and Therapeutic Role of Inoculation to Facilitate Resistance to Conspiracy Theory Beliefs." *Communication Reports, 37,* 13–27.

McCartin, Hadley R. et al. 2023. "Boys Round Here: The Relationship Between Masculine Honor Ideology, Aggressive Behavior, Race, and Regional Affiliation." *Journal of Interpersonal Violence, 38,* 5305–28.

McClelland, Heather et al. 2020. "Loneliness as a Predictor of Suicidal Ideation and Behaviour: A Systematic Review and Meta-Analysis of Prospective Studies." *Journal of Affective Disorders, 274,* 880–96.

McCourt, Alexander D. et al. 2020. "Purchaser Licensing, Point-of-Sale Background Check Laws, and Firearm Homicide and Suicide in 4 US States, 1985–2017." *American Journal of Public Health, 110(10).*

McGinty, Emma E., and Daniel W. Webster. 2016. "Gun Violence and Serious Mental Illness." In *Gun Violence and Mental Illness*, edited by Liza H. Gold and Robert I. Simon. American Psychiatric Association.

McGough, Matt et al. *Child and Teen Firearm Mortality in the US and Peer Countries.* 2023. KFF. https://www.kff.org/mental-health/issue-brief/child-and-teen-firearm-mortality-in-the-u-s-and-peer-countries/#.

McGuire, William J., and Demetrios Papageorgis. 1961. "The Relative Efficacy of Various Types of Prior Belief Defense in Producing Immunity Against Persuasion." *Journal of Abnormal and Social Psychology, 62,* 327–37.

McIntire, Mike et al. 2022. "How Gun Makers Harness Fear to Supercharge Sales." *New York Times*, June 19.

McIntire, Mike, and Jodi Kantor. 2024. "The Gun Lobby's Hidden Hand in the 2nd Amendment Battle." *New York Times*, June 18.

McIntosh, K. et al. 2010. "Principles of Sustainable Prevention: Designing the Scale-up of School-wide Positive Behavior Support to Promote Durable Systems." *Psychology in the Schools, 47,* 5–21.

McKinley, Jesse et al. 2024. "N.R.A. Stung by Corruption Verdict Tied to Millions of Misspent Dollars." *New York Times*, February 23.

McKinnon, Britt et al. 2016. "Adolescent Suicidal Behaviours in 32 Low- and Middle-Income Countries." *Bulletin of the World Health Organization, 94,* 340–50.

McRaney, David. 2022. *How Minds Change: The Surprising Science of Belief, Opinion, and Persuasion.* New York: Penguin.

McWhirter, Cameron, and Zusha Elinson. 2023. *American Gun: The True Story of the AR-15.* New York: Farrar, Straus and Giroux.

Mencken, F. Carson, and Paul Froese. 2019. "Gun Culture in Action." *Social Problems, 66,* 3–27.

Merino, Stephen M. 2018. "God and Guns: Examining Religious Influences on Gun Control Attitudes in the United States." *Religions, 9,* 189.

Meza, Jocelyn I. et al. 2023. "Practitioner Review: Common Elements in Treatments for Youth Suicide Attempts and Self-Harm—a Practitioner Review Based on Review of Treatment Elements Associated with Intervention Benefits." *Journal of Child Psychology and Psychiatry, 64,* 1409–21.

Miller, C. B. 2009. "Yes, We Did! Basking in Reflected Glory and Cutting Off Reflected Failure in the 2008 Presidential Election." *Analyses of Social Issues and Public Policy, 9,* 283–96.

Miller, Matthew et al. 2021. "Firearm Purchasing During the COVID-19 Pandemic: Results from the 2021 National Firearms Survey." *Annals of Internal Medicine, 175,* 219–25.

Miller, Matthew, and Deborah Azrael. 2022. "Firearm Storage in US Households with Children: Findings from the 2021 National Firearm Survey." *JAMA Network Open, 5(2),* e2148823.

Miller, Ted R., and Bruce Lawrence. 2019. "Analysis of CDC Fatal Injury: 2019 and HCUP Nonfatal Injury." Everystat.org.

Milov, Sarah. 2019. *The Cigarette: A Political History.* Cambridge, MA: Harvard University Press.

Molock, Sherry D. et al. 2008. "Developing Suicide Prevention Programs for African American Youth in African American Churches." *Suicide and Life-Threatening Behavior, 38,* 323–33.

Moments That Survive. 2024. *Luc-John.* https://momentsthatsurvive.org/tribute/luc -john/.

Moore, Russell. 2023. *Losing Our Religion: An Altar Call for Evangelical America.* New York: Sentinel.

Morris-Perez, Pamela et al. 2023. "Preventing Adolescent Suicide: Recommendations for Policymakers, Practitioners, Program Developers, and Researchers." *SRCD Social Policy Report, 36,* 2–32.

Mueller, Anna S. 2017. "Does the Media Matter to Suicide? Examining the Social Dynamics Surrounding Media Reporting on Suicide in a Suicide-Prone Community." *Social Science & Medicine, 180,* 152–59.

National Center for Health Statistics. 2023. *CDC Annual Mortality Data Files for WISQARS Fatal Data.* National Center for Health Statistics. https://wisqars.cdc.gov/ reports/.

Naughton, Felix et al. 2013. Dissonance and Disengagement in Pregnant Smokers. *Journal of Smoking Cessation, 8,* 24–32.

Neigenfind, Keith L. 2020. "Is Nonviolence and Pacificism in Christian and Buddhist Ethics Obligatory or Supererogatory?" *Buddhist-Christian Studies, 40,* 387–401.

Nierenberg, Andrew A. et al. 2023. "Diagnosis and Treatment of Bipolar Disorder: A Review." *JAMA, 330,* 1370–80.

Nisbett, Richard E. 1993. "Violence and U.S. Regional Culture." *American Psychologist, 48,* 441–49.

Nosek, Brian A. et al. 2007. "Pervasiveness and Correlates of Implicit Attitudes and Stereotypes." *European Review of Social Psychology, 18,* 36–88.

O'Gorman, Angie, ed. 1990. *The Universe Bends Toward Justice: A Reader on Christian Nonviolence in the U.S.* Gabriola Island, BC: New Society Publishers.

Öhman, A., and Susan Mineka. 2001. "Fears, Phobias, and Preparedness: Towards an Evolved Module of Fear and Fear Learning." *Psychological Review, 108,* 483–522.

Oliphant, Stephen N. 2023. "Bullying Victimization and Weapon Carrying: A Partial Test of General Strain Theory." *Youth & Society, 55,* 122–42.

Oppenheimer, Mark. 2021. *Squirrel Hill: The Tree of Life Synagogue Shooting and the Soul of a Neighborhood.* New York: Knopf.

O'Toole, Megan, and Mackey O'Keefe. 2023. *The Changing Demographics of Gun Homicide Victims and How Community Violence Intervention Programs Can Help.* Every townresearch.org.

Ougrin, Dennis et al. 2015. "Therapeutic Interventions for Suicide Attempts and Self-Harm in Adolescents: Systematic Review and Meta-Analysis." *Journal of the American Academy of Child and Adolescent Psychiatry, 54,* 97–107.

Ozer, Simon et al. 2020. "Group Membership and Radicalization: A Cross-National Investigation of Collective Self-Esteem Underlying Extremism." *Group Processes & Intergroup Relations, 23,* 1230–48.

Paik, H., and G. Comstock. 1994. "The Effects of Television Violence on Antisocial Behavior: A Meta-Analysis." *Communication Research, 21,* 516–46.

Paolini, Stefania et al. 2021. "Intergroup Contact Research in the 21st Century: Lessons Learned and Forward Progress If We Remain Open." *Journal of Social Issues, 77,* 11–37.

Parent, Mike C. et al. 2019. "Social Media Behavior, Toxic Masculinity, and Depression." *Psychology of Men & Masculinity, 20,* 277–87.

Paris, Joel. 2021. "Can We Predict or Prevent Suicide? An Update." *Preventive Medicine, 152,* 106353.

Pascoe, C. J. 2007. *Dude, You're a Fag: Masculinity and Sexuality in High School.* Oakland: University of California Press.

Patterson, G. R. et al. 1989. "A Developmental Perspective on Antisocial Behavior." *American Psychologist, 44,* 329–35.

Patton, Desmond U. et al. 2019. "Guns on Social Media: Complex Interpretations of Gun Images Posted by Chicago Youth." *Palgrave Communications 5:119.*

Peterson, Jillian K. et al. 2022. "Psychosis and Mass Shootings: A Systematic Examination Using Publicly Available Data." *Psychology, Public Policy, and Law, 28,* 280–91.

Petri, Alexandra. 2023. "The Problem Is the Human Heart. It's Not Guns." *Washington Post,* October 27, 2023.

Pew Research Center. 2014. *Religious Landscape Study.* https://www.pewresearch.org/religion/religious-landscape-study/.

———. 2023. *For Most U.S. Gun Owners, Protection Is the Main Reason They Own a Gun.* August 16. https://www.pewresearch.org/politics/2023/08/16/for-most-u-s-gun-owners-protection-is-the-main-reason-they-own-a-gun/.

Phadke, Meghan et al. 2024. "Arming Teachers: Who Will Bear the Burden?" *Educational Studies.* https://doi.org/10.1080/00131946.2024.2308696.

Pierre, Joseph M. 2019. "The Psychology of Guns: Risk, Fear, and Motivated Reasoning." *Palgrave Communications, 5,* 159. https://doi.org/10.1057/s41599-019-0373-z.

Pike, Sarah M. 2009. "Dark Teens and Born-Again Martyrs: Captivity Narratives After Columbine." *Journal of the American Academy of Religion, 77,* 647–79.

Plant, E. Ashby, and Janet S. Hyde et al. 2000. "The Gender Stereotyping of Emotions." *Psychology of Women Quarterly, 24,* 81–92.

Pleck, Joseph R. 1981. *The Myth of Masculinity.* Cambridge, MA: MIT Press.

———. 1995. "The Gender Role Strain Paradigm: An Update." In *A New Psychology of Men,* edited by R. F. Levant and W. S. Pollack, 11–32. New York: Basic Books.

Polner, Murray, and Naomi Goodman, eds. 1994. *The Challenge of Shalom: The Jewish Tradition of Peace and Justice.* Gabriola Island, BC: New Society Publishers.

Pope Alexander VI. 1493. *Inter Caetera.* www.nim.nih.gov/nativevoices/timeline/171.html.

Post, Lori et al. 2021. "Impact of Firearm Surveillance on Gun Control Policy: Regression Discontinuity Analysis." *JMIR Public Health and Surveillance, 7,* e26042, https://doi.org/10.2196/26042.

Pratt, Erich. 2022. "The Bible, Guns, and the Second Amendment." Gunowners.org.

Pritchard, Colin et al. 2023. "USA Suicides Compared to Other Western Countries in the 21st Century: Is There a Relationship with Gun Ownership?" *Archives of Suicide Research*, 27, 135–47.

Privor-Dumm, Lois, and Terris King. 2020. "Community-Based Strategies to Engage Pastors Can Help Address Vaccine Hesitancy and Health Disparities in Black Communities." *Journal of Health Communication*, 25, 827–30.

Purvis, Rachel S. et al. 2023. "Key Conversations and Trusted Information Among Hesitant Adopters of the COVID-19 Vaccine." *Journal of Health Communication*, 28, 595–604.

Rabbinical Assembly. 2016. *Resolution on American Gun Violence.* https://www.rabbinical assembly.org/story/resolution-american-gun-violence.

Ranney, Megan et al. 2019. "What Are the Long-Term Consequences of Youth Exposure to Firearm Injury, and How Do We Prevent Them? A Scoping Review." *Journal of Behavioral Medicine*, 42, 724–40.

Reeping, Paul et al. 2022. "State Firearm Laws, Gun Ownership, and K–12 School Shootings: Implications for School Safety." *Journal of School Violence*, 21, 132–46.

Reese, Thomas. 2022. "The Catholic Bishops Support Gun Control. Why Don't We Hear More About It?" *National Catholic Reporter.* June 14, 2022. https://www .ncronline.org/news/opinion/catholic-bishops-support-gun-control-why-dont-we -hear-more-about-it.

Reinbergs, Erik J. et al. 2024. "Firearm Carrying and Adolescent Suicide Risk Outcomes Between 2015 and 2021 Across Nationally Representative Samples." *Suicide and Life-Threatening Behavior*, 54, 302–9.

Religious Action Center of Reform Judaism. 2023. *Gun Violence Prevention.* https:// rac.org/issues/gun-violence-prevention?_gl=1*e2n7ma*_ga*OTU3Mzk2N jcxLjE2OTkxNDIwOTY.*_ga_6WX143SJW5*MTY5OTE0MjA5NS4xL jEuMTY5OTE0MjEzMi4yMy4wLjA.

Reyna, Christine et al. 2022. "The Psychology of White Nationalism: Ambivalence Toward a Changing America." *Social Issues and Policy Review*, 16, 79–124.

Ribeiro, Jessica D. et al. 2018. "Depression and Hopelessness as Risk Factors for Suicide Ideation, Attempts and Death: Meta-Analysis of Longitudinal Studies." *British Journal of Psychiatry*, 212, 279–86.

Richards, Adam S. et al. 2021. "Freedom-Prompting Reactance Mitigation Strategies Function Differently Across Levels of Trait Reactance." *Communication Quarterly*, 69, 238–58.

Roberts, Steven O., and M. T. Rizzo. 2021. "The Psychology of American Racism." *American Psychologist*, 76, 475–87.

Robertson, Campbell et al. 2023. "In Philadelphia, a Mass Shooting Leaves Five Dead." *New York Times*, July 4.

Romer, Dan et al. 2023. "Media Influences on Children and Advice for Parents to Reduce Harmful Exposure to Firearm Violence in Media." *Pediatric Clinics of North America*, 70, 1217–24.

Roozenbeek, Jon et al. 2022. "Psychological Inoculation Improves Resilience Against Misinformation on Social Media." *Science Advances*, 8, eabo6254.

Roozenbeek, Jon, and Sander van der Linden. 2024. *The Psychology of Misinformation.* New York: Cambridge University Press.

Rosenberg, Rosalind. 1983. *Beyond Separate Spheres: Intellectual Roots of Modern Feminism.* New Haven: Yale University Press.

Rossin-Slater, Maya et al. 2020. "Local Exposure to School Shootings and Youth Antidepressant Use." *PNAS, 117,* 23484–89.

Rudd, M. David et al. 2015. "Brief Cognitive-Behavioral Therapy Effects on Post-Treatment Suicide Attempts in a Military Sample: Results of a Randomized Clinical Trial with 2-Year Follow-Up." *American Journal of Psychiatry, 172,* 441–49.

Sadler, Melody, and Thierry Devos. 2020. "Ethnic Diversity Matters: Putting Implicit Associations Between Weapons and Ethnicity in Context." *Group Processes and Intergroup Relations, 23,* 285–300.

Savage, Joanne, and Christina Yancey. 2008. "The Effects of Media Violence Exposure on Criminal Aggression: A Meta-Analysis." *Criminal Justice and Behavior, 35,* 772–91.

Schell, Terry L. et al. 2020. "Changes in Firearm Mortality Following the Implementation of State Laws Regulating Firearm Access and Use." *PNAS, 117,* 14906–10.

Schenck, Robert. 2020. Foreword to *God and Guns in America*, by Michael W. Austin. Grand Rapids, MI: Wm. B. Eerdmans Publishing Co.

Schildkraut, Jaclyn et al. 2020. "Locks, Lights, Out of Sight: Assessing Students' Perceptions of Emergency Preparedness Across Multiple Lockdown Drills." *Journal of School Violence, 19,* 93–106.

Schneider, Mary-Jane. 2021. *Introduction to Public Health*, 6th ed. Burlington, MA: Jones & Bartlett.

Schonfeld, David J. et al. 2020. "Participation of Children and Adolescents in Live Crisis Drills and Exercises." *Pediatrics, 146,* e2020015503.

Schutten, Nathaniel et al. 2023. "Understanding Gun Ownership in the Twenty-First Century: Why Some Americans Own Guns, But Most Do Not." *Justice Quarterly, 40,* 27–250.

Schwadel, Philip. 2014. "Are White Evangelical Protestants Lower Class? A Partial Test of Church-Sect Theory." *Social Science Research, 46,* 100–116.

Seidler, Zac E. et al. 2024. "A Randomized Wait-List Controlled Trial of Men in Mind: Enhancing Mental Health Practitioners' Self-Rated Clinical Competencies to Work with Men." *American Psychologist, 79,* 423–36.

Septier, Mathilde et al. 2019. "Association Between Suicidal Spectrum Behaviors and Attention-Deficit/Hyperactivity Disorder: A Systematic Review and Meta-Analysis." *Neuroscience and Biobehavioral Reviews, 103,* 109–18.

Serra, Giulia et al. 2022. "Suicidal Behavior in Juvenile Bipolar Disorder and Major Depressive Disorder Patients: Systematic Review and Meta-Analysis." *Journal of Affective Disorders, 311,* 572–81.

Seto, Christopher H., and Laura Openieks. 2023. "Under God and Under Threat: Christian Nationalism and Conspiratorial Thinking as Links Between Political Orientation and Gun Ownership." *Justice Quarterly, 41,* 291–316.

Shapira, Harel, and Samantha J. Simon. 2018. "Learning to Need a Gun." *Qualitative Sociology, 41,* 1–20.

Sharkey, Patrick. 2010. "The Acute Effect of Local Homicides on Children's Cognitive Performance." *PNAS, 107*, 11733–38.

Shaw, Daniel S., and E. C. Shelleby. 2014. "Early-Onset Conduct Problems: Intersection of Conduct Problems and Poverty." *Annual Review of Clinical Psychology, 10*, 503–28.

Silva, Jason R., and Emily A. Greene-Colozzi. 2024. "Assessing Leakage-Based Mass Shooting Prevention: A Comparison of Foiled and Completed Attacks." *Journal of Threat Assessment and Management, 11(4)*, 203–17.

Silver, James et al. 2018. *A Study of the Pre-Attack Behaviors of Active Shooters in the United States between 2000–2013*. Federal Bureau of Investigation, US Department of Justice.

Sim, Jessica J. et al. 2013. "Understanding Police and Expert Performance: When Training Attenuates (vs. Exacerbates) Stereotypic Bias in the Decision to Shoot." *Personality and Social Psychology Bulletin, 39*, 291–304.

Simon, Gregory E. 2024. "Management of Depression in Adults: A Review." *JAMA, 332*, 141–52.

Simon, Samantha J. 2024. *Before the Badge: How Academy Training Shapes Police Violence*. New York University Press.

Simon, Thomas R. et al. 2001. "Characteristics of Impulsive Suicide Attempts and Attempters." *Suicide and Life-Threatening Behavior, 32(supp)*, 49–59.

Sivaraman, Josie J. et al. 2019. "Association of State Firearm Legislation with Female Intimate Partner Homicide." *American Journal of Preventive Medicine, 56*, 125–33.

Slemaker, Alexandra. 2023. "Studying Mass Shooters' Words: Warning Behavior Prior to Attacks." *Journal of Threat Assessment and Management, 10*, 1–17.

Slotkin, Richard. 1973. *Regeneration Through Violence: The Mythology of the American Frontier, 1600-1860*. Norman: University of Oklahoma Press.

———. 1992. *Gunfighter Nation: The Myth of the Frontier in Twentieth-Century America*. Harper Perennial.

Small Arms Survey. 2020. "Global Firearms Holdings." Smallarmssurvey.org.

Smart, Rosanna et al. 2023. *The Science of Gun Policy: A Critical Synthesis of Research Evidence on the Effects of Gun Policies in the United States*, 3rd ed. RAND Corporation. https://www.rand.org/pubs/research_reports/RRA243-4.html.

Song, Zirui et al. 2023. "The Clinical and Economic Impact of Child and Adolescent Firearm Injuries on Survivors and Family Members." *Journal of General Internal Medicine, 38(Suppl2)*, S97–S98.

Sorenson, Susan B., and Rebecca A. Schut. 2018. "Nonfatal Gun Use in Intimate Partner Violence: A Systematic Review of the Literature." *Trauma, Violence, & Abuse, 19*, 431–42.

Spencer, Chelsea M., and Sandra M. Stith. 2020. "Risk Factors for Male Perpetration and Female Victimization of Intimate Partner Homicide: A Meta-Analysis." *Trauma, Violence, and Abuse, 21*, 527–40.

Sprinkle, Preston. 2021. *Nonviolence: The Revolutionary Way of Jesus*. Colorado Springs: David C Cook.

Stretesky, Paul B. and Mark R. Pogrebin. 2007. "Gang-Related Gun Violence: Socialization, Identity, and Self." *Journal of Contemporary Ethnography, 36,* 85–115.

Stroebe, Wolfgang et al. 2022. "When Mass Shootings Fail to Change Minds About the Causes of Violence: How Gun Beliefs Shape Causal Attributions." *Psychology of Violence, 12,* 305–13.

Stroud, Angela. 2012. "Good Guys with Guns: Hegemonic Masculinity and Concealed Handguns." *Gender & Society, 26,* 216–38.

———. 2015. *Good Guys with Guns: The Appeal and Consequences of Concealed Carry.* Chapel Hill: University of North Carolina Press.

Studdert, David M. et al. 2022. "Homicide Deaths Among Adult Cohabitants of Handgun Owners in California, 2004 to 2016." *Annals of Internal Medicine, 175,* 804–11.

Susmann, Mark W. et al. 2022. "Correcting Misperceptions of Gun Policy Support Can Foster Intergroup Cooperation Between Gun Owners and Non-Gun Owners." *PLOS ONE, 17(6),* e0268601.

Swift, Joshua K. 2021. "The Effectiveness of the Collaborative Assessment and Management of Suicidality (CAMS) Compared to Alternative Treatment Conditions: A Meta-Analysis." *Suicide and Life-Threatening Behavior, 51,* 882–96.

Swim, Janet K. et al. 1995. "Sexism and Racism: Old-Fashioned and Modern Prejudices." *Journal of Personality and Social Psychology, 68,* 199–214.

Tajfel, Henri, and J. C. Turner. 1986. "The Social Identity Theory of Intergroup Behavior." In *Psychology of Intergroup Relations,* edited by S. Worchel and W. G. Austin, 7–24. Newton, MA: Nelson-Hall.

Targoff, Ramie. 2024. *Shakespeare's Sisters: How Women Wrote the Renaissance.* New York: Knopf.

Tocci, Charles et al. 2023. "Statement on the Effects of Law Enforcement in School Settings." *American Journal of Community Psychology,* 1–18.

Trivellato, Francesca. 2019. *The Promise and Peril of Credit: What a Forgotten Legend About Jews and Finance Tells Us About the Making of European Commercial Society.* Princeton: Princeton University Press.

TSA. 2024. "TSA Intercepted More Than 1,500 Firearms at Airport Checkpoints Nationwide During the First Quarter of 2024." Press release. April 11. https://www.tsa.gov/news/press/releases/2024/04/11/tsa-intercepted-more-1500-firearms-airport-checkpoints-nationwide.

Tulchinsky, Theodore, and Elena Varavikova. 2014. "A History of Public Health." *The New Public Health,* 1–42. https://doi.org/10.1016%2FB978-0-12-415766-8.00001-X.

Tversky, Amos, and Daniel Kahneman. 1974. "Judgment Under Uncertainty: Heuristics and Biases." *Science, 185,* 1124–31.

US Surgeon General. 2024. *Firearm Violence: A Public Health Crisis in America.* https://www.hhs.gov/surgeongeneral/priorities/firearm-violence/index.html.

Valente, Rob, and Rachel Graber. 2022. "Firearms, Domestic Violence, and Dating Violence: Abusers' Use of Firearms Violence to Exert Coercive Control and Commit Intimate Partner Homicides. In *Handbook of Interpersonal Violence and Abuse Across the Lifespan,* edited by R. Geffner et al., 2815–37. Springer.

Van Damme, Stefaan et al. 2008. "Attentional Bias to Threat: A Perceptual Accuracy Approach." *Emotion, 8,* 820–27.

VanSickle, Abbie. 2024. "Supreme Court Rejects Trump-Era Ban on Gun Bump Stocks." *New York Times,* June 14.

Vegter, Abigail, and Kevin R. den Dulk. 2021. "Clinging to Guns and Religion? A Research Note Testing the Role of Protestantism in Shaping Gun Identity in the United States." *Politics and Religion, 14,* 809–824.

Vescio, Theresa K. et al. 2025. "Masculinity Threats Sequentially Arouse Public Discomfort, Anger, and Positive Attitudes Toward Sexual Violence." *Personality and Social Psychology Bulletin, 51(1),* 96–109.

Wallace, Lacey N. 2019. "Implied Threat or Part of the Scenery: Americans' Perceptions of Open Carry." *Journal of Risk Research, 22,* 817–32.

Wallace, Maeve E. et al. 2021. "Firearm Relinquishment Laws Associated with Substantial Reduction in Homicide of Pregnant and Postpartum Women." *Health Affairs, 40,* 1654–62.

Wallin, Mikaela A. et al. 2022. "The Association of Federal and State-Level Firearm Restriction Policies with Intimate Partner Homicide: A Re-Analysis by Race of the Victim." *Journal of Interpersonal Violence, 27(17–18).*

Webster, Daniel W. et al. 2023. *Estimating the Effects of Safe Streets Baltimore on Gun Violence.* Center for Gun Violence Solutions, Johns Hopkins University, Bloomberg School of Public Health. https://publichealth.jhu.edu/sites/default/files/2023–03/estimating-the-effects-of-safe-streets-baltimore-on-gun-violence-march-2023.pdf.

Whaley, Arthur L. 2022. "The Cultural Ecology of Gun Violence: Culture of Honor and Code of the Street." *Du Bois Review, 19,* 193–203.

Whippman, Ruth. 2024. *BoyMom: Reimagining Boyhood in an Age of Impossible Masculinity.* New York: Harmony.

White, Stephen G., and J. Reid Meloy. 2016. WAVR-21™, 3rd ed. https://www.wavr21.com.

Whitehead, Andrew L. et al. 2018. "Gun Control in the Crosshairs: Christian Nationalism and Opposition to Stricter Gun Laws." *Socius, 4,* 1–13.

White House. 2021. *Reducing Military and Veteran Suicide: Advancing a Comprehensive, Cross-Sector, Evidence-Informed Public Health Strategy.* https://www.whitehouse.gov/wp-content/uploads/2021/11/Military-and-Veteran-Suicide-Prevention-Strategy.pdf.

Whitlock, Janis et al. 2014. "Connectedness and Suicide Prevention in Adolescents: Pathways and Implications." *Suicide and Life-Threatening Behavior, 44,* 246–72.

Willer, Robb et al. 2013. "Overdoing Gender: A Test of the Masculine Overcompensation Thesis." *American Journal of Sociology, 118,* 980–1022.

Witkowski, Terrence H. 2020. "Guns for Christmas: Advertising in *Boys' Life* Magazine, 1911–2012." *Journal of Macromarketing, 40,* 396–414.

Wolfe, Elizabeth, and Artemie Moshtaghian. 2023. "Authorities Investigating Online Threats of Violence Against Jewish Students at Cornell University, School's President Says." CNN. October 30. https://www.cnn.com/2023/10/29/us/cornell-university-antisemetic-threats-online-investigation/index.html.

Wolfram, Joel, and Campbell Robertson. 2023. "Suspect Showed Troubling Signs Before Philadelphia Rampage, D.A. Says." *New York Times*, July 5.

World Economic Forum. 2024. *The Global Risks Report 2024*, 19th ed. www3.weforum.org.

Xiao, Yunyu et al. 2024. "Decoding Suicide Decedent Profiles and Signs of Suicidal Intent Using Latent Class Analysis." *JAMA Psychiatry, 81*, 595–605.

Zainal, Nur Hani. 2024. "Is Combined Antidepressant Medication (ADM) and Psychotherapy Better Than Either Monotherapy at Preventing Suicide Attempts and Other Psychiatric Serious Adverse Events for Depressed Patients? A Rare Events Meta-Analysis." *Psychological Medicine, 54*, 457–72.

Zalewski, Maureen et al. 2023. "Integrating Dialectical Behavior Therapy with Child and Parent Training Interventions: A Narrative and Theoretical Review." *Clinical Psychology: Science and Practice, 30*, 365–76.

Zeineddin, Suhail et al. 2023. "Disfiguring Firearm Injuries in Children in the United States." *The American Surgeon, 89*, 2070–72.

Zeoli, April M. et al. 2016. "Risks and Targeted Interventions: Firearms in Intimate Partner Violence." *Epidemiologic Review, 38*, 125–39.

Zeoli, April M. et al. 2018. "Analysis of the Strength of Legal Firearms Restrictions for Perpetrators of Domestic Violence and Their Associations with Intimate Partner Homicide." *American Journal of Epidemiology, 187*, 2365–71.

Zeoli, April M. et al. 2022. "Effectiveness of Firearm Restriction, Background Checks, and Licensing Laws in Reducing Gun Violence." *Annals of the American Academy of Political and Social Science, 704*, 118–36.

Zick, Timothy. 2018. "Arming Public Protests." *Iowa Law Review, 104*, 223–85.

INDEX

active shootings: active shooter attacks, 45, *185*; active shooter drills, 8, 23–24, 95, 161, 177; active shooter games, 172. *See also* mass shootings
"Addressing the Mental Health Crisis in Youth" (Aftab/Druss), 25
aggrieved entitlement, 68
air rifles, 13
AK-47 semiautomatic rifles, 59, *124*, 126
Alberta, Tim, 83
Alexander VI, Pope, 62
alexithymia, 41, 42
Alito, Samuel, 152
Allport, Gordon, 59
ALS Association, 54–55
American Academy of Pediatrics, 24, 41–42, 116
American Federation of Teachers (AFT), 24, 176
American Indians, 9, 61–65, 71
American Rifleman (periodical), 85–86, 119, 120–21, 148
"America's First Freedom" slogan, 120
Anderson, Carol, 143
Anderson, Casey, 120
Anti-Defamation League (ADL), 91
antidepressants, 22, 111
anti-Semitism, 91–92
antisocial behavior, 169, 170, 171
AR-15 semiautomatic rifles, 11, 12, 48, 132, 138, 162; bump stock enhancement, 152–53; JR-15 as a child-size version, 129; in mass shootings, 1, 58, 125, 128, 154–55,

156, 158; as a semiautomatic weapon, *124*, 128, 152; Sporter as a modified version, 126–27
ArmaLite company, *124*, 126
armed citizenry, 4, 128
armed individualism, 121, 122, 123
Armslist, 16, 155
Arm up Ladies (Czubek), 16
Articles of Confederation, 144–45
assault weapons, 1, 37, 59, 76, 125, 161; banning sales of, 3, 58, 84, 153–54, 157, 163; Bushmaster assault rifles, 127; civilian ownership of, 12, 186; Daniel Defense as manufacturing, 163; progun activist arguments for, *185*
Assessing and Treating Emotionally Inexpressive Men (Levant/Pryor), 41
ATF. *See* Bureau of Alcohol, Tobacco, Firearms, and Explosives
at-risk youth, 27
attentional bias, 131–32
Austin, Michael W., 88–89, 90
Australia, 3, 5
automatic rifles, *124*, 127

background checks, 54, 56–57, 84, 152, 155–56, 159, 167, 186
Bad News (video game), 141, 177
Baldwin, Alec, 135
Baldwridge, Marsha, 21–22
Bandura, Albert, 26–27
banks, holding accountable, 135, 138
basking in reflected glory (BIRGing), 67